MW01596270

辜鸿铭 英译经典 —— 中英双语评述本

大学 中庸

辜鸿铭 英译

王京涛 评述

Higher Education

The Universal Order or Conduct of Life

中华书局

图书在版编目(CIP)数据

辜鸿铭英译经典：大学 中庸：中英双语评述本/辜鸿铭英译；王京涛评述. —北京：中华书局，2017.1
ISBN 978-7-101-11917-6

Ⅰ.辜… Ⅱ.①辜…②王… Ⅲ.①儒家②《大学》-译文-汉、英③《中庸》-译文-汉、英 Ⅳ.B222.1

中国版本图书馆 CIP 数据核字(2016)第 142184 号

书　　名　辜鸿铭英译经典：大学 中庸(中英双语评述本)
英 译 者　辜鸿铭
评 述 者　王京涛
责任编辑　王　芳
出版发行　中华书局
　　　　　(北京市丰台区太平桥西里 38 号　100073)
　　　　　http://www.zhbc.com.cn
　　　　　E-mail:zhbc@zhbc.com.cn
印　　刷　北京瑞古冠中印刷厂
版　　次　2017 年 1 月北京第 1 版
　　　　　2017 年 1 月北京第 1 次印刷
规　　格　开本/880×1230 毫米　1/32
　　　　　印张 10⅜　插页 2　字数 240 千字
印　　数　1-6000 册
国际书号　ISBN 978-7-101-11917-6
定　　价　42.00 元

出 版 说 明

　　《大学》《中庸》的英文翻译,在历来"四书五经"的翻译中一直是比较少的。早期,有英国传教士马礼逊(Robert Morrison)和马士曼(Joshua Marshman)的《大学》英译本(分别出版于1812年和1814年),英国传教士柯大卫(David Collie)的"四书"全译本(1828年),以及后来集大成的英国传教士、汉学家理雅各(James Legge)的《中国经典》(*Chinese Classic*)(其第一卷包括《大学》《中庸》《论语》,出版于1861年)。一直以来,这些儒家经典的英译工作都是西方传教士垄断的,直至辜鸿铭英译本的出现。

　　辜鸿铭(1857—1928)是中国近代著名学者,学贯中西,精通英、法、德、拉丁、希腊、马来文等9种语言文字,他是第一个独立完成《大学》《中庸》《论语》三部儒家经典英译的中国人。不同于理雅各等传教士,辜鸿铭翻译儒家经典的目的是要向西方传播中国文化和儒家思想。尽管精通西方文化,但辜鸿铭并不认为西方文化优于中国文化。他希望他的译介工作,能够改变西方对中国文化的不公正态度,重新认识中国。正如其《中庸》英译本(1906年)序言中所说:"如果这本来自中国旧学的书能够偶然地帮助那些欧美人，特别是那些现在在中国的人，更好地理解'道德法则'，拥有更清楚、更深刻的道德义务感，以便他们在对待中国及中国人时，能用道德法则替代欧洲的'炮舰'与'暴力'文明的精神和态度；在与每个中国人及整个中华民族的各种关系中，去尊重并服从道德义务感——那么，我就会感到这么多年来我用于研究和翻译这本书的精力，没有白费。"他的译本不仅面向学者，也面向广大不懂中文、对中国文化感到陌生的一般西方读者，行文努力按照一个受过教育的普通英国人的思维方式来表达。比如，他将《大学》书名译为"高等教育"；模仿基督教的宣教传统，将《中庸》称为一本"教义手册"；采用视"中庸"的内涵为"中的原则"的解释，"中的原则"也是亚里士多德哲学中常见的提法，为西方大众所熟知。

此次出版的辜鸿铭的《大学》《中庸》英译本，以中英双语形式呈现，包括英译文、《大学》《中庸》原文、中文今译三部分。《大学》英译文采自《神学季刊》1930—1931年连载的版本（与辜氏英译《大学》1915年初版基本一致），《中庸》英译文采自其1906年初版；《大学》《中庸》原文采自《四书章句集注》（中华书局，1983），即本书宋体字部分；中文今译则译自辜鸿铭的英译文，即本书楷体字部分。另外，全书每一节后附有译者的评述，让读者更好地了解辜鸿铭对《大学》《中庸》独到的理解与译法。

中华书局编辑部

2016年5月

2

目　录

HIGHER EDUCATION　大　学

THE UNIVERSAL ORDER OR CONDUCT OF LIFE　中　庸

HIGHER EDUCATION

大 学 ①

① 辜鸿铭译《大学》书名为"高等教育"（Higher Education）。本书所采用的《大学》辜氏译本，为《神学季刊》杂志于1930年7月至1931年4月连载的版本。据吴思远研究，《神学季刊》杂志所刊载的这个版本，除了部分删节和微调之外，内容与辜鸿铭正式出版的英译《大学》一致，而该书由上海《文汇西报》社出版于1915年（《辜鸿铭与英译〈大学〉出版之谜》，《中华读书报》2015年9月16日18版）。辜鸿铭在英译《大学》时几乎彻底打乱了《大学》原文的顺序。

INTRODUCTORY NOTE

The following is a new translation of one of the four books in the Confucian Bible which has been translated by Dr. Legge as the "Great Learning". This *Ta Hsüeh* (大学①), the "Method of Higher Education", together with the *Chung Yung* (中庸), the "Universal Order or Conduct of Life", forms what may be called the "Catechism of the Confucian Teaching". When first publishing my translation of the *Chung Yung* some ten years ago, I said: "It was my intention to publish these two books together; but I have not been able to bring my translation of the other book into a shape to satisfy the standard at which I aim at in my translation." Now the present translation is, in my humble opinion, fit to be presented to the public. I therefore venture to offer it to the consideration of educated men who are really and sincerely interested in the cause of education in China and in the world.

In order to make the sequence of thought more intelligible, I have ventured to slightly rearrange the text as adopted by the great Chinese commentator Chu Hsi (朱熹) and followed by Dr. Legge. The book consists of the text of Confucius and commentary or explanation of the text by a disciple.

Ku Hung-ming, Peking, 1915

---

① 中文字为原书所标示,下同。

引　言

　　以下是对儒家圣经"四书"里其中一部的新译，它被理雅各博士称为"伟大的学问"。这本《大学》也即"高等教育的方法"，与《中庸》即"普遍秩序或生活指导"，一起构成了我们所说的"孔子学说的教义手册"。数年前，当我初次出版我的《中庸》译本时，我说："我的目的是把这两本书一起出版，但按照我的翻译标准，我还未能让另一本书的译文达到让我满意的程度。"但现在依我的浅见，这个翻译适合出版了。因此，我冒险地把它推荐给那些受过教育并真正对中国及世界的教育事业感兴趣的人们，供其思考。

　　为使脉络更加清晰，我冒险地调整了伟大的中国注释家朱熹所采用的文本顺序，而是采用了理雅各的顺序。这本书由"孔子的文本"及"一位弟子对文本的注释"两部分构成。

辜鸿铭，北京，1915

第一章^①

---

① 辜鸿铭将《大学》的文本分成两段："孔子的文本"及相应的"一位弟子对文本的注释"，
这里译者作了分章，下同。

THE TEXT OF CONFUCIUS

The object of a Higher Education is to bring out（明）[1] the intelligent（明）moral power（德）of our nature; to make a new and better society (lit. people); and to enable us to abide in the highest excellence.

When a man has a standard of excellence before him, and only then, will he have a fixed and definite purpose; with a fixed and definite purpose, and only then, will he be able to have peace and tranquillity of mind; with[2] tranquillity of mind, and only then, will he be able to have peace and tranquillity[3] of soul; with peace and serenity of soul, and only then, can he devote himself to deep, serious thinking and reflection; and it is only by deep, serious thinking and reflection that a man can attain true culture.

COMMENTARY

I

1. The *Commission of Investiture to Prince K'ang* says: "He (the Emperor Wen) succeeded in making manifest the power of his moral nature."

---

① 原文即为汉字,下同。
② 原文如此,此处或漏 "peace and"。
③ 原文如此,此处 "tranquillity" 或应为下文中的 "serenity"。

孔 子 的 文 本

大学之道,在明明德,在亲民,在止于至善。

知止而后有定,定而后能静,静而后能安,安而后能虑,虑而后能得。

高等教育的目标①在于阐明(明)我们本性中智慧的(明)道德力量(德),在于建设一个更新和更好的社会(字面意思指"人民"),在于使我们遵守最高的美德。

只有当一个人拥有了关于美德的标准,唯有此时,他才会拥有一个固定而明确的目的;而只有有了固定而明确的目的,唯有此时,他才能拥有宁静而安稳的心灵;只有有了宁静而安稳的心灵,唯有此时,他的灵魂才能心神静谧;只有有了心神静谧的灵魂,唯有此时,他才能致力于深刻而严肃的思考;而只有通过深刻而严肃的思考,唯有此时,一个人才能获得真正的修养。

注　释

一

1.《康诰》曰:"克明德。"

　　《康诰》上说:"他(周文王)在彰显自身道德品格的力量方面是成功的。"

---

① 即"大学之道"。

2. In the *Address of the Minister I-Yin to the Emperor T'ai Chia*, it is said: "He (the great Emperor T'ang) kept constantly before him the clear Ordinance of God."

3. In the *Memorial Record of the Emperor Yao*, it is said: "He succeeded in making manifest the lofty sublimity of his moral nature."

4. Thus all these men made manifest the intelligent moral power of their nature.

[This section explains what "to bring out the intelligent power of our nature" means.]

II

1. The *Inscription on the Emperor T'ang's Bath* says: "Be a new man each day; from day to day be a new man; every day be a new man."

2. The *Commission of Investiture to Prince K'ang* says: "Create a new society."

2.《大甲》曰:"顾諟天之明命。"

　　在《大甲》中,他说:"他(伟大的帝王汤)不断地提醒自己上帝明确的训令。"

3.《帝典》曰:"克明峻德。"

　　《帝典》上说:"他在彰显其自身道德品格的崇高上是成功的。"

4. 皆自明也。

　　因此,所有这些人彰显了他们本性中智慧的道德力量。

[这一节解释了"阐明我们本性中智慧的道德力量"的含义。]①

二

1. 汤之《盘铭》曰:"苟日新,日日新,又日新。"

　　帝王汤的《盘铭》上说:"每天做个新人;一天一天都要做新人;每一天都要做个新人。"

2.《康诰》曰:"作新民。"

　　《康诰》上说:"创造一个新社会。"

---

① 这句话是辜鸿铭对以上4节文字的总结,下同。

3. The *Book of Songs* says: "Although the Royal House of Chou was an old State, a new Mission was given to it."

4. Therefore whatever a gentleman finds for his hands to do, he doeth with all his might.

[This section explains what "to make a new and better society" means.]

III

1. The *Book of Songs* says: "The Imperial Domain was a thousand li wide; within it all the people found their abode."

2. The *Book of Songs*, again, says: "The twittering yellow bird has found its abode on the side of a little hill."

Confucius commenting on this said: "In choosing their abode, even the birds know what to choose. Can it be that man is less intelligent than birds?"

3. The *Book of Songs* says: "Profoundly serious was the Emperor Wen. Ah! how earnestly he strove to realize his ideals."

As a ruler, his ideal was to love mankind. As a subject, his ideal was to respect authority. As a son, his ideal was to

3. 《诗》曰:"周虽旧邦,其命惟新。"

　　《诗经》上说:"周朝虽是旧国家,新使命却赋予它。"

4. 是故君子无所不用其极。

　　因此,无论一位绅士要着手做什么,他总是会竭尽全力。

[这一节解释了"建设一个更新和更好的社会"的含义。]

三

1. 《诗》云:"邦畿千里,惟民所止。"

　　《诗经》上说:"帝国疆域千里阔,人民居家各有所。"

2. 《诗》云:"缗蛮黄鸟,止于丘隅。"子曰:"於止,知其所止,可以人而不如鸟乎!"

　　《诗经》上还说:"呢喃的黄鸟,在山侧找到栖巢。"

　　孔子对此评论说:"在寻找居所上,即使小鸟都知道该如何选择。难道人还不如小鸟聪明吗?"

3. 《诗》云:"穆穆文王,於缉熙敬止!"为人君,止于仁;为人臣,止于敬;为人子,止于孝;为人父,止于慈;与国人交,止于信。

　　《诗经》上说:"多么认真啊,文王。啊!他热切地努力去实现理想。"

　　作为统治者,他的理想就是去守护人民。作为臣民,

be a dutiful son. As a father, his ideal was to be kind to his children. In intercourse with his fellow men, his ideal was to be faithful and true.

4. The *Book of Songs* says:

> Look where the river forms a nook,
> How trim the fresh green bamboos are;
> So full of grace is he, — our Prince,
> Like ivory finely cut and filed;
> Like a gem chiselled, ground and ground again.
> Oh! how distinguished and calm he looks,
> Oh! how majestic and grand his air;
> So full of grace is he, — our Prince,
> Oh! His glory will never end.

The words "cut and filed" refer to the care that he took to improve his knowledge. The words "chiselled and ground" refer to the care that he took to make himself perfect. The words "how distinguished and calm he looks" show the seriousness of his mind. The words "how majestic and grand his air" show the dignity of his manners. Lastly, the words, "So full of grace is he, — our Prince, Oh! His glory will never end," means that when glorious moral qualities are brought to such perfection, the people will never forget them.

他的理想就是去尊重权威。作为儿子,他的理想就是去做个孝顺的儿子。作为父亲,他的理想就是要对孩子们仁慈。与他的同胞交往,他的理想就是忠实和真诚。

4. 《诗》云:"瞻彼淇澳,菉竹猗猗。有斐君子,如切如磋,如琢如磨。瑟兮僩兮,赫兮喧兮。有斐君子,终不可喧兮!"如切如磋者,道学也;如琢如磨者,自修也;瑟兮僩兮者,恂栗也;赫兮喧兮者,威仪也;有斐君子,终不可喧兮者,道盛德至善,民之不能忘也。

《诗经》上说:"看那河流在何处回旋,齐整的翠竹明亮光鲜。多有魅力,我们君王,就如象牙被精心打磨,又像宝石一遍遍磨研。噢!他多显耀而庄严,噢!庄重而气度不凡;多有魅力,我们君王,噢!其荣耀无穷无疆。"

"精心打磨"这个词指的是他致力于提升自身知识水平的努力。"一遍遍磨研"这个词指的是他致力于让自己趋于完美的努力。"他多显耀而庄严"显示了他思想的严肃。"庄重而气度不凡"显示了他仪态的尊贵。最后,"多有魅力,我们君王,噢!其荣耀无穷无疆"这句话的意思是,一旦伟大的道德品格达到如此完美的境界,人民将永不会忘记他们。

5. The *Book of Songs* says: "Ah, the former kings are not forgotten!"

The higher classes appreciate their great moral qualities and love them. The lower classes are made happier and enjoy the benefits derived from their work. In this way they attain immortality.

[This section explains what "to abide in the highest excellence" means.]

5. 《诗》云:"於戏,前王不忘!"君子贤其贤而亲其亲,小人乐其乐而利其利,此以没世不忘也。

《诗经》上说:"啊,以前的君王们并未被遗忘!"

较高等级的人赞赏他们伟大的道德品格,并热爱他们。较低等级的人因受益于他们的工作而感到幸福快乐。如此,他们获得了不朽的名声。

[这一节解释了"使我们遵守最高的美德"的含义。]

孔 子 的 文 本

本段首先阐明了《大学》的主旨,而辜鸿铭也曾在著作中多次阐释过自己对《大学》主旨的理解。

"大学"一词,正如对本书标题的翻译,辜鸿铭译为"Higher Education","高等教育"。他认为理雅各将"大学"译为"Great Learning"(伟大的学问)是不对的。在《中国古典的精髓》的一篇文章中,辜鸿铭就说:"所谓大学,并不像理雅各博士所译成的那样是'伟大的学问',而实际上指的是高等的教育。"(黄兴涛主编,《辜鸿铭文集·下卷》,海南出版社,1996,第329页)可见,他认为理雅各并没有理解"大学"的真正含义。那么,其含义是什么呢? 在《东西文明异同论》的一篇演讲中,辜鸿铭说:"我们东洋的教育,不仅能使我们的子弟适应现代社会的生活,而且还能促使现代世界向着更美好的方向发展。孔子说:教育的目的在于称作'大学'的根本上。那就是'大学之道,在明明德',也就是发现人们所固有的辨别道德的能力,这就是教育的目的。必须成为一个为社会所推崇的人,成为一个聪慧的人,也就是说,教育的目的,在于为了明德,在于为了创造一个新的更好的社会而培养人才。《大学》中的'作新民'之'民'不是指人民,而是指社会,创造新的更好的社会是高等教育的目的,这才是孔子的本意。"(同上,第306页)还是在《中国古典的精髓》一文中,他同样强调:"近代欧洲的进步重点放在产业和机械工业的发达,而古代中国则侧重于人的进步,人的灵魂的、理智的进步,《大学》中尤其强调创造一个新的更美好的社会是高等教育的最终目的。"(同上,第329页)

对此,辜鸿铭在脚注中还引用孟德斯鸠的言论:

> 促使我们去学习的第一动机,就是我们试图加强天性中的优秀,使智慧的本性更加智慧。

同时,他还引用了马修·阿诺德的言论加以进一步说明:

> 关于文化,还有另一种观点——在其中,我们对世人所有的爱,对消除人类错误的欲望,清除人类的困惑以及减轻人类的不幸、使世界更加美好与幸福的崇高愿望——诸如我们称之为"社会性"的动机——作为文化的一种背景,并构成其主要与突出的那部分。因此,文化并不被认为源于好奇心,而是被恰当地描述为源于对完美的热爱;是对完美的学习。

辜鸿铭认为,"大学"或曰"高等教育"的主旨,就在于"为了创造一个新的更好的社会而培养人才",最终使社会更加美好。这是我们理解辜鸿铭英译《大学》的基础。

所以,在文中,他将"明明德"中第一个"明"译为"bring out","阐明";"明德"译为"the intelligent moral power of our nature","我们本性中智慧的道德力量"。而"亲民",则译为"make a new and better society","建设一个更新和更好的社会"。其中,"民",他认为指整个社会而言,虽然字面意思是"人民"。"止于至善"译为"to enable us to abide in the highest excellence","使我们遵守最高的美德"。

后文"知止而后有定,定而后能静,静而后能安,安而后能虑,虑而后能得"一句是对"美德"的进一步讨论。句中,关键词分别为"止""定""静""安""虑""得",它们分别代表着一种心境,且构成一种层层递进的逻辑关系。

其中,"止"译为"has a standard of excellence before him","拥有一个关于美德的标准"。"定",译为"have a fixed and definite purpose","拥有一个固定而明确的目的"。"静"译为"be able to have peace and tranquillity of mind","拥有宁静而安稳的心灵"。"安"译为"be able to have peace and serenity of soul","灵魂心神静谧"。"虑"译为"devote himself to deep, serious thinking and reflection","致力于深刻而严肃的思考"。"得"译为"attain true culture","获得真正的修养"。以上这些指一个人从致力于美德的追求而至于获得真正修养的过程。对此,辜鸿铭引用歌德的言论注释说:"宗教的虔诚并非目的,只是意味着通过心灵完全的平静与安宁,而达到最高的修养。"

注　释

一

辜鸿铭认为这是孔子弟子对前面孔子文本的注释。根据他在翻译中的说明,这一节是对"明明德"的解释,即何谓"阐明我们本性中智慧的道德力量"。文中列举了三个事例说明。

其中,《康诰》为《尚书·周书》中的一篇,是周公封康叔为"卫君"时做的文告,康叔是周公的弟弟。《康诰》,辜鸿铭译为"Commission of Investiture to Prince K'ang",即"康王的任命书"。

"克明德",译为"He (the Emperor Wen) succeeded in making manifest the power of his moral nature","他(周文王)在彰显自身道德品格的力量方面是成功的"。其中,"克"为"成功"之意。这句话说的是周文王的道德。

《大甲》为《尚书·商书》中的篇名,描述的是商王太甲的为政生涯及丞相伊尹对他的告诫，辜鸿铭译为 "Address of the Minister I-Yin to the Emperor T'ai Chia"，"伊尹向帝王太甲的陈述"。"顾諟天之明命" 一句中，"顾" 原为 "看、视" 之意，辜鸿铭译为 "kept constantly before him"，"不断地提醒自己"。"諟" 通 "是"，为代词。后面 "天之明命" 译为 "the clear Ordinance of God"，"上帝明确的训令"。这句话表现了商汤对自己的道德要求。

《帝典》即《尚书·虞夏书》中的《尧典》，记述的是帝尧的事迹。辜鸿铭译为 "Memorial Record of the Emperor Yao"，"关于帝尧的记录"。"克明峻德" 一句中，"明" 译为 "making manifest"，"使彰显" 之意。"峻德" 译为 "the lofty sublimity of his moral nature"，"道德品格的崇高"。这句话说的是帝尧的道德境界。

二

辜鸿铭认为，这一节解释了 "在亲民" 的含义，即何谓 "建设一个更新和更好的社会"。文中同样列举了三个例子予以说明。

《盘铭》译为 "Inscription on the Emperor T'ang's Bath"，"帝王汤的浴盆上的铭文"。"苟日新，日日新，又日新"，辜鸿铭认为三句话是在重复强调同一个意思，即每天都要做一个 "新人"。

"作新民" 译为 "create a new society"，"创造一个新社会"。把 "民" 译为 "社会"，请见上文对 "孔子的文本" 的评述。

"周虽旧邦，其命惟新" 一句中，"命" 译为 "Mission"，指使命。

"君子无所不用其极" 译为 "whatever a gentleman finds for his hands to do, he doeth with all his might"，"无论一位绅士要着手做什么，他总是会竭尽全力"。

三

辜鸿铭认为，这一节解释了 "止于至善" 即 "遵守最高的美德" 的含义，文中列举了5处《诗经》的诗句予以说明。

首先是1、2小段中的 "邦畿千里，惟民所止" 与 "缗蛮黄鸟，止于丘隅" 两句诗。其中的 "止" 字，辜鸿铭均译为 "abode"，"居所"。第3小段 "穆穆文王，於缉熙敬止" 一句诗中，他把 "止" 译为 "ideal"，"理想"。"缉熙敬止"，译为 "strove to realize his ideals"，"努力去实现理想"。辜鸿铭认为，"止" 在文中分别代表这两个含义。下文 "为人君，止于仁；为人臣，止于敬；为人子，止于孝；为人父，止于慈；与国人交，止于信" 中，"止" 均为 "理想" 之意，指做人的道德理想。

接下来是诗句"瞻彼淇澳，菉竹猗猗。有斐君子，如切如磋，如琢如磨。瑟兮僴兮，赫兮喧兮。有斐君子，终不可喧兮"。"淇澳"译为"forms a nook"，指河流"形成拐角"。"猗猗"译为"trim"，"整齐、修长"之意。"有斐君子"译为"So full of grace is he, — our Prince"，"多有魅力，我们君王"。其中，"斐"译为"full of grace"，"充满魅力"。"君子"指国君。

"瑟兮僴兮，赫兮喧兮"译为"Oh! how distinguished and calm he looks, / Oh! how majestic and grand his air"，"噢！他多显耀而庄严，/噢！庄重而气度不凡"。

再接下来是对这句诗的分解。"道学"译为"improve his knowledge"，"提升自身知识水平的努力"。"自修"译为"make himself perfect"，"让自己趋于完美"。"恂栗"译为"the seriousness of his mind"，指"思想的严肃"。"威仪"译为"the dignity of his manners"，"仪态的尊贵"。总的来看，"瞻彼淇澳"这段诗表现了"止于至善"的完美境界。

最后一小段中引用了"於戏，前王不忘"一句诗，辜鸿铭译为"the former kings are not forgotten"，"以前的君王们并未被遗忘"。而下文则阐释他们为何未被遗忘。"君子贤其贤而亲其亲"，译为"The higher classes appreciate their great moral qualities and love them"，"较高等级的人赞赏他们伟大的道德品格，并热爱他们"。其中，"君子"指较高等级的人。"其"指前文所说的"前王"们。下文"小人乐其乐而利其利"中，"小人"译为"the lower classes"，"较低等级的人"。"其"同样指"前王"们。

"此以没世不忘也"，译为"In this way they attain immortality"，"如此，他们获得了不朽的名声"。说明达到这样"止于至善"即达到"最高的美德"的道德境界，将是不朽的。

第二章

THE TEXT OF CONFUCIUS

Men in old times when they wanted to further the cause of enlightenment and civilization in the world began first by securing good government in their country. When they wanted to secure good government in their country, they began first by putting their house in order. When they wanted to put their house in order, they began first by ordering their conversation aright. When they wanted to put their conversation aright, they began first by putting their minds in a proper and well-ordered condition. When they wanted to put their minds in a proper and well-ordered condition, they began first by getting true ideas. When they wanted to have true ideas, they began first by acquiring knowledge and understanding. The acquirement of knowledge and understanding comes from a systematic study of things.

After a systematic study of things, and only then, knowledge and understanding will come. When knowledge and understanding have come, and only then, will men have true ideas. When men have true ideas, and only then, will their minds be in a proper and well-ordered condition. When men's minds are in a proper and well-ordered condition, and only then, will their conversation be ordered aright. When men's conversations are ordered aright, and only then, will their houses be kept in order. When men's houses are kept in order, and only then, will there be good government in the country. When there is good government in all countries, and only then, will there be peace and order in the world.

孔子的文本

古之欲明明德于天下者,先治其国;欲治其国者,先齐其家;欲齐其家者,先修其身;欲修其身者,先正其心;欲正其心者,先诚其意;欲诚其意者,先致其知;致知在格物。

物格而后知至,知至而后意诚,意诚而后心正,心正而后身修,身修而后家齐,家齐而后国治,国治而后天下平。

古代的人们,当他们想促进世间的教化与文明事业时,他们首先会在国内确保好的统治。而当他们想在国内确保好的统治时,他们首先会赋予家族以秩序。当他们想赋予家族以秩序时,他们首先会拥有恰当的谈吐。而当他们想拥有恰当的谈吐时,他们首先会使自己的心灵处于一个适当而有序的状态。当他们想使自己的心灵处于一个适当而有序的状态时,他们首先要获得真实的思想。而当他们想要获得真实的思想时,他们首先要获取知识与智慧。而知识与智慧来自系统地研究事物。

在系统地研究事物之后,唯有此时,知识与智慧才会到来。而当知识与智慧到来之后,唯有此时,人们才会产生真实的思想。当人们产生真实的思想,唯有此时,他们的心灵才会处于一个适当而有序的状态。当人们的心灵处于适当而有序的状态,唯有此时,他们的谈吐才会恰当。当人们的谈吐是恰当的,唯有此时,他们的家族才会拥有秩序。而当人们的家族拥有了秩序,唯有此时,国家才会拥有好的统治。当国家拥有了好的统治,唯有此时,世间才会实现和平与秩序。

COMMENTARY

IV

1. In physical nature, there are causes and effects. In human affairs, there are springs of actions and consequences. When a man knows that he must first attend to the one before he can deal with the other, he is then not far from the truth. From the Emperor down to the lowest of the common people, the one thing that all must do is to make the ordering of their conversation aright, the foundation for everything. When the foundation is in disorder, that which is built on it will not be in order. When that which is essential is neglected, that which is not essential can never be properly attended to.

2. Confucius says: "In deciding lawsuits, I am not better than other men. But what I make it a point to do is — I try to make lawsuits impossible. Men who come before me without a just cause have nothing to say for themselves."
Watch therefore with fear and trembling over the hearts of the people. That is the root of the matter in knowledge. That is the highest knowledge.

注 释

四

1. 物有本末，事有终始，知所先后，则近道矣。自天子以至于庶人，壹是皆以修身为本。其本乱而末治者否矣，其所厚者薄，而其所薄者厚，未之有也！

在自然界是存在因果的，在人类事务中，同样存在原因和结果。当一个人懂得他必须首先致力于一件事，然后才能处理其他的事，这时，他才算离真理不远。从帝王一直到最底层的普通人，所有人都必须先做的，就是拥有恰当的谈吐，这是所有事情的基础。当基础是无序的，那么，它的上层建筑也不会有序。当必要的东西恰恰是被忽视的，那么，致力于不必要的事情就是不恰当的。

2. 子曰："听讼，吾犹人也，必也使无讼乎！"无情者不得尽其辞。大畏民志，此谓知本。此谓知本，此谓知之至也。

孔子说："在裁决诉讼上，我并不比别人强。但我决心去做的是——使诉讼变得不可能。来到我面前的人，如果没有正当理由，他将变得无话可说。"

因此，要以敬畏与忐忑之心看待人民的意志。这就是知识的本质。这就是最高的知识。

V

1. Now what is meant by "to have true ideas" is to have no self-deception, as when one hates a bad smell or loves what is beautiful. That is what is called self-detachment. Therefore a gentleman watches diligently over his secret thought.

2. When he is alone, there is no evil which an immoral man will not do; but when he sees a gentleman, he immediately disguises himself and conceals what is evil and shows off what is good within him. But men see through us as though our hearts and reins lay open to them. What is the use then of concealing? That is what is meant by the saying that what is truly within will surely show without. Therefore a gentleman watches diligently over his secret thought.

3. The disciple of Confucius, Tseng-tzu, says: "When you know that ten eyes are looking upon you and ten fingers are pointing at you, is it not awful?"

4. Wealth embellishes a house, but moral qualities embellish the person. When the mind is free and easy, the body will grow in

五

1. 所谓诚其意者：毋自欺也，如恶恶臭，如好好色，此之谓自谦，故君子必慎其独也！

   那么，所谓"拥有真实的思想"，就是不自欺，正如一个人厌恶臭味而喜爱美丽的事物一样。这就是所谓的自我超脱。因此，一位绅士总是孜孜不倦地审视他隐秘的念头。

2. 小人闲居为不善，无所不至，见君子而后厌然，揜其不善，而著其善。人之视己，如见其肺肝然，则何益矣。此谓诚于中，形于外，故君子必慎其独也。

   一个不道德的人在独处时，没有什么邪恶的事他不会去做；而当他见到一个绅士，他马上又会伪装自己，隐瞒他内心的邪恶而卖弄他好的一面。但人们已经看穿了我们，仿佛我们的心脏和肺腑就暴露在他们面前。那么，隐瞒又有何用呢？这就是所谓的真实的内在必然会显露于外。因此，一位绅士会孜孜不倦地审视他隐秘的念头。

3. 曾子曰："十目所视，十手所指，其严乎！"

   孔子的学生曾子说："当你知道有十只眼睛盯着你，十根手指指着你，这不是很可怕的吗？"

4. 富润屋，德润身，心广体胖，故君子必诚其意。

   财富会修饰一间屋子，而道德品格会修饰一个人。当

27

flesh. Therefore a gentleman must have true ideas.

VI

1. Now what is meant by saying that the ordering of one's conversation aright depends upon putting the state of the mind in a proper and well-ordered condition, is this. When a person is under the influence of passion, his mind is not in a proper and well-ordered condition. When he is under the influence of fear and terror, his mind is not in a proper and well-ordered condition. When he is under the influence of pleasure and amusement, his mind is not in a proper and well-ordered condition. When he is under the influence of sorrow and distress, his mind is not in a proper and well-ordered condition.

2. When the mind is absent, we look, but do not see; we hear but do not understand; we eat, but do not know the taste of that which we eat.

3. This is what is meant by saying that the ordering of one's conversation aright depends upon putting the state of the mind in a proper and well-ordered condition.

你的心灵是自由和轻松的，身体就会变得丰腴。因此，一位绅士必须拥有真实的思想。

六

1. 所谓修身在正其心者，身有所忿懥，则不得其正；有所恐惧，则不得其正；有所好乐，则不得其正；有所忧患，则不得其正。

    那么，所谓的一个人拥有恰当的谈吐取决于使自己的心灵处于一个恰当而有序的状态，就是这个意思。当一个人被情欲左右，他的心灵将不会处于一个恰当而有序的状态。当他处于害怕与恐惧之中，他的心灵将不会处于一个恰当而有序的状态。当他沉浸于愉快与娱乐之中，他的心灵将不会处于一个恰当而有序的状态。当他深陷悲伤与痛苦之中，他的心灵将不会处于一个恰当而有序的状态。

2. 心不在焉，视而不见，听而不闻，食而不知其味。

    当心灵是茫然的，我们睁眼睛看，却看不见；我们竖耳朵听，却听不懂；我们大口吃，却尝不出味道。

3. 此谓修身在正其心。

    这就是所谓的一个人拥有恰当的谈吐取决于使自己的心灵处于一个恰当而有序的状态。

VII

1. Now what is meant by saying that putting one's house in order depends upon the ordering of his conversation aright, is this. Men are biassed towards those for whom they feel love and affection; biassed towards those of whom they despise and dislike; towards^① those for whom they feel pity and compassion; biassed towards those towards whom they feel arrogance and pride. Wherefore it is that there are few men in the world who love and yet know the bad qualities of those whom they love; who hate and yet know the good qualities of those whom they hate.

2. Hence it is said in the common adage: "No man knows the wickedness of his son, no man knows the richness of his crops."

3. This is what is meant by saying that unless you order your conversation aright, you cannot put your house in order.

---

① 原文如此,或应为 "biassed towards"。

七

1. 所谓齐其家在修其身者：人之其所亲爱而辟焉，之其所贱恶而辟焉，之其所畏敬而辟焉，之其所哀矜而辟焉，之其所敖惰而辟焉。故好而知其恶，恶而知其美者，天下鲜矣！

　　那么，所谓的使家族处于秩序中取决于他拥有恰当的谈吐，是这样的意思。人们总是对那些他们所热爱与喜爱的人有所偏爱；总是对那些他们所鄙视与厌恶的人抱有偏见；①总是对那些他们所怜悯与同情的人有所偏向；而对那些会让他们感到傲慢与自大的人，他们往往会相当抵触。因此，世界上只有很少的人会热爱他们所爱的人，但同时也知道他们坏的品质；只有很少的人会憎恨那些他们所憎恨的人，然而却也知道他们好的品质。

2. 故谚有之曰："人莫知其子之恶，莫知其苗之硕。"

　　因此，有一句谚语这样说："没人知道自己儿子的不好，没人知道自己庄稼的富饶。"

3. 此谓身不修不可以齐其家。

　　这就是所谓的除非你拥有恰当的谈吐，否则不会给家族带来秩序。

---

① 原文中有"之其所畏敬而辟焉"一句，意为"总是对那些他们所敬畏的人有所偏敬"。辜鸿铭此处漏译。

VIII

1. Now what is meant by saying that in order to have good government in the country, one must first put one's house in order, is this. He who cannot teach the members of his own family to be good, can never teach other people to be good. Hence the moral man, without going out of his house, can learn the duties which he owes to the State. The duties of a good son will teach him how to serve his Sovereign. The duties of subordination in the family will teach him to respect authority. The kindness of a father to his children will teach him how to treat the multitude.

2. The *Commission of Investiture to Prince K'ang* says: "Watch over the people as a mother watches over her new born child."
   A mother who seeks with her whole heart the good of her child, although she makes mistakes, will never go wholly wrong. No girl ever had to learn how to take care of her child before marriage.

3. When there is kindness and humanity in one family, the whole nation will grow kind and humane. When there is courtesy and politeness in one family, the whole nation will all become polite and courteous. The ambition and perversity of one man, on

八

1. 所谓治国必先齐其家者，其家不可教而能教人者，无之。故君子不出家而成教于国：孝者，所以事君也；弟者，所以事长也；慈者，所以使众也。

    那么，所谓的为了在一国内拥有好的统治，他必须首先使家族拥有秩序，就是这个意思。他如果不能教育他自己的家人向善，就不可能教其他人向善。因此，一个有道德的人即使不出家门，他依然能够学习他对于国家的义务。作为一个孝子的义务会教给他如何为他的君王服务。在家族中顺从的义务会教给他如何去尊重权威。父亲对孩子们的慈爱，会教给他如何对待人民大众。

2. 《康诰》曰"如保赤子"，心诚求之，虽不中不远矣。未有学养子而后嫁者也！

    《康诰》上说："照看人民就如一位母亲照料她刚出生的孩子。"

    一位母亲全身心地寻求如何善待孩子，尽管她会犯错，但不会完全地错。没有女孩会在出嫁之前就已学会如何去照料孩子。

3. 一家仁，一国兴仁；一家让，一国兴让；一人贪戾，一国作乱；其机如此。此谓一言偾事，一人定国。

    当一个家族拥有了仁慈与人道，那么，整个国家就会渐渐变得仁慈而人道。当一个家族拥有礼节与文雅，那么，

the other hand, may bring to confusion and anarchy the whole nation. Such is the power of influence. Hence the saying: "One word can ruin everything; one man can save a nation."

4. The Emperors Yao and Shun set up humanity as their principle in governing the Empire, and the people responded and became humane. The Emperors Chieh and Chou set up cruelty as their principle in governing the Empire, and the people responded and became cruel. When rulers give orders which are contrary to that which they themselves love to practise, the people will not obey them. Therefore, before requiring any moral quality of the people, the ruler must himself have that moral quality; before condemning any vice in the people, he must himself be free of that vice. A man who does not consider his own moral condition can never influence others for good.

5. Therefore government in a country depends upon putting one's house in order.

6. The *Book of Songs* says:

> The peach tree is tender and fair,
> With its leaves all in bloom;
> The girl is going to her new home,
> She will rightly order her household.

整个国家就会渐渐变得礼貌而文雅。另一方面,一个人的野心与乖戾,可能导致整个国家的混乱与无序。这就是感染的力量。因此,有谚语说:"一句话能毁掉一切,一个人能拯救国家。"

4. 尧舜帅天下以仁,而民从之;桀纣帅天下以暴,而民从之;其所令反其所好,而民不从。是故君子有诸己而后求诸人,无诸己而后非诸人。所藏乎身不恕,而能喻诸人者,未之有也。

帝尧和帝舜在统治帝国时建立起了人道的原则,人民积极响应也变得人道。帝王桀和纣在统治帝国时建立起了残忍的原则,人民也积极响应,并变得残忍。当统治者下的命令与他们所实际乐于遵循的正好相反,人民就不会遵从他们。因此,在对人民的道德品格做出任何要求之前,统治者自身必须拥有那种道德品格;在谴责人民拥有某种恶习之前,他自身必须免于那种恶习。一个不重视自身道德约束的人,不可能引导别人向善。

5. 故治国在齐其家。

因此,一个国家的统治取决于让家族拥有秩序。

6.《诗》云:"桃之夭夭,其叶蓁蓁;之子于归,宜其家人。"宜其家人,而后可以教国人。

《诗经》上说:"桃树柔而美,树叶亮而翠;女孩赴新家,家人受教化。"

Only when there is order in the household, is it possible to teach the people of the nation to be good.

7. The *Book of Songs* says: "Do your duty to your elder brothers, Do your duty to your younger brothers."

Only when a man has done his duty to his brothers at home, can he teach the people of the nation to be good.

8. The *Book of Songs* says: "His manners were without reproach. He therefore brought the whole nation to order."

Thus only when the ruler is fit to be to his people a model father, a model son and a model brother, will the people take him as their model.

9. This is, then, what is meant by saying that good government in a country depends upon putting one's house in order.

IX

1. Now what is meant by saying that peace and order throughout the world depends upon having good government in one's own country, is this. When those in authority honour old age, the people will become dutiful sons. When those in authority

只有当家族拥有秩序，才有可能教化一国的人民
向善。

7.《诗》云："宜兄宜弟。"宜兄宜弟，而后可以教国人。

《诗经》上说："为你长兄尽责，为你幼弟尽责。"

只有当一个人在家里为他的兄弟们尽责，他才会教给
一国的人民向善。

8.《诗》云："其仪不忒，正是四国。"其为父子兄弟足法，
而后民法之也。

《诗经》上说："他仪态雅致免于责辱，带来秩序给国
家民族。"

因此，对人民而言，只有当统治者适合做一个模范的
父亲、一个模范的儿子和模范的兄弟，人民才会把他视为
一个榜样。

9. 此谓治国在齐其家。

这就是所谓的一个国家良好的统治取决于家族拥有
秩序。

九

1. 所谓平天下在治其国者：上老老而民兴孝，上长长而民兴
弟，上恤孤而民不倍，是以君子有絜矩之道也。

那么，所谓世间的和平与秩序取决于国家的良好统

respect and obey their superiors, the people will all become good citizens. When those in authority take care of the poor and helpless, the people will not neglect them. Thus a gentleman has a self-measuring rule.

2. What a man hates in the conduct of those who are above him, let him not show it in his treatment of those who are under him. What he hates in the conduct of those who are under him, let him not show it when doing his duty to those who are above him. What he hates in the conduct of those who go before him, let him not be the first to show in dealing with those who come after him. What he hates in the conduct of those who come after him, let him not follow their example and show in dealing with those who go before him. What he hates in the conduct of those who are on the right hand of him, let him not show in dealing with those who are on the left hand of him. What he hates in the conduct of those who are on the left hand of him, let him not show in dealing with those who are on the right hand of him. This is what is called a self-measuring rule.

3. The *Book of Songs* says: "How the people love the prince who is a father and a mother to the people."
To love what the people love and to hate what the people hate: that is what is meant by being a father and a mother to the people.

治，是这样的意思。如果当权者尊敬老人，人民就会成为孝子。如果当权者都尊重并服从他们的上级，人民就会成为优秀的公民。如果当权者悉心照顾贫穷与无助的人，人民就不会疏远他们。因此，一位绅士总会有一个自我衡量的准则。

2. 所恶于上，毋以使下；所恶于下，毋以事上；所恶于前，毋以先后；所恶于后，毋以从前；所恶于右，毋以交于左；所恶于左，毋以交于右：此之谓絜矩之道。

　　如果一个人厌恶他的上级对他的行为，他就不要如此对他的下属。如果他厌恶他的下属对他的行为，他就不要在为上级服务时也如此这般。如果他厌恶那些先行者的某些行为，他就不要如此对待他的后来者。如果他厌恶他的后来者的某些行为，它就不要模仿后来者的行为而如此对待他的先行者们。如果他厌恶那些在他右手边的人的某些行为，他就不要如此对待他的左手边的人。如果他厌恶他的左手边的人的某些行为，他就不要如此对待他的右手边的人。这就是所谓的自我衡量的准则。

3.《诗》云："乐只君子，民之父母。"民之所好好之，民之所恶恶之，此之谓民之父母。

　　《诗经》上说："君主对民如父母，人民多么热爱他。"

　　爱人民之所爱，恨人民之所恨：这就是所谓的待人民如父母。

4. The *Book of Songs* says:

> Lofty like the southern hill,
>
> With its rugged mass of rocks;
>
> Awful you are, my lord of Yin,
>
> The people all look up to you.

Those who are responsible for the government of a nation cannot be too careful in what they do. The least mistake on their part will have awful consequences to the world.

5. The *Book of Songs* says:

> Before the Yin rulers had lost the hearts of the people,
>
> They found favour in the sight of God;
>
> Take warning then from the House of Yin,
>
> The great High Mission is not easy to hold.

This means that when a ruler gains the heart of the people, he will gain the kingdom; when he loses the hearts of the people, he will lose the kingdom.

4. 《诗》云："节彼南山，维石岩岩；赫赫师尹，民具尔瞻。"有
   国者不可以不慎，辟则为天下僇矣。

   《诗经》上说：

   > 高耸如南山，
   > 满山崎岖岩；
   > 师尹多可畏，
   > 人民举头看。

   那些有统治国家的义务的人，对自身的行为不能不
   谨慎。就他们而言，最小的错误都会给世间带来可怕的
   后果。

5. 《诗》云："殷之未丧师，克配上帝；仪监于殷，峻命不易。"
   道得众则得国，失众则失国。

   《诗经》上说：

   > 殷朝丧失民心前，
   > 上帝赐予恩泽厚；
   > 前车教训须借鉴，
   > 伟大使命常守难。

   这是说，当统治者赢得了民心，他就会赢得整个王国；
   而当他丧失民心，他将失掉王国。

6. Therefore the first care of the ruler is to make sure that he has the moral qualities. Who has the moral qualities, has the people; who has the people, has the land; who has the land, has the revenue; who has the revenue, has the power to use it.

7. Moral qualities are the foundation of a nation. Wealth is but the means. When the ruler mistakes the end for the means and the means for the end, the result will be rapine and scrambling for wealth among the people. Therefore the accumulation of wealth in a few hands leads to the dissolution of Society, while the distribution of wealth among the many contributes to the stability of Society.

8. Hence it is said: "Words spoken in violence will return again with violence, and wealth gotten by violence will be taken away by violence."

9. The *Commission of Investiture to Prince K'ang* says: "The Divine Mission is not given us for ever." That is to say, if we are good, we shall win it; if we are not good, we shall lose it.

6. 是故君子先慎乎德。有德此有人,有人此有土,有土此有财,有财此有用。

　　因此,统治者最关心的是确信他拥有道德品格。拥有了道德品格,就拥有了人民;拥有了人民,就拥有了土地;拥有了土地,就拥有了收益;拥有了收益,就拥有了使用它的权力。

7. 德者本也,财者末也,外本内末,争民施夺。是故财聚则民散,财散则民聚。

　　道德品格是一国之基础,财富只是手段。当统治者错把目的当作手段,而把手段当作目的,结果就是,人民很快就会陷入财富的争抢。因此,财富若聚集到少数人手中,就会导致社会的崩溃,而若把财富分配给大多数,将有助于社会的稳固。

8. 是故言悖而出者,亦悖而入;货悖而入者,亦悖而出。

　　因此说:"在暴力中说的话,会再引发暴力,而用暴力获得的财富,也会被暴力夺走。"

9. 《康诰》曰:"惟命不于常!"道善则得之,不善则失之矣。

　　《康诰》中说:"神圣使命并不会永远赐予我们。"

　　就是说,如果我们是善的,就会赢得它;如果不善,就会失去它。

10. In the *History of the Kingdom of C'hu*, it is said: "There is naught that the people of C'hu deem precious; goodness alone they deem precious."

11. Fan, the uncle of Duke Wen of the Kingdom of T'sin, while the Duke was in exile abroad, said: "Our Prince now in exile considers nothing as precious; he only holds as precious his love for his parents."

12. In his speech from the Throne, the Duke of T'sin said: "Let me have as my Minister a plain and simple man who has absolutely no other qualification except a free and open mind and a broad and tolerant spirit; who regards the possession of abilities by others as if he possessed them himself; who shows his broad and tolerant spirit by taking the same delight in the superior intelligence of others as he would were it his own. Such a man will be able to protect our children and grandchildren, the black-haired people. He will benefit us in every way. A man, on the other hand, who, when he sees others possessing abilities, is envious of and hates them; who, when he sees superior intelligence in others, shows his narrow and intolerant spirit by putting difficulties in their way, so that they cannot get known,

10.《楚书》曰："楚国无以为宝,惟善以为宝。"

　　《楚书》上说:"楚国的人民没有视作珍宝的,只把善良视为珍宝。"

11.舅犯曰:"亡人无以为宝,仁亲以为宝。"

　　晋文公的舅舅犯,当晋文公流放国外时,他说:"如今我们国君在流放中,他并不把什么当作珍宝,只把对父母的爱当作珍宝。"

12.《秦誓》曰:"若有一个臣,断断兮无他技,其心休休焉,其如有容焉。人之有技,若己有之,人之彦圣,其心好之,不啻若自其口出,寔能容之,以能保我子孙黎民,尚亦有利哉。人之有技,媢疾以恶之,人之彦圣,而违之俾不通,寔不能容,以不能保我子孙黎民,亦曰殆哉。"

　　在他的王位演讲中,秦公[①]说:"让我拥有一个朴实而单纯的人做我的大臣,他除了拥有自由和开放的心灵以及广博而宽容的精神,并无其他长处;他把其他人拥有的能力,看作好像他自己拥有;他为别人卓越的智慧而高兴,就像他自己拥有,这显示出他广博与宽容的精神。这样一个人,将能够保护我们的子孙以及广大黎民百姓。他将在各个方面使我们受益。另一方面,如果一个人看到别人拥有能力而嫉妒他们,并憎恨他们;如果他看到别人拥有卓越的智慧,却通过给他们偷偷设置阻碍而不使他们显名,

---

① 辜鸿铭此处误译为前面的"晋"(T'sin),依原文为"秦公"。

45

such a man will not be able to protect our children and grandchildren, the black-haired people. He will in every way be a man dangerous to us all."

13. It is the duty of all good men to banish such a man and drive him to live among the uncivilized heathen, not to allow him to live with us in China. This is what is meant by saying: "It is only the truly good and moral man who can love or hate others."

14. To see men of worth and not be able to raise them to office, but to keep them in a subordinate position under you, that is gross neglect of duty. To see bad and unworthy men and not be able to remove them, — that is weakness.

15. To love and like those whom all men hate and dislike; to hate and dislike those whom all men love and like; that is to outrage the natural feeling of men. Calamities will be sure to overtake a person who thus acts.

16. Thus in life there is one great law for a gentleman. If faithful and trustworthy, he is sure to succeed; if proud and careless, he is sure to fail. In the same manner in the production of wealth there is one great law. When there are many who produce and few who consume; when those who work, work

这显示出他狭隘与不宽容的精神。这样一个人，将不能保护我们的子孙以及广大黎民百姓。他在各个方面对我们来说都是危险的。"

13. 唯仁人放流之，迸诸四夷，不与同中国。此谓唯仁人为能爱人，能恶人。

    所有善良的人，都有义务将这样一个人驱逐出去，把他赶到未开化的野蛮部落去生活，不允许他跟我们一起在中国生活。这就是这句谚语所说的："只有真诚与有道德的人才能爱憎他人。"

14. 见贤而不能举，举而不能先，命也；见不善而不能退，退而不能远，过也。

    看到有价值的人却不能晋升他们，而是把他们放在从属于你的位置，这是显而易见的失职。看到卑劣而且不合适的人而不能开除他们——这就是软弱。

15. 好人之所恶，恶人之所好，是谓拂人之性，灾必逮夫身。

    去热爱与喜爱那些人们所憎恨和厌恶的人；去憎恨和厌恶那些人们所热爱与喜爱的人；这就违背了人们的自然情感。灾害一定会降临在这样行事之人的身上。

16. 是故君子有大道，必忠信以得之，骄泰以失之。生财有大道，生之者众，食之者寡，为之者疾，用之者舒，则财恒足矣。

    因此，对于绅士来说，在生活中有一条重大的法则。

hard, and those who spend, spend slowly; then there will always be plenty of wealth in the nation.

17. Moral men make money to live. Immoral men live to make money.

18. You will never find where the rulers are human and kind that the people do not love honour and duty. You will never find where the people in a nation love honour and duty, that the affairs of that nation do not prosper, and that the wealth in the nation does not belong to the ruler.

19. The noble Lord Meng Hsien said: "The man who keeps horses and carriages, does not look after fowls and pigs. The family that stores ice in the house, does not rear oxen and sheep. In the same manner the ruler of a nation should not keep a minister whose sole aim is to exact as much money as he can from the people. Rather than have such a minister, it were better to have a minister who openly robs him."

This is what is meant by saying that what really makes a nation prosperous is not wealth and material prosperity, but honour and duty.

若忠诚可靠,他必将成功;若傲慢冷漠,他必将遭败。同样,在财富的创造中,也存在一条重要的法则。如果多数人生产而少数人消费,如果工作者工作努力而消耗者消耗缓慢,那么,这个国家将总是拥有充足的财富。

17. 仁者以财发身,不仁者以身发财。

有道德的人为了生活而去挣钱。不道德的人生活就是为了挣钱。

18. 未有上好仁而下不好义者也,未有好义其事不终者也,未有府库财非其财者也。

你永远不会发现,如果统治者是人道而良善的,人民却不热爱荣誉与责任。你永远不会发现,如果一国之民热爱荣誉与责任,而那个国家却不繁荣昌盛,以及一国的财富不属于统治者。

19. 孟献子曰:“畜马乘不察于鸡豚,伐冰之家不畜牛羊,百乘之家不畜聚敛之臣,与其有聚敛之臣,宁有盗臣。”此谓国不以利为利,以义为利也。

贵族孟献子说:“那些拥有马匹和马车的人,不会去照料鸡和猪。在屋里储存冰的人家,不会饲养牛和羊。同理,一国的统治者也不应该任用把竭力聚敛人民之财作为唯一目标的大臣。与其有这样一个大臣,还不如有一个公开抢劫他的大臣。”

这就是所谓的真正使一个国家繁荣的,并非财富与物质的成功,而是荣誉与责任。

20. When a ruler who wishes to make his nation prosperous and great, devotes his attention only to questions of finance and revenue, he is surely under the influence of some base and ignoble person. When such a base and ignoble person directs the affairs of a nation, even though he be a man of ability, calamities and disaster will follow, and then even a good man who comes after him, will be able to do nothing. This, then, is what is meant by saying that what really makes a nation prosperous is not wealth and material prosperity, but honour and duty.

20. 长国家而务财用者，必自小人矣。彼为善之，小人之使为国家，灾害并至。虽有善者，亦无如之何矣！此谓国不以利为利，以义为利也。

　　如果一个统治者试图让他的国家繁荣而伟大，但他仅仅专注于金融与财政方面的问题，他必然是受到了一些卑鄙可耻之徒的影响。一旦如此卑鄙可耻之徒管理国家事务，哪怕他是个有能力的人，不幸和灾祸也将随之而至，在这之后，即使继承他的是一个良善的人，也将无能为力。那么，这就是所谓的真正使一个国家繁荣的，并非财富与物质的成功，而是荣誉与责任。

孔 子 的 文 本

本段系统地阐述了从"格物"到"明明德于天下"或"平天下"的逻辑关系。

此处对"明明德"一词的翻译与开头稍有不同,前一个"明"字,译为"further","促进,增进"之意。"明德"译为"the cause of enlightenment and civilization","教化与文明事业"。"天下"译为"the world","世间"。指在人世间促进"明德",即促进人类文明的发展。

"治其国"译为"securing good government in their country","在国内确保好的统治"。"齐其家"译为"putting their house in order","赋予家族以秩序"。"修其身"译为"ordering their conversation aright","拥有恰当的谈吐"。"正其心"译为"putting their minds in a proper and well-ordered condition","使自己的心灵处于一个适当而有序的状态"。"诚其意"译为"getting true ideas",即"获得真实的思想"。此处,辜鸿铭在脚注中进一步注释说:"关于他们自己以及世界的真实思想。汉语中'诚意'这个词相当于苏格拉底所说的'认识你自己'。"也就是说,这里所谓的"真实",首先是对自我的认识,同时,也是指对世界的真正的认知。

接下来,"致其知"译为"acquiring knowledge and understanding","获取知识与智慧"。"格物"译为"asystematic study of things",即"系统地研究事物"。

在辜鸿铭看来,这一段详细地讲述了教育应该遵循的逻辑与次序,即良好的教育应该始于对事物的研究,进而形成对自我及人世间的真实认知,而最终促进人类文明的发展。而在《何谓文化教养》一文中,他对这一问题有进一步的阐述,他说:"像孔子所著的《论语》《大学》等等,表明有教养的人拥有的知识不是暧昧模糊的知识,而是系统的、科学的知识,它是通过'格物'而得到的知识。所谓'格物致知'的'物',即是与存在相关的、脉络整然的科学知识,'物'在汉语中的意思,不仅仅是物质性的事物,它含有物质、精神两方面的内容。也就是说大凡存在的一切就是'物','物'也就是存在。"(黄兴涛主编,《辜鸿铭文集·下卷》,第288—289页)其中,他认为,"格物"的"物"含有"物质、精神两方面的内容",也即"存在"本身。换言之,教育的起点,又可以说在于对"存在"本身的系统研究。

注 释

四

辜鸿铭认为,这两段是对前一节"孔子的文本"中所阐明的教育逻辑的注释,即在了解了教育的逻辑之后，进一步强调遵循事物发展次序的重要性。所以，它首先指出了"本末"和"终始"的关系。"物有本末，事有终始"一句中，"本末"译为"causes and effects"，"因果"。"终始"译为"actions and consequences"，也是指原因和结果。其中，"物"译为"physical nature"，指自然界。"事"译为"human affairs"，指人类事务。指不管自然界还是人类社会，万事都存在它的原因和结果。

"知所先后，则近道矣"一句中，"先后"译为"he must first attend to the one before he can deal with the other"，"他必须首先致力于一件事，然后才能处理其他的事"。"道"译为"the truth"，"真理"。在指出世界万物都存在"因果"之后，这一段强调了在做事上应该考虑做事的先后。

"壹是皆以修身为本"译为"the one thing that all must do is to make the ordering of their conversation aright, the foundation for everything"，"拥有恰当的谈吐，这是所有事情的基础"。这一句进而指出对于芸芸大众来讲，什么才是最先应该做的，那就是"修身"，这是"本"（基础）。换言之，在"修身"的基础之上，有这样的"因"，才会达成"齐家""治国""平天下"这些"果"。

下文"听讼"一段讲的则是何谓"致知"中的"知"。

文中首先列举了孔子对于"诉讼"的一段话："听讼，吾犹人也，必也使无讼乎！"其中，"听讼"译为"deciding lawsuits"，"裁决诉讼"。"使无讼"译为"make lawsuits impossible"，"使诉讼变得不可能"。紧接着的"无情者不得尽其辞"译为"men who come before me without a just cause have nothing to say for themselves"，"来到我面前的人，如果没有正当理由，他将变得无话可说"。"无情"即"没有正当理由"，"不得尽其辞"指无话可说。指除非有正当理由，否则无法提起诉讼。这显示了孔子对于"诉讼"的敬畏之心。

接下来，文章指出要"大畏民志"，译为"watch therefore with fear and trembling over the hearts of the people"，"以敬畏与忐忑之心看待人民的意志"。"知本"译为"the root of the matter in knowledge"，"知识的本质"。"此谓知之至也"一句中，"知之至"译为"the highest knowledge"，"最高的知识"。即，所谓"知识"，其本质与最高状态即在于对人民的敬畏。

五

本段是对"诚其意"的诠释。

"诚其意"，与前文一样，辜鸿铭在翻译中强调"true ideas"，即拥有"真实的思想"。就像在前文中所指出的，所谓"真实的思想"，主要是人对自我与人世间的真实认知。

在此段中，辜鸿铭再次强调了这一含义。

"恶恶臭，好好色"译为"hates a bad smell or loves what is beautiful"，"厌恶臭味而喜爱美丽的事物"，即反映了一种最为自然、天然的状态。"自谦"译为"self-detachment"，"自我超脱"。辜鸿铭在此注释说："为了拥有真实的自我，马修·阿诺德说，你必须'按目标的本来面目，审视它'，并且为了能做到如此，'你必须放空自己'。也是指真实地面对自己，拥有真实的自我。"

然而，要达到这种境界并非易事，它会受到隐秘思想的干扰。因此，文中指出"君子必慎其独"，"慎其独"译为"watches diligently over his secret thought"，"孜孜不倦地审视他隐秘的念头"。意思是，因为要做真实的自我，所以，应该时刻审视内心产生了哪些干扰的因素。

而"小人"则往往做不到"慎独"。"小人闲居为不善"一句中，"小人"译为"an immoral man"，"不道德的人"。"闲居"译为"alone"，指独处的时候。"不善"译为"evil"，"邪恶的事，坏事"。后面，"厌然"译为"disguises himself"，"伪装自己"。"揜其不善，而著其善"译为"conceals what is evil and shows off what is good within him"，"隐瞒他内心的邪恶而卖弄他好的一面"。这说明了不道德的人面对"自我"时是不真实的。

但这样的伪装并不能成功，也就是下文所说的，"人之视己，如见其肺肝然"，"诚于中，形于外"。前一句译为"men see through us as though our hearts and reins lay open to them"，"人们已经看穿了我们，仿佛我们的心脏和肺腑就暴露在他们面前"。后一句译为"what is truly within will surely show without"，"真实的内在必然会显露于外"。都是指隐瞒和伪装是徒劳的。

曾子一句中"其严乎"的"严"，译为"awful"，糟糕、可怕之意。指人如果不面对真实的自我而选择伪装，其实恰如赤裸裸地被人看，被人指，是很可怕的。

"富润屋，德润身"的"润"字，译为"embellish"，修饰之意。"心广体胖"的"广"，译为"free and easy"，指心灵自由与轻松的状态。而只有做到"真实"，才能达到这种"自由"的状态。

六

本段讲的是"修身"首先取决于"正心"。"修身"，正如辜鸿铭在本书中的翻译，指一个人拥有恰当的谈吐，"正心"指一个人的心灵处于恰当而有序的状态。

"身有所忿懥，则不得其正；有所恐惧，则不得其正；有所好乐，则不得其正；有所忧患，则不得其正"一段中，"忿懥"译为"under the influence of passion"，"被情欲所左右"。"恐惧"译为"under the influence of fear and terror"，"处于害怕与恐惧中"。"好乐"

译为"under the influence of pleasure and amusement","沉浸于愉快与娱乐之中"。"忧患"译为"under the influence of sorrow and distress","深陷悲伤与痛苦之中"。即,在这四种心灵状态下,是无法"正心"的,即心灵无法达到恰当而有序的状态。

这一段所表达的含义与《中庸》"喜怒哀乐之未发,谓之中"是相同的,那一句辜鸿铭译为"when the passions, such as joy, anger, grief and pleasure, have not awakened, that is our true self(中)or moral being","当诸如喜悦、愤怒、悲伤与快乐等激情尚未唤起时,就是我们真实的自我(中)或道德本性"。其中,辜鸿铭把"中"同样译为"真实的自我",也就是此处所说的"正心"。

"心不在焉,视而不见,听而不闻,食而不知其味"一句是对上述道理的形象化比喻。其中,"心不在焉"译为"the mind is absent","当心灵是茫然的",也即处于上述四种状态时。

七

本段讲的是"齐其家"取决于"修其身"。

文中"人之其所亲爱而辟焉,之其所贱恶而辟焉,之其所畏敬而辟焉,之其所哀矜而辟焉,之其所敖惰而辟焉"一句中,"辟"译为"biassed towards",有偏向之意。即,文中列举了人们对五种人的态度往往是不真实的,分别是"所亲爱"、"所贱恶"、"所畏敬"、"所哀矜"、"所敖惰"。辜鸿铭漏掉了对"所畏敬"的翻译,剩下四种分别译为"for whom they feel love and affection","他们所热爱与喜爱的人"(所亲爱);"of whom they despise and dislike","他们所鄙视与厌恶的人"(所贱恶);"for whom they feel pity and compassion","他们所怜悯与同情的人"(所哀矜);"towards whom they feel arrogance and pride","那些会让他们感到傲慢与自大的人"(所敖惰)。

因为人们拥有这五种"偏向",所以,很难会做到"好而知其恶,恶而知其美"。此句译为"who love and yet know the bad qualities of those whom they love; who hate and yet know the good qualities of those whom they hate",即"热爱他们所爱的人,但同时也知道他们坏的品质;憎恨那些他们所憎恨的人,然而却也知道他们好的品质"。也就是说,能够不受主观情绪的影响而对人有真实的认识,这样就是"修身"。后面列举的谚语是表达同一个意思。

八

本段讲了"治国"如何首先取决于"齐家",即一个国家的统治如何取决于家族拥有秩序，而家族的秩序又往往取决于个人。从个人到国家，具有一以贯之的伦理关系，文中从"其家不可教"至"未有学养子而后嫁者也"即对这一伦理的阐释。

"其家不可教而能教人者，无之"译为"He who cannot teach the members of his own family to be good, can never teach other people to be good"，"他如果不能教育他自己的家人向善，就不可能教其他人向善"。

"君子不出家而成教于国"译为"the moral man, without going out of his house, can learn the duties which he owes to the State"，"一个有德之人即使不出家门，他依然能够学习他对于国家的义务"。"成教于国"指在家中学习对于国家的义务。当然，这种学习不是理论上的学习，而是在生活中掌握。那么，下面三句话就是其原则："孝者，所以事君也；弟者，所以事长也；慈者，所以使众也"，译为"The duties of a good son will teach him how to serve his Sovereign. The duties of subordination in the family will teach him to respect authority. The kindness of a father to his children will teach him how to treat the multitude"，"作为一个孝子的义务会教给他如何为他的君王服务。在家族中顺从的义务会教给他如何去尊重权威。父亲对孩子们的慈爱，会教给他如何对待人民大众"。做得了"孝""弟""慈"，也就能够使家族拥有秩序，并从中学到如何对待"君""长""众"，即扩展到整个国家社会。

"如保赤子"一句，辜鸿铭译为"watch over the people as a mother watches over her new born child"，"照看人民就如一位母亲照料她刚出生的孩子"。其中，"保"为照看、照料之意。"赤子"即刚出生的孩子。"心诚求之"译为"a mother who seeks with her whole heart the good of her child"，"一位母亲全身心地寻求如何善待孩子"。"虽不中不远矣"译为"although she makes mistakes, will never go wholly wrong"，"尽管她会犯错，但不会完全地错"。这句话是说，在对待人民时，应该悉心照料，并勇于尝试，不怕失误。

接下来，"一家仁，一国兴仁；一家让，一国兴让；一人贪戾，一国作乱"一句则说明了，在上述伦理之中，个人的道德品行对于整个国家的影响。"仁"译为"kindness and humanity"，即拥有"仁慈与人道"；"让"译为"courtesy and politeness"，拥有"礼节与文雅"；"贪戾"译为"ambition and perversity"，"野心与乖僻"；"作乱"译为"bring to confusion and anarchy"，"导致混乱与无序"。"其机如此"的"机"译为"the power of influence"，指以上家族与个人对整个国家的感染。"一言偾事"译为"one word can ruin everything"，"一句话能毁掉一切"。"一人定国"译为"one man can save a nation"，"一个人能拯救国家"。

"尧舜帅天下以仁，而民从之；桀纣帅天下以暴，而民从之"一句，则举例说明了统治者个人品德对人民的影响，并说明了"君子有诸己而后求诸人，无诸己而后非诸人"的道理，辜鸿铭译为"before requiring any moral quality of the people, the ruler must himself have that moral quality; before condemning any vice in the people, he must himself be free of that vice", "在对人民的道德品格做出任何要求之前,统治者自身必须拥有那种道德品格;在谴责人民拥有某种恶习之前,他自身必须免于那种恶习"。这表现了统治者应以身作则的原则。

下文引用了《诗经》里的三首诗,进一步阐述"治国"取决于"齐家"的道理。

"桃之夭夭,其叶蓁蓁;之子于归,宜其家人"一句中,"桃"译为"the peach tree","桃树"。"夭夭"译为"tender and fair","柔而美"。"蓁蓁"译为"in bloom","亮而翠"。"之子于归"译为"The girl is going to her new home","女孩赴新家",指出嫁。"宜其家人"译为"She will rightly order her household","家人受教化",即她将给她的家人带来秩序。

"宜兄宜弟"译为"Do your duty to your elder brothers, / Do your duty to your younger brothers","为你长兄尽责,/为你幼弟尽责"。其中,"宜"为尽义务、尽责任之意。

"其仪不忒,正是四国"译为"His manners were without reproach. / He therefore brought the whole nation to order","他仪态雅致免于责辱,/带来秩序给国家民族"。其中,"仪"指仪态、态度。"不忒"指不被指责、免于受辱。"正是四国"指给整个国家带来秩序。

"其为父子兄弟足法,而后民法之也"一句中,"足法"译为"to be to his people a model","为他的人民做榜样"。"民法之"指人民以之为榜样。强调的是统治者个人的道德品格对人民的影响。

九

本段讲的是"平天下"取决于"治其国",也即整个世界的和平与秩序取决于每个国家的良好统治。具体到如何"治其国",根据辜鸿铭的翻译,本文重点讲述了以下六个方面,概括如下:1."絜矩之道"——每个个人尤其是治国者的行为准则;2.治国者要做"民之父母";3."德"与"财"的关系;4."善"的问题;5."臣"的问题——任用何种人才治国;6.治国的"义"与"利"的问题。

分别来看:

"絜矩之道",辜鸿铭译为"self-measuring rule","自我衡量的准则"。文章首先指出,"上老老而民兴孝,上长长而民兴弟,上恤孤而民不倍",这是治国者对"民"的直接影响,指拥有权力的人通过自己的行为而做出示范,以及民众会产生的效应。

其中,"上老老"译为"those in authority honour old age","当权者尊敬老人"。"长长"译为"respect and obey their superiors","尊重并服从他们的上级"。"恤孤"译为

"take care of the poor and helpless"，"悉心照顾贫穷与无助的人"。"弟"译为"become good citizens"，"成为优秀的公民"。"倍"译为"neglect"，"疏远"。

文章认为，如果治国者尊敬老人、服从上级、照顾贫弱，那么，人民就会在家变得孝顺、在外成为好的公民，并亲近治国者。那么，治国者如何才能达到这样的状态呢？那就是遵循"絜矩之道"。文中的解释就是"所恶于上，毋以使下；所恶于下，毋以事上；所恶于前，毋以先后；所恶于后，毋以从前；所恶于右，毋以交于左；所恶于左，毋以交于右"。

其中，"恶"译为"hates in the conduct of"，指"憎恨某人的行为"。在整个一段中，"恶"都是指憎恨之意。"上"译为"those who are above him"，指上级。"下"译为"those who are under him"，"下级"。"使"译为"show it in his treatment"，指像对待上级那样对待下级。

"前"译为"those who go before him"，"先行者"。"后"译为"those who come after him"，"后来者"。"从"译为"be the first to show in dealing with"，指用同样的方式对待后来者。

"右"译为"on the right hand of him"，"右边的人"。"左"译为"on the left hand of him"，"左边的人"。"交"译为"show in dealing with"，指用同样的方式对待。

即，在上下级之间以及对待前后左右的人，你都应该避免对任何人做出你本来所厌恶的行为。

接下来是谈治国者要做"民之父母"。文章引用《诗经》的诗句"乐只君子，民之父母"，辜鸿铭译为"how the people love the prince who is a father and a mother to the people"，指"君主对民如父母，人民多么热爱他"。文章又进一步说"民之所好好之；民之所恶恶之。此之谓民之父母"。

而对于统治者而言，文章又进一步指出，"辟则为天下僇矣"，译为"the least mistake on their part will have awful consequences to the world"，即"就他们而言，最小的错误都会给世间带来可怕的后果"。指统治者自身的道德言行意义重大，稍有不慎即会引发灾难。并引用了《诗经》中的诗句予以说明："节彼南山，维石岩岩；赫赫师尹，民具尔瞻。"译为"Lofty like the southern hill, /With its rugged mass of rocks; /Awful you are, my lord of Yin, /The people all look up to you"，直译就是：像南山般高耸，山上布满崎岖的岩石，师尹多么可畏，人民全都仰望他。其中，"节"为高耸之意，"岩岩"为崎岖之意，"赫赫"为可畏之意，"瞻"为仰望之意。

然后，就是应赢得"民心"的问题。文章举例《诗经》的诗句："殷之未丧师，克配上帝；仪监于殷，峻命不易。"译为"Before the Yin rulers had lost the hearts of the people, / They found favour in the sight of God; / Take warning then from the House of Yin, / The

58

great High Mission is not easy to hold",直译就是:在殷朝还未丧失民心之前,上帝赐予他们恩惠,那么,吸取殷朝的教训,要想守住伟大的使命并非易事。其中,"丧师"为丧失民心之意,"克配上帝"指上帝赐予他们恩惠,"峻命不易"指守住上帝伟大的使命不易,这里说明了赢得"民心"是至关重要的。

对于治国来讲,财政是个重要方面,然而,文章认为应该认清它与"德"的关系。文章指出,"君子"应"先慎乎德"。这里的"君子"译为"the ruler"指统治者。"慎乎德"译为"he has the moral qualities",指拥有道德品格。然后又论证说:"有德此有人,有人此有土,有土此有财,有财此有用。"译为"Who has the moral qualities, has the people; who has the people, has the land; who has the land, has the revenue; who has the revenue, has the power to use it","拥有了道德品格,就拥有了人民;拥有了人民,就拥有了土地;拥有了土地,就拥有了收益;拥有了收益,就拥有了使用它的权力"。其中,"人"指人民,"土"指土地,"财"指财政收入,"用"指支配财政收入的权力。

这是说明,"德"比"财"更为优先,也更为重要。所以,下文接着说"德者本也,财者末也",译为"Moral qualities are the foundation of a nation. Wealth is but the means","道德品格是一国之基础,财富只是手段"。其中,"本"指一个国家的基础、根本,"末"指手段、方法。"外本内末,争民施夺"译为"When the ruler mistakes the end for the means and the means for the end, the result will be rapine and scrambling for wealth among the people","当统治者错把目的当作手段,而把手段当作目的,结果就是,人民很快就会陷入财富的争抢"。

进而,文章由"财"的得失,指出了"善"的重要性。文章中说:"言悖而出者,亦悖而入;货悖而入者,亦悖而出。"其中,"悖",辜鸿铭译为"in violence"或"with violence"或"by violence",都指使用暴力之意。这是反对暴力的含义。

文章又引用了《康诰》的句子,"惟命不于常",译为"the Divine Mission is not given us for ever","神圣使命并不会永远赐予我们"。其中,"命"指"上帝"的神圣使命,"常"指"永远赐予我们"。意思就是下文所说的"道善则得之,不善则失之",译为"if we are good, we shall win it; if we are not good, we shall lose it",即"如果我们是善的,就会赢得它;如果不善,就会失去它"。强调"善"的重要,指只有"善"才能赢得"命",即上帝的神圣使命。后文中《楚书》的句子仍是强调这一含义。

接下来,话题转到"臣"的问题上,即应选用何样的人来治国这一问题上。文章引用《秦誓》一段话,强调治国应由有德之人。文中,"断断兮无他技,其心休休焉"译为"a plain and simple man who has absolutely no other qualification except a free and open mind and a broad and tolerant spirit","一个朴实而单纯的人,他除了拥有自由和开放的心灵以及广博而宽容的精神,并无其他长处"。其中,"断断"译为"plain and simple",

"朴实而单纯"。"其心休休焉"译为"a free and open mind and a broad and tolerant spirit"，指拥有"自由和开放的心灵以及广博而宽容的精神"。这样一个人，才能"保我子孙黎民"。而对于与此相反的人，则"不能保我子孙黎民"，并且对于这样的人，文中强调，"唯仁人放流之，迸诸四夷，不与同中国"。同时，文章又强调"唯仁人为能爱人，能恶人"，"It is only the truly good and moral man who can love or hate others"，"只有真实与有道德的人才能爱憎他人"。指要选"仁人"为臣治国。

下文则指出在相反的情况下会导致"灾必逮夫身"。"见贤而不能举，举而不能先"一句中，"举"译为"raise them to office"，指晋升他们。"不能先"译为"keep them in a subordinate position under you"，"把他们放在从属于你的位置"。"命也"译为"这是显而易见的失职"。"见不善而不能退，退而不能远"一句中，"退"译为"remove them"，指开除掉。"过也"译为"that is weakness"，"这就是软弱"。

"好人之所恶，恶人之所好，是谓拂人之性，灾必逮夫身"一句强调了在"好恶"上应与人民大众保持一致。否则就是"拂人之性"，译为"outrage the natural feeling of men"，"违背了人们的自然情感"。

下文进而把论述延伸到普通人的生活中。"君子有大道"译为"in life there is one great law for a gentleman"，"对于绅士来说，在生活中有一条重大的法则"。"必忠信以得之，骄泰以失之"，译为"If faithful and trustworthy, he is sure to succeed; if proud and careless, he is sure to fail"，"若忠诚可靠，他必将成功；若傲慢冷漠，他必将遭败"。

最后，文章落到"义"和"利"的关系上，并谈到在"义"和"利"的问题上，不同的人治国会导致不同的结果。

文章首先指出，"生财有大道"，辜鸿铭译为"in the production of wealth there is one great law"，"在财富的创造中，也存在一条重要的法则"。"道"也指一种原则、规律。下面"生之者众，食之者寡，为之者疾，用之者舒，则财恒足矣"一句阐明了这样的一种规律。

但文章立刻再次强调"仁"与"财"存在主次关系。"仁者以财发身，不仁者以身发财"译为"Moral men make money to live. Immoral men live to make money"，"有道德的人为了生活而去挣钱。不道德的人生就是为了挣钱"。还是强调"道德"应占主导与优先的地位，并且接下来一句强调"上好仁"而带来"下好义"。如此这般，则"未有府库财非其财者也"，指对仁的热爱，必然换来统治者对一国之财富的拥有。

因此，在下文引用了孟献子的话之后，文章强调"国不以利为利，以义为利也"，辜鸿铭译为"what really makes a nation prosperous is not wealth and material prosperity, but honour and duty"，"真正使一个国家繁荣的，并非财富与物质的成功，而是荣誉与责任"。

而最后一段则在于解释在治国理政中，如何才算"国不以利为利，以义为利"。文中，"长国家而务财用者，必自小人矣"译为"When a ruler who wishes to make his nation prosperous and great, devotes his attention only to questions of finance and revenue, he is surely under the influence of some base and ignoble person"，"如果一个统治者试图让他的国家繁荣而伟大，但他仅仅专注于金融与财政方面的问题，他必然是受到了一些卑鄙可耻之徒的影响"。其中，"长"译为"to make his nation prosperous and great"，指使国家繁荣伟大。"务财用"译为"devotes his attention only to questions of finance and revenue"，"仅仅专注于金融与财政方面的问题"。"自小人"译为"under the influence of some base and ignoble person"，"受到了一些卑鄙可耻之徒的影响"。

"彼为善之，小人之使为国家，灾害并至，虽有善者，亦无如之何矣"一句译为"When such a base and ignoble person directs the affairs of a nation, even though he be a man of ability, calamities and disaster will follow, and then even a good man who comes after him, will be able to do nothing"，"一旦如此卑鄙可耻之徒管理国家事务，哪怕他是个有能力的人，不幸和灾祸也将随之而至，在这之后，即使继承他的是一个良善的人，也将无能为力"。其中，"彼为善之"指在道德上卑鄙可耻的人尽管可能有实干能力，但这样的人一旦决定国家政策，则会导致灾害并至。"虽有善者，亦无如之何矣"译为"then even a good man who comes after him, will be able to do nothing"，"即使继承他的是一个良善的人，也将无能为力"。意思是，若舍弃道德而治理国家，只专注于金融和财政，终将毁掉国家。

至此，文章充分地论述了"治国"应该坚持"德""善""仁""义"为优先的治理原则，其次才是"财"与"利"。

附录 《四书章句集注·大学》[①]

　　大学之道，在明明德，在亲民，在止于至善。知止而后有定，定而后能静，静而后能安，安而后能虑，虑而后能得。物有本末，事有终始，知所先后，则近道矣。古之欲明明德于天下者，先治其国；欲治其国者，先齐其家；欲齐其家者，先修其身；欲修其身者，先正其心；欲正其心者，先诚其意；欲诚其意者，先致其知；致知在格物。物格而后知至，知至而后意诚，意诚而后心正，心正而后身修，身修而后家齐，家齐而后国治，国治而后天下平。自天子以至于庶人，壹是皆以修身为本。其本乱而末治者否矣，其所厚者薄，而其所薄者厚，未之有也！

　　《康诰》曰："克明德。"《大甲》曰："顾諟天之明命。"《帝典》曰："克明峻德。"皆自明也。

　　汤之《盘铭》曰："苟日新，日日新，又日新。"《康诰》曰："作新民。"《诗》曰："周虽旧邦，其命惟新。"是故君子无所不用其极。

　　《诗》云："邦畿千里，惟民所止。"《诗》云："缗蛮黄鸟，止于丘隅。"子曰："於止，知其所止，可以人而不如鸟乎！"《诗》云：

[①]　鉴于辜鸿铭在英译《大学》时几乎彻底打乱了《大学》原文的顺序，故附《四书章句集注》中《大学》的正文（朱熹撰，《四书章句集注》，中华书局，1983）。

"穆穆文王，於缉熙敬止！"为人君，止于仁；为人臣，止于敬；为人子，止于孝；为人父，止于慈；与国人交，止于信。《诗》云："瞻彼淇澳，菉竹猗猗。有斐君子，如切如磋，如琢如磨。瑟兮僩兮，赫兮喧兮。有斐君子，终不可喧兮！"如切如磋者，道学也；如琢如磨者，自修也；瑟兮僩兮者，恂栗也；赫兮喧兮者，威仪也；有斐君子，终不可喧兮者，道盛德至善，民之不能忘也。《诗》云："於戏，前王不忘！"君子贤其贤而亲其亲，小人乐其乐而利其利，此以没世不忘也。

子曰："听讼，吾犹人也，必也使无讼乎！"无情者不得尽其辞。大畏民志，此谓知本。

此谓知本，此谓知之至也。

所谓诚其意者：毋自欺也，如恶恶臭，如好好色，此之谓自谦，故君子必慎其独也！小人闲居为不善，无所不至，见君子而后厌然，揜其不善，而著其善。人之视己，如见其肺肝然，则何益矣。此谓诚于中，形于外，故君子必慎其独也。曾子曰："十目所视，十手所指，其严乎！"富润屋，德润身，心广体胖，故君子必诚其意。

所谓修身在正其心者，身有所忿懥，则不得其正；有所恐惧，则不得其正；有所好乐，则不得其正；有所忧患，则不得其正。心不在焉，视而不见，听而不闻，食而不知其味。此谓修身在正其心。

所谓齐其家在修其身者：人之其所亲爱而辟焉，之其所贱恶而辟焉，之其所畏敬而辟焉，之其所哀矜而辟焉，之其所敖惰而辟焉。故好而知其恶，恶而知其美者，天下鲜矣！故谚有之曰："人莫知其子之恶，莫知其苗之硕。"此谓身不修不可以齐其家。

所谓治国必先齐其家者，其家不可教而能教人者，无之。故君子不出家而成教于国：孝者，所以事君也；弟者，所以事长也；慈者，所以使众也。《康诰》曰"如保赤子"，心诚求之，虽不中不远矣。未有学养子而后嫁者也！一家仁，一国兴仁；一家让，一国兴让；一人贪戾，一国作乱；其机如此。此谓一言偾事，一人定国。尧舜帅天下以仁，而民从之；桀纣帅天下以暴，而民从之；其所令反其所好，而民不从。是故君子有诸己而后求诸人，无诸己而后非诸人。所藏乎身不恕，而能喻诸人者，未之有也。故治国在齐其家。《诗》云："桃之夭夭，其叶蓁蓁；之子于归，宜其家人。"宜其家人，而后可以教国人。《诗》云："宜兄宜弟。"宜兄宜弟，而后可以教国人。《诗》云："其仪不忒，正是四国。"其为父子兄弟足法，而后民法之也。此谓治国在齐其家。

所谓平天下在治其国者：上老老而民兴孝，上长长而民兴弟，上恤孤而民不倍，是以君子有絜矩之道也。所恶于上，毋以使下；所恶于下，毋以事上；所恶于前，毋以先后；所恶于后，毋以从前；所恶于右，毋以交于左；所恶于左，毋以交于右：此之谓絜矩之道。《诗》云："乐只君子，民之父母。"民之所好好之，民之所恶恶之，此之谓民之父母。《诗》云："节彼南山，维石岩岩；赫赫师尹，民具尔瞻。"有国者不可以不慎，辟则为天下僇矣。《诗》云："殷之未丧师，克配上帝；仪监于殷，峻命不易。"道得众则得国，失众则失国。是故君子先慎乎德。有德此有人，有人此有土，有土此有财，有财此有用。德者本也，财者末也，外本内末，争民施夺。是故财聚则民散，财散则民聚。是故言悖而出者，亦悖而入；货悖而入者，亦悖而出。《康诰》曰："惟命不于常！"道善则得之，不善则失之矣。《楚书》曰："楚国无以为宝，惟善以为宝。"舅犯曰："亡人无以为宝，仁亲以为宝。"《秦誓》曰："若有一个臣，断断兮无他技，其心休休焉，其如有容焉。人之有技，若己有之，人之彦圣，其心好之，不啻若自其口出，寔能容之，以能保我子孙黎民，尚亦有利哉。人之有技，媢疾以恶之，人之彦圣，而违之俾不通，寔不能容，以不能保我子孙黎民，亦曰殆哉。"唯仁人放流之，迸诸四夷，不与同中国。此谓唯仁人为能爱人，能恶人。见贤而不能举，举而不能先，命也；见不善而不能退，退而不能远，过也。好人之所恶，恶人之所好，是谓拂人之性，灾必逮夫身。是故君子有大道，必忠信以得之，骄泰以失之。生财有大道，生之者众，食之者寡，为之者疾，用之者舒，则财恒足矣。仁者以财发身，不仁者以身发财。未有上好仁而下不好义者也，未有好义其事不终者也，未有府库财非其财者也。孟献子曰："畜马乘不察于鸡豚，伐冰之家不畜牛羊，百乘之家不畜聚敛之臣，与其有聚敛之臣，宁有盗臣。"此谓国不以利为利，以义为利也。长国家而务财用者，必自小人矣。彼为善之，小人之使为国家，菑害并至。虽有善者，亦无如之何矣！此谓国不以利为利，以义为利也。

THE UNIVERSAL ORDER

OR

CONDUCT OF LIFE

中　庸[①]

PREFACE

THE present volume is a translation of one of the four Confucian canonical books called the *Chung Yung*, which has been translated by Dr. Legge as the "Doctrine of the Mean". The Chinese word *Chung* means central, — hence right, true, fair and square; and *Yung* means common, ordinary, — hence universal. The two Chinese words therefore mean the true, fair and square universal standard of right; in short, the common sense of right.

This book, together with another book translated by Dr. Legge as the "Great Learning " or, as it should be properly translated, "Higher Education" — these two books form what may be called the Catechism of the Confucian teaching. It was my intention to publish these two books together. But I have not been able to bring my translation of the other book into a shape to satisfy the standard which I aim at in my translation. My aim in translation, after I have thoroughly mastered the meaning, is not only to reproduce the *matter*, but also the *manner* of the original. For, as Wordsworth says of all literature of really intrinsic value, — "to be sure, it is the manner, but the matter always comes out of the manner." But to be able to reproduce the manner, what in literature is called the *style*, of the great and wise men of the past, one must try to put oneself in the same state of temper and mind in which they were, — a thing one finds not easy to attain, living in this modern world of the "civilisation of progress."

Most people now believe that the old order of things in China is passing away and they hail the coming era of the new learning and of

序　言

本书是对儒家"四书"之一《中庸》的翻译,理雅各博士(Dr. Legge)将它译为"中的学说"(Doctrine of the Mean)。中文的"中"字意思是中间,指正确、真实、公正、公平;"庸"字意思是普通、平常,指普遍之意。因此,这两个汉字的意思,就是对于正确的真实、公正而且公平的普遍标准;概言之,就是关于正确的常识。

这本书与被理雅各博士译为"伟大的学问"或应被恰当地译为"高等教育"的另一本书①一起,可以称为儒家学说手册。我原本想把两本书放在一起出版,但我还没法让另一本书的译文达到让我满意的标准。我做翻译的目标是,当我完全弄懂它的意思之后,不仅仅要再现它的内容②本身,而且要展现它原本的风格。正如华兹华斯所说的,所有文学价值的真实本质在于:"确实,它仅仅是风格,但内容往往产生于风格。"但为了能再现过去伟大而明智的人的风格——在文学上被称为文风——作为译者,你必须把自己置于与他们在性情与思想上相同的状态,一种对于生活在当代"进步文明"世界的人来讲,并不容易达到的状态。

如今,大多数人相信,中国的旧秩序正在渐渐逝去,他们为正在到来的新学时代,以及这个国家的文明的进步而欢呼。但以我

---

① 指《大学》,理雅各译为 "Great Learning" , 即 "伟大的学问"。而辜鸿铭则主张应译为 "Higher Education" , 即 "高等教育"。

② 此处原文辜鸿铭设为斜体,下同。

the civilisation of progress into this country. I for one do not believe that the old order of things in China can pass away. The reason is because I know that the old order of things, the Chinese civilisation and Chinese social order, is a moral civilisation and a true social order; and being that, it cannot, in the nature of things, pass away.

But people will say to me what do you mean by "moral" and "immoral"? Indeed speaking one day with an educated foreigner on the comparative morality of Chinese and foreigners in Shanghai, my foreign friend said that it depended altogether upon the "point of view". In order therefore that there may be no misunderstanding arising from the "point of view", let us here take an action which will be regarded by Chinese and foreigners alike as a moral action and analyse it to see what it is that constitutes its morality?

In 1853, when the Taiping rebels captured the native city of Shanghai, troubles arose between the Imperial Chinese authorities and foreigners, in consequence of which the foreign Consuls seized the Shanghai Custom-house. But when the troubles were over, the foreign Consuls not only handed back to the Chinese all the money they had collected as duties, but rendered an exact account for every cent they had collected. A Chinese literati living then in Hunan, who afterwards rose to be the great Marquis *Tseng Kuo-fan*, when he heard of this last action of the foreign Consuls in Shanghai, wrote to a friend saying: "They (these foreigners) too really can act or conduct themselves like moral men (彼亦有君子之行)." (君子之行 mean moral conduct, and 君子之道 translated by Dr. Legge as "the way of the superior man", mean moral law, same as 道 the law.)

Now what is the principle in the action of the foreign Consuls which

的观点,我并不相信中国的旧秩序将会逝去。原因就是,事物旧有的秩序、中国文明以及中国的社会秩序,是一种道德文明和一种真实的社会秩序。正因如此,从事物的本性上来说,旧秩序不会逝去。

但人们会问我,你所谓的"道德"和"不道德"是什么意思呢? 确实,有一次,我跟一位受过教育的外国朋友在上海聊天,不管从中国还是外国的角度,他都可以称为有道德的人。我的外国朋友说,道德和不道德的意思完全取决于你的"观点"如何。那么,为了不对"观点"产生可能的误解,在此,让我们看一下,哪种行为会被中国人和外国人视为道德的,再分析一下,看看什么东西构成了道德。

1853年,当太平天国的叛乱者占领上海时,中华帝国当局与外国人之间产生了纷争,结果,外国领事们占领了上海海关。但当纷争平息之后,外国领事们不仅归还了他们义务征收到的所有关税,而且提供了一个精确到每一分的统计。那时湖南的一位文人,即后来伟大的曾国藩侯爵,在听说了外国领事们在上海的行为后,给一个朋友写信说:"他们(那些外国人)确实能像有道德的人那样行为处事。"(彼亦有君子之行)("君子之行"的意思是有道德的行为,而被理雅各博士译为"上等人之道"的"君子之道"意思是道德法则,道就是法则。)

那么,被曾国藩侯爵视为构成道德或道德行为的、外国领事们行为的原则,到底是什么呢? 是这样的。外国领事们之所以归还

the Marquis Tseng Kuo-fan recognised at once as constituting morality or moral conduct? It is this. The foreign Consuls restored the money, not because there was any outside force to compel them to do it, nor because by doing it they would get any profit or benefit in any shape from it; they did it because it was right to do it, and because it would be wrong not to do it, from the sense of right and wrong, the sense of moral obligation. A moral action is therefore to do as a free agent what is right, from the pure and simple sense of moral obligation, and morality is the recognition of and obedience to this sense of moral obligation.

Now it is this sense of moral obligation in human conduct that makes not only civilisation, but human society possible. Just think of a state of society where everybody disregards this sense of moral obligation in every relation of life. It is impossible to imagine that such a state of society could exist for one single hour or one single instant. Think on the other hand of a state of society where everybody acts solely and in perfect accordance with this sense of moral obligation. That would be a perfect society in which not only police but all government would be unnecessary.

I say therefore that the Chinese civilisation is a moral and true civilisation because, in the first place, it not only recognises this moral obligation as the fundamental basis of its social order, but it makes the perfect attainment of this sense of moral obligation in men its sole aim; consequently, in the social order, the method of education, the method of government, and all social appliances have for their aim and object to educate men to the sense of this moral obligation; and all those habits, tastes, modes, and pursuits of life alone are encouraged which are calculated to make it easy for men to obey the moral obligation. In short the ideal goal which Chinese civilisation sets

关税，并非因为有什么外力强迫他们如此，也不是因为他们会由此而获得什么利益和好处，他们之所以如此，是因为这样做是对的，而不这样做是错的，他们是在对与错的意义上、在道德义务的意义上来做的。因此，一个有道德的举动是因正确的动因而做出的，源自一种单纯、朴素的道德义务，而道德就是对这种道德义务的认知及服从。

正是人类行为中的这种道德义务感，使得不仅文明而且人类社会的存在，变得可能。试想一下，如果一个社会，每个人在生活的所有关联中都忽视这种道德义务感，难以想象，这样的社会状态能够存在哪怕一个小时，或者只是瞬间。想一想另一种社会状态，那里每个人都纯粹地并完全地与这种道德义务感保持一致，那将是一个完美的社会，不仅警察，甚至所有的政府都是没有必要的。

因此，我要说，中国文明是一种有道德的、真正的文明，首先，它不仅把这种道德义务感视为社会秩序的根本基础，而且，它把达到这种道德义务感的完美状态，作为人们的唯一目的。因而，在社会秩序中，教育方式、统治方式，以及所有的社会构成，都以培养人们拥有这种道德义务感为目标。而生活中备受鼓励的一切习惯、品味、风尚以及追求，都旨在让人们更易于遵从这种道德义务。简言之，中国文明为人类追求进步提供了理想的目标，它并非要限制每个人的快乐，即限制个人的嗜好和让每个人拥有愉快的时光，而是指"对人类真实的道德本性——义务感——以及道德秩序的认

before mankind towards which they are to progress forward, is not infinite happiness for everybody, which means infinite self-indulgence and having a good time for everybody, but the complete and perfect "realisation of true moral being — the sense of obligation — and moral order in mankind so that the Universe shall become a cosmos and all things can attain their full growth and development".

I am well aware how very far the Chinese as a nation and as individuals are at present from the realisation of the high ideal of their civilisation. But at the same time I think it right to say here that even now, looking upon the present demoralised state of things in China, the Chinese civilisation, if one would take the trouble to interpret and look into the inside of facts, — cannot be considered a failure. If you judge a civilisation by the standard to what extent men living under that civilisation, who have money, can enjoy themselves, can have a good time of it, then the Chinese civilisation is certainly a failure. But if you judge a civilisation by the standard of strength and effectiveness of the sense of moral obligation in the nation living under that civilisation, then I think I can show that the Chinese civilisation even now is not a failure, but, on the contrary, a wonderful success.

Now it is well known that in many parts of China at the present moment the greater portion of the population are living on the verge of starvation. It is also well known, or at least should be known, that the local authorities in China have no police, or any military force worth speaking of, to keep order. Nevertheless I think it can be shown that taking the same area and size of population in any of the worst parts of these famine stricken districts, there will be found there a smaller ratio of lawlessness, breaches of public order and crime than there is to be found, say in the

识的"完全与完美，"如此，宇宙将变成一个有序的整体，而万物能够实现充分的生长与发展"。

我非常清楚，中国人无论作为一个民族还是个人，目前距离实现他们最高的文明理想还多么遥远。但与此同时，我认为，即使看到中国目前令人沮丧的事态，如果你能不厌其烦地领会并深入考察事实的本质，中国文明并不能被视为失败。如果你通过人们在多大程度上拥有金钱、能娱乐自己并由此而获得愉快这样的标准来判断一个文明，那么，中国文明的确是失败的。但是，如果你通过一个国家的道德义务感的程度与效果这样的标准来衡量一个文明，那么，我觉得我能证明，中国文明不仅不是个失败，相反，它是一个非常美妙的成功。

此刻，在中国的许多地方，众多人口正生活在饥饿的边缘，这是众所周知的。而同时众所周知，或人们至少应该知道的是，中国的地方当局并没有值得一提的警察或任何军力来维持秩序。然而，就相同的范围和人口数量来说，拿这些灾区里任何一个灾难深重的地区，与富有和繁荣的上海外国租界来比，你将发现，那里违法乱纪、破坏公共秩序和犯罪的行为更少见，而上海外国租界每年的警力则都需花费五十万两白银。阿瑟·史密斯牧师说："儒教的答案就是中国。"我回答说：是的，儒教的答案就是中国，但我只想说，你必须从本质与道德的角度而非仅仅从电灯的角度来看中国。

实际上，如果需要更多的证据来证明我所说的中国文明是种

wealthy and prosperous foreign model settlement of Shanghai where there is a police force costing half a million taels a year. The Revd. Arthur Smith says: "The answer to Confucianism is China." I reply: Yes, the answer to Confucianism is China, only I say, you must look at China from the essential, moral side and not merely from the electric-light side.

Indeed if anything more is needed to prove what I have said that the Chinese civilisation is a wonderful success, this one other fact alone should prove it beyond any doubt or cavil: the fact, namely, that not withstanding the present demoralised state of the stricken condition of the people, the Chinese Government is still able to keep its public engagements with the foreign Powers for the disgraceful Boxer indemnity. For what force is this upon which the mandarins in China depend, to make each unit of these four hundred millions hungry people in China pay up for a debt with which they individually have had nothing to do? This force in China, it is well known, is not police or physical force. This force in China is the force of the highly developed law-abiding instinct of the Chinese people. Whence does it come —this highly developed law-abiding instinct of the Chinese people which is now standing so well the test under the strain of the present hard and difficult conditions? It comes from the strong sense of moral obligation in the Chinese people. But where do the Chinese people get this — their strong sense of moral obligation? The answer is: from the Chinese civilisation. I say therefore that the Chinese civilisation is a wonderful success.

In the following translation then will be found the enunciation and elucidation of the sense of moral obligation which forms the basis of human conduct and social order in human society in the scheme of the Chinese civilisation. There is of course no "new learning" in all this, but what is

美妙的成功，单单这一件事，就可以消除任何疑惑或吹毛求疵：尽管当前中国公共事务的状态令人沮丧，人民也在挨饿，中国政府还是能够遵守与外国列强就拳乱而签订的可耻的赔偿条约。中国的高级官员们依赖的是什么力量，使得四万万挨饿的中国人去偿还那个跟他们每一个个人都毫无关系的债务呢？中国的这种力量，众所周知，并非警察或武力。中国的这种力量，恰恰是中国人高度发达的守法本能。而中国人的这种在眼下如此艰难的条件下，却仍然能够保持得如此良好的、高度发达的守法本能，究竟从何而来呢？它来自于中国人的强烈的道德义务感。而中国人又是从哪里获得这种强烈的道德义务感的呢？答案就是，来自中国文明。因此，我说，中国文明是一个美妙的成功。

而在下面的这些译文中，你将找到对这种在中国文明框架下、构成了人类组织与社会秩序之基础的道德义务感之来源的阐明。当然，其中完全没有"新学"存在，而是有着更好的"真"学。这种对道德义务感的阐述，也会在每一个拥有文明的民族其最好的文学中，以不同形式找到，而最显著的是，正如我在对译文文本的附加说明①中所展现的，这本写于两千年之前的书里，以如此的形式与语言而进行的阐述，也可以在近期最优秀和伟大的欧洲思想家的作品中发现。而让这本书具有特殊价值的是——就我有限的知识而言，就我所知——在欧洲文学中，不管是古代还是现代，都没

---

① 指《中庸》的"附录"四篇。

better, there is *true* learning in it. The enunciation of the sense of moral obligation in some form or other is to be found in the best literature of every nation that has ever had a civilisation; and what is most remarkable, as I have shown in the notes I have appended to the translation of the text, the enunciation in the same form and language as it is in this book, written two thousand years ago, is to be found in the latest writings of the best and greatest thinkers of modern Europe. But what makes the peculiar merit of this book is this. As far as my limited knowledge goes, there is no book in all European literature, ancient or modern, that I know of, in which is to be found so simple, clear, to the point, succinct and at the same time so complete and comprehensive a statement of the sense of moral obligation or moral law as is to be found in this little book.

In conclusion, I wish to say here that if this little book from the old learning of China will peradventure contribute to help the people of Europe and America, especially those who are now in China, to a better understanding of the "moral law", to a clearer, and deeper sense of moral obligation, so that they will be enabled when dealing with China and the Chinese to substitute, for the spirit and attitude of the civilisation of the "gunboat" and "the mailed fist" of Europe, the moral law; in their every relation with the Chinese as individuals and as a nation, to respect and obey the sense of moral obligation then I shall feel that I have not spent in vain the labour of many years in understanding and translating this book.

Ku Hung-ming

有一本书像这本小书这样，对道德义务感或道德法则阐述得如此通俗、清晰、扼要、简明，而且同时又如此完整且综合。

作为结论，我在此想说，如果这本来自中国旧学的书能够偶然地帮助那些欧美人，特别是那些现在在中国的人，更好地理解"道德法则"，拥有更清楚、更深刻的道德义务感，以便他们在对待中国及中国人时，能用道德法则替代欧洲的"炮舰"与"暴力"文明的精神和态度；在与每个中国人及整个中华民族的各种关系中，去尊重并服从道德义务感——那么，我就会感到这么多年来我用于研究和翻译这本书的精力，没有白费。

辜鸿铭

I.
第一章①

<hr />

① 辜鸿铭英译《中庸》分章与朱熹《四书章句集注·中庸》分章大体一致,译者这里标以相对应的《四书章句》中《中庸》的章节编号。

The ordinance of God is what we call the law of our being（性①）. To fulfill the law of our being is what we call the moral law（道）. The moral law when reduced to a system is what we call religion（教）.

The moral law is a law from whose operation we cannot for one instant in our existence escape. A law from which we may escape is not the moral law. Wherefore it is that the moral man（君子）watches diligently over what his eyes cannot see and is in fear and awe of what his ears cannot hear.

［Modern Science, which is supposed to teach Materialism, on the contrary really teaches the existence, reality and inexorability of law, which is not material but something which the eyes cannot see and the ears cannot hear. It is because he knows and is impressed with the reality and inexorability of law that the moral man lives a spiritual life and thereby becomes a moral man.］②

There is nothing more evident than what cannot be seen by the eyes and nothing more palpable than what cannot be perceived by the senses. Wherefore the moral man watches diligently over his secret thoughts.

---

① 原文即为汉字,下同。
② 方括号中的文字,为辜鸿铭原书中对上面文字的解读,依辜鸿铭英译《中庸》的原书位置排印,下同。

天命之谓性，率性之谓道，修道之谓教。

道也者，不可须臾离也，可离非道也。是故君子戒慎乎其所不睹，恐惧乎其所不闻。

上帝的法令，就是我们所说的我们本性的法则（性）；服从我们本性的法则，就是我们所说的道德法则（道）；当道德法则被归纳成一个体系时，就是我们所说的宗教（教）。

道德法则是一种我们在生存中片刻也无法逃避其作用的法则。一种我们能够逃避的法则，就不是道德法则。因此，有道德的人会坚持不懈地审视他的眼睛所看不到的东西，并对他的耳朵所听不到的东西感到畏惧与敬畏。

［现代科学被假定为教人以唯物主义，实际上正相反，是教人以法则的存在、真实与严酷，这些不是物质，而是眼睛无法看见、耳朵无法听见的东西。正因为有道德的人懂得并深深地了解法则的真实与严酷，他才会过一种精神上的生活，从而成为一个有道德的人。］

莫见乎隐，莫显乎微，故君子慎其独也。

没有比用眼睛无法看见的东西更明显的，也没有比用感官无法感觉到的东西更明白的。因此，有道德的人坚持不懈地审视着他的隐秘的思想。

["Keep thy heart with all diligence, for out of it are the issues of life." — *Prov.* IV]

When the passions, such as joy, anger, grief and pleasure, have not awakened, that is our true self (中) or moral being. When these passions awaken and each and all attain due measure and degree, that is the moral order (和). Our true self or moral being is the great reality (大本 lit. great root) of existence, and moral order is the universal law (达道) in the world.

["our true self" — literally our central (中) inner self, or as Mr. Matthew Arnold calls it, "the central clue in our moral being which unites us to the universal order." Mr. Arnold also calls it our "permanent self". Hence, the text above says, it is the root of our being. Mr. Arnold says, "All the forces and tendencies in us are like our proper central moral tendency, in themselves beneficent, but they require to be harmonised with this central (moral) tendency." — *St.Paul and Protestantism*]

When true moral being and moral order are realised, the universe then becomes a cosmos and all things attain their full growth and development.

［"你要切切保守你心,因为一生的果效,是由心发出。"(箴4:23)^①］

喜怒哀乐之未发,谓之中;发而皆中节,谓之和。中也者,天下之大本也;和也者,天下之达道也。

当诸如喜悦、愤怒、悲伤与快乐等激情尚未唤起时,就是我们的真实自我(中)或道德本性。当这些激情被唤起并且它们都达到了恰当的标准与程度时,就是道德秩序(和)。我们的真正自我或道德本性就是存在的伟大的真实(大本,字面意思是伟大的根基),而道德秩序就是世界上的普遍的法则(达道)。

［"我们的真实自我"——字面意思是我们"中心的内在自我",或如马修·阿诺德先生所说的,"我们道德本性中把我们与普遍秩序相连的中心线索"。阿诺德先生也称之为"永恒的自我"。因此,上面这一段是说,这是我们本性的根基。阿诺德先生说:"我们内心所有的力量与趋向,就像我们恰当的中心道德趋向,它们本身是仁慈的,但它们需要与这个中心的(道德的)趋向相和谐。"——《圣保罗与新教》］

致中和,天地位焉,万物育焉。

当实现了真实的道德本性与道德秩序时,宇宙就会变成一个和谐统一的宇宙,而万物则会达到充分的生长与发展。

---

① 本书新旧约译文均摘自《圣经》(金边拇指索引),中国基督教三自爱国运动委员会、中国基督教协会出版发行,2008。

【评述】

　　本章为开篇第一章，交代了若干关键词。了解这些关键词的含义，是了解整部《中庸》主旨的基础。这些关键词包括：天命、性、道、教、君子、中、和。

　　首先，看"天命"一词。辜鸿铭译为"the ordinance of God"，"上帝的法令"。在此词中，关键词又在于"天"字，辜鸿铭翻译的是"God"，"神，上帝"，当然，也可以回译为"上天"。今天通常是将"天"译为"Heaven"，"上天，苍天"，大写"H"时也有"上帝"之意，但两者都不同于自然意义上的"sky"，而具有宗教意味。辜鸿铭只在《论语·子张第十九》中的第25节"陈子禽谓子贡"里将"天"译为"sky"，仅只一次。这句话是："子贡曰：'夫子之不可及也，犹天之不可阶而升也。'"辜鸿铭译为："Now Confucius cannot be equalled, just as no man can climb up to the sky." 因而，可以说，此处译"天"为"God"就使"天"具有了一种含有神秘色彩的超越自然的非凡意义。

　　其实，辜鸿铭对于"天命"与"上帝"概念的理解已有过自己的描述。他认为，"上帝"的存在毋庸置疑，然而与一般人所理解的"上帝"概念不同，它是"神圣的宇宙秩序"的代名词。他在《中国人的精神（在北京东方学会上所宣讲的论文）》中说："所有伟人，所有富有智慧的人们，通常都信仰上帝。孔子也信奉上帝，虽然他很少提及它。……然而，富于智慧的人们，其心中的上帝有别于常人。他们对上帝的信仰，就是斯宾诺莎所说的对神圣的宇宙秩序的信仰。孔子曾说过：'五十而知天命。'——懂得神圣的宇宙秩序。富于智慧的人们为这种宇宙秩序起了不同的名称。德国哲学家费希特称之神圣的宇宙观。在中国的哲学语言中，它被称之为'道'。但是无论被赋予了什么名字，它只是一种关于神圣的宇宙秩序的知识。这种知识使富于智慧的人们认识到，道德规范或'道'属于宇宙秩序的一部分，所以必须遵守。"（夏丹等选编，《辜鸿铭作品精选·中国人的精神》，长江文艺出版社，2004，第49页）在这段话中，他是将"上帝""天命""神圣的宇宙秩序"，包括"道"，基本画了等号的，而这些词都是"一种关于神圣的宇宙秩序的知识"，这种知识"属于宇宙秩序的一部分，所以必须遵守"。

　　当然，在这里，辜鸿铭还未就"天命"与"道"进行明确的区分。

　　其次，看"性"一词。辜鸿铭译为"the law of our being"，"我们本性的法则"。意思是，人类本性的法则，就是上帝的法令（也可以指体现出来的"神圣的宇宙秩序"）。人要遵循这一秩序而存在。

　　在《中国札记》系列文章中，辜鸿铭对"天命之谓性"的"性"也解释为"上帝的唯一真正的法律"。他说："真正的教会并不是基督教传教士的教会。真正的教会始终是宣扬真正的法律或天命的教会。真正的国家或政体并不是现代法学家的宪政。真正的国家始终是制定和颁布符合上帝的正义的真正法律的国家。但上帝的真正法律，符合上帝的正义的真正法律是什么呢？中国人说：'天命之谓性。'因此，'性'是上帝的唯一真正法律。然而，这里所说的'性'并不是指市井小民之'性'或卑鄙无耻者之'性'。这里的'性'，诚如爱默生所言，是指世界上'纯朴无瑕者'之'性'。这一点永远是上帝的唯一真正的法律。代表纯朴无瑕者的传教士或法学家就是真正的传教士、真正的法学家或政治家。愿意并且能够接受各民族的纯朴无瑕者的智慧、愿望和抱负的影响与指导的国家就是真正的国家。简言之，尽管真正的教会，当今真正现实的天主教会，并不是由各民族最有文化教养的人，由最纯朴无瑕的人正式创立的，但这些人都是上述教会的成员。'有教无类'，这就是兼爱的含义。"（汪堂家编译，《乱世奇文·尊王篇·中国札记之五·三八》，上海人民出版社，2002，第120—121页）

再看"道"一词。辜鸿铭译为"the moral law"，"道德法则"。意思是，遵循了"我们本性的法则"，就是"道德法则"。也就是说，道德其实即来自于"神圣的宇宙秩序"。"神圣的宇宙秩序（天命）"是首先通过赋予人，而成为人的"本性的法则"，而人们对这种本性法则的遵守，即"道德法则"。在《孔教研究之二》中，辜鸿铭有过类似的解说："'道'这个字在孔子的学说中指的是本性的法则。而本性的法则又是'天命'的体现。因此，中国人所谓的自由是一种自由的灵魂——是实现人生本质的法则。因此这种自由是道德的自由。是服从'天命'。'我欢快地漫游，因为我在寻找您的旨义。'（《旧约》）"（夏丹等选编，《辜鸿铭作品精选·呐喊》，第368页）这一翻译背后是条明晰的逻辑线索。

再看"教"。辜鸿铭译为"religion"，"宗教"。"修道之谓教"即"The moral law when reduced to a system is what we call religion"（当道德法则被归纳成一个体系时，就是我们所说的宗教）。他还是承接着自己上面的逻辑，每个人都被"上帝"（上天）赋予了关于"神圣的宇宙秩序"的知识，这是人们本性的法则，而道德法则指的是对这种本性法则的服从与遵循。而当这些道德法则被归纳为一个体系时，就成了"宗教"。这是从"神圣的宇宙秩序"到"宗教"的一个逻辑关系。辜鸿铭是具有很深的宗教情结的，在《中国人的精神（在北京东方学会上所宣讲的论文）》中，他曾论述宗教含义说："就广义而言，我们所说的宗教是指带有行为规范的教育系统，它是被许多人所接受并遵守的准则，或者说至少是为一个民族中的大多数人所接受并遵守的准则。"（夏丹等选编，《辜鸿铭作品精选·中国人的精神》，第38页）正是在这个意义上，他将中国的儒学称为"国教"，起名"好公民宗教"（The Religion of Good-citizenship）。换言之，他其实是将儒学塑造为一个文明型的、有效用的理论体系和行为规范，即广义上的"宗教"。而《中庸》此章，则是他对"宗教"的一个哲学定义。

再看"君子"一词。辜鸿铭译为"the moral man"，"有道德的人"。其实还是遵循他的逻辑。因为"道德法则"指的是对"神圣的宇宙秩序"所赋予的"本性法则"的遵循，那么，"君子"即遵循这一"道德法则"的有道德的人。简言之，君子即遵循神圣宇宙秩序的人。

再看"中"字。辜鸿铭译为"our true self（中）or moral being"，"我们的真实自我或道德本性"。在此，辜鸿铭依然延续了上面的逻辑，这句话"喜怒哀乐之未发，谓之中"，译为"When the passions, such as joy, anger, grief and pleasure, have not awakened, that is our true self（中）or moral being"（当诸如喜悦、愤怒、悲伤与快乐等激情尚未唤起时，就是我们的真实自我［中］或道德本性）。即，所谓"中"，即完全遵循"道德法则"的状态。

再看"和"字。辜鸿铭译为"the moral order"，"道德秩序"。"发而皆中节，谓之和"，译为"When these passions awaken and each and all attain due measure and degree, that is the moral order（和）"（当这些激情被唤起并且它们都达到了恰当的标准与程度时，就是道德秩序［和］）。也就是说，他延续前面的逻辑，认为人在完全遵循道德法则的情况下是"真实自我或道德本性"的，而如果他的激情表达恰当，则属于"道德秩序"的一种表现。也就是说，"中"是道德"静"时的一种表述，"和"则是道德"动"时的一种表述。在《中国古典的精髓》一文中，辜鸿铭曾引用此句用来阐述"进步"的概念，认为要"进步"必须首先确立道德的秩序：

> 欧美的许多无识之辈动辄断言，中国的学说里缺少"进步"的概念。然而，我的看法恰恰相反，我深信，表现在中国古典学说中的中国文化的精髓正是"秩序和进步"。四书里的《中庸》一篇，若我将其英译就是"Universal Order"（普遍的秩序），《中庸》有这样一句："致中和，天地位焉，万物育焉。"
>
> 因此，依照孔子的教义，即便将此句解释为"文化的目的，不仅在于人类，而且在于使所有被创造的事物都能得到充分的成长和发展"，也并不算过分。在这里，难道看不出真正的发展、进步的精神吗？只有先确立秩序——道德秩序，然后，社会的发展就会自然地发生，在无秩序——无道德秩序的地方，真正的或实际的进步是不可能有的。
>
> 欧洲人以前犯过，至今仍在犯的错误就在于他们抛开道德秩序去追求进步，就像建造巴比伦塔的古代人一样，他们一心将他们摩天大楼式的文明往高处一个劲地筑，而无视自然法则的存在，结果正如我们现在所看到的，他们的那种摩天楼式的文明正在走向崩溃了。

黄兴涛编译，《辜鸿铭文集·下卷》，第328—329页

到此为止，辜鸿铭就描述完了从"神圣的宇宙秩序"到人间"道德秩序"的逻辑链条，大致是：神圣的宇宙秩序（天命）—［遵循这种秩序即］人类本性的法则（性）—

［遵循人类本性的法则即］道德法则（道）—［道德法则被归纳为一个体系即为］宗教（教）—［遵循道德法则即为］君子—［完全遵循"道德法则"的"静"的状态即］真实自我或道德本性（中，也即文中的"大本"）—［抒发激情而程度恰当或遵循"道德法则"的"动"的状态即］道德秩序（和，也即文中的"达道"）。

　　这是理解《中庸》的逻辑上的主线和基础——其实，也可以说是理解辜鸿铭的哲学思想的一个主线与基础——但这并非全部的《中庸》精神，而仅仅是打开了它的一扇门。"道也者，不可须臾离也，可离非道也。是故君子戒慎乎其所不睹，恐惧乎其所不闻。莫见乎隐，莫显乎微，故君子慎其独也。"这一句非常重要。如果说上述的那条逻辑线索是主干的本然面目，这句话则是对它的修饰与发散。这种"神圣的宇宙秩序"所赋予人间的"道德法则"，虽然看不见也感觉不到，却是人们所无法逃避的，是人类社会运行的内在法则——能被人所逃避的法则必然不是这一根本法则。所以，"有道德的人"（君子）总是"坚持不懈地审视着他的隐秘的思想"（慎独），这是达到"中""和"状态所必需的。

Ⅱ.
第二章

Confucius remarked: "The life of the moral man is an exemplification of the universal moral order. The life of the vulgar person, on the other hand, is a contradiction of the universal moral order.

"The moral man's life is an exemplification of the universal order, because he is a moral person who constantly lives his true self or moral being. The vulgar person's life is a contradiction of the universal order, because he is a vulgar person who in his heart has no regard for, or fear of, the moral law."

["The fool hath said in his heart, There is no God."]

仲尼曰："君子中庸，小人反中庸。

"君子之中庸也，君子而时中；小人之中庸也，小人而无忌惮也。"

孔子说："有道德的人的生活，就是普遍道德秩序的一个范例。与之相反，粗俗下流之人的生活，就是普遍道德秩序的一个反例。

"有道德的人的生活是普遍秩序的一个范例，是因为他是一个有道德的人，不断地以真实自我或道德本性的状态生活。粗俗下流之人的生活是普遍秩序的一个反例，是因为他是一个粗俗下流的人，在心中没有注意到或畏惧道德的法则。"

［"愚蠢的人在心中说，根本没有上帝。"］

【评述】

此章是拿"君子"与"小人"两种人的行为进行了对比，实则是拿后者反衬前者，也是拿前者批判后者。辜鸿铭的译文，则大大加强了批判的意味。"小人"译为"the vulgar person"（粗俗下流的人），在文末的解读中，辜鸿铭还引用了一句话："The fool hath said in his heart, There is no God."（愚蠢的人在心中说，根本没有上帝。）这句话他在《中国人的精神（在北京东方学会上所宣讲的论文）》中也引用过（见夏丹等选编，《辜鸿铭作品精选·中国人的精神》，第49页）。在此句中，他又将"小人"称为"the fool"（蠢人）。事实上，他在翻译《论语》时，大多数时候也是将"小人"译为"蠢人"（a fool）的。

"君子"与"小人"是儒学思想中两个最为常见的对立概念，人们一般意义上的理解，也通常认为指人的道德品质而言。那么，从根本上来说，"君子"与"小人"的区别何在呢？在儒学语境中，《中庸》此段应该是答案。

先说"君子"。君子作为"the moral man"（有道德的人），在第一章中已有论述，即遵循"道德法则"（道）的人。而且，遵循道德法则有两种状态：一静一动。"静"者为"中"，"动"者为"和"。本段的"君子之中庸也，君子而时中"一句里，"时中"，辜鸿铭译为"constantly lives his true self or moral being"（不断地以真实自我或道德本性的状态生活），说的是君子遵循道德法则的"静"的表现"中"即真实自我或道德本性，这一点在第一章的论述中已经说明。从辜鸿铭的翻译看，这句表现的是：君子的生活之所以处于"中庸"的状态，是因为他达到了"时中"的境界。此处，"中庸"一词译为"the universal moral order"（普遍道德秩序）。也就是说，因为君子能够"时中"（不断地以真实自我或道德本性的状态生活），所以，他的生活状态是"中庸"（普遍道德秩序）的一个典范表现。那么，"时中"就是达到"中庸"的一个条件。君子就是因能达到"时中"（真实自我或道德本性）境界而处于"中庸"（普遍道德秩序）生活状态的人。这应该是儒学语境中"君子"的哲学含义。

再说"小人"。"小人反中庸"，辜鸿铭译为"The life of the vulgar person, on the other hand, is a contradiction of the universal moral order"（粗俗下流之人的生活，就是普遍道德秩序的一个反例）。也就是说，小人与君子恰恰相反，是正与"中庸"（普遍道德秩序）原则相违的。小人与中庸相违的表现是什么呢？即"小人而无忌惮也"，辜鸿铭译为"he is a vulgar person who in his heart has no regard for, or fear of, the moral law"（他是一个粗俗下流的人，在心中没有注意到或畏惧道德的法则）。也就是说，他作为一个"小人"，与"君子"的"中""和""慎独"等做法正好相反，他根本不在乎、不畏惧、不相信"道德的法则"，或者如辜鸿铭文末的解读中所说的，认为"根本没有上帝"（因为道德的法则,也即神圣的宇宙规律,其实就是"上帝")。这就是"小人"的真正含义,也是小人被认为"不道德"的真正原因。

这段话告诉我们,区分"君子""小人"的根本分水岭,其实就是对"中庸"原则的态度。还有一点值得注意的是:"中庸"一词在本章首次出现,并且成为评价人品德状况的一个根本性原则。

Ⅲ.
第三章

Confucius remarked: "To find and get into the true central (中) balance of our moral being, *i.e.*, our true moral ordinary (庸) self, that indeed is the highest human attainment. People are seldom capable of it for long."

[Emerson says: "From day to day the capital facts of human life are hidden from our eyes. Suddenly the mist rolls up and reveals them, and we think how much good time is gone that might have been saved had any hint of these things been shown."]

子曰:"中庸其至矣乎! 民鲜能久矣! "

孔子说:"找到并进入我们道德本性的真正的中心(中)平衡,也即,我们真正的、道德的普通(庸)自我,这确实是人类最高的境界。人们很少能够长久地如此。"

[爱默生说:"日复一日,人类生活的首要事实在我们眼前被隐藏起来。突然,迷雾散去,显露出了它们,我们就想,有多少对这些东西有所征兆的本来可以节省的美好时光白白荒废了呀! "]

【 评述 】

本章是对"中庸"的另一种解说,并表达了中庸之"难"。

"中庸"一词,在第二章中辜鸿铭译为"the universal moral order"(普遍的道德秩序)。此处辜鸿铭做了不同的翻译。他其实是分别翻译了"中"和"庸"两个字——"中"存在于"the true central(中)balance of our moral being"(我们道德存在的真正的中心[中]平衡)之中,其中,按照辜鸿铭在句中的安排来看,"中"的意思就是"中心";"庸"字存在于"our true moral ordinary(庸)self"(我们真正的、道德的普通[庸]自我)之中,"庸"的意思就是"普通"。但是,"中庸"一词绝对不可能是简单的"中心、普通"之意,而应理解为这两句话的结合,即"道德存在的真正的中心(中)平衡"与"我们真正的、道德的普通(庸)自我";中间用了"i.e."(也即)连接,表明两者含义相同。换言之,此处"中庸"的意思是:心中真正的平衡,也即处于真正的、道德的普通自我的一种状态。第二章中辜鸿铭译"中庸"为"普遍的道德秩序","君子中庸",意即君子的生活状态合乎普遍的道德秩序。那么,这里"中庸"的意思,我们也可以进一步理解为:心中真正的平衡,即处于真正的、道德的普通自我的一种状态,达到了这种平衡,即合乎了普遍的道德秩序。"中",在第二章"时中"中辜鸿铭的翻译是"true self or moral being"(真实自我或道德本性),与此处"中庸"的含义相近。可以说,此处"中庸"的概念比第二章"中"的概念多了"中心平衡"的一层含义以及"普通"这一定语,是对后者概念上的一种深化与细化。当然,对"中""庸""中庸"这些字眼,每处的翻译未必完全相同,也未必像数字一样精确,但仔细考究,却包含着同样或相近的含义。另外,"普遍"一词的含义,在下面第四章有解读。

Ⅳ.
第四章

Confucius remarked: "I know now why there is no real moral life. The wise mistake moral law to be something higher than what it really is; and the foolish do not know enough what moral law really is. I know now why the moral law is not understood. The noble natures want to live too high, high above their moral ordinary self; and ignoble natures do not live high enough, *i.e.*, not up to their moral ordinary true self.

"There is no one who does not eat and drink. But few there are who really know the taste of what they eat and drink."

[Goethe says: "O needless strictness of morality while nature in her kindly way trains us to all that we require to be! O strange demand of society which first perplexes and misleads us, then asks of us more than Nature herself!" — The moral law is the law of life, *i.e.*, the law of our moral nature; and moral nature, what we call our moral being, is nothing else but our true moral ordinary self. To live a moral life therefore means to *live*; to live, not as angels nor as brutes, but as natural ordinary reasonable human beings. But men in trying to to live too high, "to be unco' guid" , to be more than nature requires them to be, lose the sense of reality, live in a world of self delusion so that they really do not live; in fact, do not know the taste of what they eat and drink.]

子曰："道之不行也,我知之矣,知者过之,愚者不及也;道之不明也,我知之矣,贤者过之,不肖者不及也。

"人莫不饮食也,鲜能知味也。"

孔子说:"我现在知道为何没有真正的道德生活了。明智的人将道德法则误解为比它实际上更高深的东西;而愚蠢的人,则并没有充分地了解道德法则实际上是什么。我现在知道为何道德法则不被了解了。天性高贵的人希望生活得更崇高,高于他们道德的普通自我;而天性卑鄙的人则生活得不够崇高,也即,没有达到他们道德上的普通的真实自我。

"没人不吃不喝。但很少有人真正懂得他们所吃所喝的东西的味道。"

[歌德说:"当本性通过仁慈的方式训练我们需要成为的全部时,道德准则的严格是不必要的!首先迷惑并误导我们,然后比本性自身更多地要求我们,这是社会奇怪的要求!"——道德法则就是生活的法则,即我们道德本性的法则;而道德本性,我们所称作的道德存在,不是别的,正是我们真正的、道德上的普通自我。去过一种道德的生活,因此就意味着去生活;去生活,既不作为天使也不作为禽兽,而是作为本性的、普通的、理性的人类存在。但那些试着过太过崇高的生活的人,"做一个刻极清高的人",远超过本性要求他们所成为的,就丧失了对现实的感知,生活在一个自我欺骗的世界里,以至于他们并没有真正地生活;其实,他们不懂得他们所吃所喝的东西的味道。]

【评述】

根据辜鸿铭的翻译，本章的核心在"ordinary"（普通）一词。而围绕这个核心，则有两层意思递进展开：第一层意思是"道"为何"不行"——即不被人实行；第二层意思是"道"的"不明"——即不被人了解。

"道"，辜鸿铭译为"the moral law"（道德法则）。也就是说，此段讨论的是有关"道德法则"的问题——"不行"即"真正的道德生活"为何难以实现（即"道德法则"难以践行）；"不明"即"道德法则"为何难以被人理解。根据第一章的翻译，我们知道，"道德法则"也即"率性之谓道"的"道"，是对"人类本性法则"的遵循，而"人类本性法则"则是对"神圣的宇宙秩序"（天命）的遵循。

那么，为何"真正的道德生活"难以实现？"知者过之，愚者不及也"，辜鸿铭译为"The wise mistake moral law to be something higher than what it really is; and the foolish do not know enough what moral law really is"（明智的人将道德法则误解为比它实际上更高深的东西；而愚蠢的人，则并没有充分地了解道德法则实际上是什么）。也就是说，"知者"与"愚者"都没有正确地认识"道"：前者过于聪明，后者不够聪明。

而"道德法则"又为何难以被人认识和了解呢？"贤者过之，不肖者不及也"，辜鸿铭译为"The noble natures want to live too high, high above their moral ordinary self; and ignoble natures do not live high enough, *i.e.*, not up to their moral ordinary true self"（天性高贵的人希望生活得更崇高，高于他们道德的普通自我；而天性卑鄙的人则生活得不够崇高，也即，没有达到他们道德上的普通的真实自我）。即，"贤者"对自己的要求高过了"道德上的普通自我"，"不肖者"对自己的要求，则过低，低于"道德上的普通的真实自我"。

这两者在程度上一高一低，而都没有做到最关键的——"普通"。那么，什么是"普通"呢？这一点辜鸿铭在下面的解读中讲得比较明白："去生活，既不作为天使也不作为禽兽，而是作为本性的、普通的、理性的人类存在。"意思是，"贤者"希望做一个天使，"不肖者"则近乎禽兽，都是偏离人类普通本性的。即使是"那些试着过太过崇高的生活"的"贤者"，实则"丧失了对现实的感知，生活在一个自我欺骗的世界里"，而没有品味真正的生活味道。

在解读中，辜鸿铭给"live"加了斜体，实则是强调"生活"才是人的根本。辜鸿铭认为，儒学教给人的最主要的道理，就是去懂得如何生活，好好生活。在《孔教研究之二》中，他就此问题也有过详细的论述："如果奉行孔子的教诲，像他教导的那样去进行自我修养，努力做一名好学生，那么就会在孔子弟子的言语中找到孔子学说中关于怎样生活、怎样真正地生活之真谛。要弄清我们应该怎样生活，首先我们必须对这样一个问题有个明确的概念，即我们为何而活？我们必须知道，基督教教义关于人类最主要的目标是这样表达的：'人类之根本目的，乃赞美上帝。'这样理解或许不错，但却是不确定的。在这点上，正如我们所看到的，孔子的学说非常清楚明白而不存在任何歧义。'孝弟也者，其为仁之本与？'……佛教和基督教告诉人们，如果人们想成为一名好人，一名上帝之子，人们只需思索灵魂的状态及对上帝的义务，而不必思考现实世界。作为另一种学说的儒教认为，为了保持良好的心境，思考灵魂的状态是很有必要的，但同时还必须思考上帝把人类置于其间的人世，以根据上帝的意愿完成其功业。……换言之，本来意义上的宗教如佛教和基督教是一种为人们谋划怎样隐迹于山林荒野，以及为那些在北戴河避暑的小屋里，不干别事，只对其灵魂之状态和对上帝之义务进行思索的人设立的宗教。孔子学说的精义却与此大相径庭。如果人们乐意，可以称之为宗教，也可以称之为道德体系，它告诉人们作为公民应如何生活，即是为那些卡莱尔说的'要纳税、付租金和有烦恼'的人所设的宗教。"（夏丹等选编，《辜鸿铭作品精选·呐喊》，第361—362页。）

事实上，作为"要纳税、付租金和有烦恼"的人去生活，而不是像"贤者"那样要求"太过崇高"而"生活在一个自我欺骗的世界里"，以及像"不肖者"那样要求"不够崇高"，既是"普通"的含义所在，也是"道"（道德法则）的精义所在。

V.
第五章

Confucius remarked: "There is in the world now really no moral social order at all."

[The word *tao* here means the moral law finding its expression in social order. Confucius in his time, as Carlyle or Ruskin in modern Europe, considered the world to have gone on a wrong track; the ways of men and constitution of society to be radically wrong.]

子曰："道其不行矣夫！"

孔子说："在今天的世界上，真的根本没有道德的社会秩序。"

［"道"这个字此处是指在社会秩序中表现出来的道德法则。孔子在他的时代，如同卡莱尔或罗斯金在现代的欧洲，认为世界走上了错误的轨道；人类的发展方向与社会结构是完全错误的。］

【评述】

这句话是孔子对"道"难以实行的叹息。在解读中,辜鸿铭对"道"的解释如同前面,是"the moral law"(道德法则)。辜鸿铭在解读中说"孔子……认为世界走上了错误的轨道",可见,"道"(道德法则)实则是社会秩序的根本法则。

VI.

第六章

Confucius remarked: "There was the Emperor Shun. He was perhaps what may be considered a truly great intellect.Shun had a natural curiosity of mind and he loved to inquire into near facts (literally 'near words' meaning here ordinary topics of conversation in every day life). He looked upon evil merely as something negative; and he recognised only what was good as having a positive existence. Taking the two extremes of negative and positive, he applied the mean between the two extremes in his judgement, employment and dealings with people. This was the characteristic of Shun's great intellect."

[What is here said of the Emperor Shun in ancient China may be also said of the two greatest intellects in modern Europe, — Shakespeare and Goethe. The greatness of Shakespeare's intellect is to be seen in this: that in all his plays there is not one essentially bad man. Seen through Shakespeare's intellect, such a monster of wickedness of the popular imagination as King Richard the Hunchback, becomes not a villain who makes "damnable faces" , not even a really despicably bad man, but on the contrary, a brave heroic soul who is driven by his strong ill-regulated vindictive passions to awful acts of cruelty and finally himself to a tragic end. In fact, the tragedy of all Shakespeare's tragedies, as it is of real human life, is not the misery resulting from evil in man's nature; not the misery of essentially bad wicked men who do not exist except in the imagination of the man of small vulgar intellect; but the tragedy is the pitiful, pitiable misery and suffering of good brave heroic noble-minded men who are driven by their ill-regulated passions to tragic courses and to a tragic end. Herein then lies the greatness of Shakespeare's intellect.

子曰:"舜其大知也与! 舜好问而好察迩言,隐恶而扬善,执其两端,用其中于民,其斯以为舜乎!"

孔子说:"有一位帝王舜。他或许可被视为一位真正伟大的智者。舜具有一种天生的求知欲,并且喜欢查问近旁的事(字面意思是'近旁的话',此处指每天生活中谈论的普通话题)。他将恶仅仅视为某些消极的事情;而将善仅仅视为具有一种积极的存在。对待消极与积极这两种极端,他在评判、雇用及对待人民时,使用这两种极端的中间情绪。这就是舜的伟大才智的特征。"

[此处对古代中国的帝王舜的评论,或许也可以用在现代欧洲两位伟大的智者身上——莎士比亚与歌德。莎士比亚的伟大才智可以这样来认识:在他所有的戏剧中,从未有过一个本质上的坏人。用莎士比亚的才智来看,诸如"驼背者理查德"这样一个公众所幻想出来的恶棍,不会变成一个"面目可憎"的罪犯,甚至不会是一个真正卑劣的坏人,而相反是一个勇敢的、英勇的人——只是被他强烈的病态式报复激情所驱使而做了可怕、残忍的行为,并使他自己最后落得个悲惨的结局。其实,莎士比亚所有悲剧作品中体现的悲剧,就如同真正的人类生活一样,并非源于人们本性中的邪恶;也并非仅仅存在于那些微不足道的、卑鄙下流的人们幻想中的、本质上邪恶的人的苦难;而是那些被病态激情驱入悲惨过程并导致悲惨结局的,具有英勇、勇敢的高贵品质的人们的那些令人同情、可怜的不幸与痛苦。这里,蕴含着莎士比亚伟大的才智。

那么,如果说在莎士比亚的才智看来,一个邪恶的恶棍仅仅就是一个具有强烈的病态激情的人;那么,通过伟大歌德的伟大才智来看,魔鬼不会成为一个遭受地狱磨难的恶棍,甚至不是一个邪恶的精神,而仅仅是一

Now, if seen through the intellect of Shakespeare, a human monster of wickedness becomes merely a man with strong ill-regulated passions; the very Devil seen through the great intellect of the great Goethe, becomes not a monster of fire and brimstone, not even an evil spirit, but merely a spirit of negation (ein Geist der vermeint), in fact, merely a partial, incompletely developed nature. Goethe elsewhere says: "What we call evil in human nature is merely a defective or incomplete development, a deformity or malformation-absence or excess of some moral quality rather than anything positively evil." We can see now how deep and true is the insight of Confucius in pointing out in the text above that the true characteristic of a great intellect is ability to see only good and not evil in the nature of things.

Emerson also says: "We judge of a man's wisdom by the largeness of his hope." If this is true, then the prevalence of what is called pessimism in individuals as in nations is a sure sign of the unsoundness, defect or deformity of intellect.*See Appendix A.]

个否定的精神（ein Geist der vermeint），实际上，仅仅是部分的、不充分发展的本性。歌德在另一个地方说："我们所称作人类本性中的恶的，仅仅是一种有缺陷或不充分的发展，一种丑陋或畸形——欠缺或过度地拥有某种道德特性，而不是绝对的邪恶。"现在我们可以看出，孔子在上文中指出伟大才智的真正特性是一种仅仅看到事物本性的善而不是恶的能力，是多么深刻与真实。

爱默生也说："我们判断一个人的智慧，是通过看他的希望的广度。"如果这是真实的，那么，在个体与民族中盛行的悲观主义，就是一种智力不健全、缺陷或畸形的明确征兆。＊见附录A[①]]

---

① 即本书的《中庸》附录，下同。

【评述】

本章的核心是"知"字，辜鸿铭译为"intellect"（智者），或者确切地说，应该指"truly great intellect"（真正伟大的智者）。而怎样才算"舜"那样的真正伟大的智者呢？文中给出的答案有这三点：1."好问而好察迩言"，即"had a natural curiosity of mind and he loved to inquire into near facts"（具有一种天生的求知欲，并且喜欢查问近旁的事）；2."隐恶而扬善"，即"He looked upon evil merely as something negative; and he recognised only what was good as having a positive existence"（他将恶仅仅视为某些消极的事情；而将善仅仅视为具有一种积极的存在）；3."执其两端，用其中于民"，即"Taking the two extremes of negative and positive, he applied the mean between the two extremes in his judgement, employment and dealings with people"（对待消极与积极这两种极端，他在评判、雇用及对待人民时，使用这两种极端的中间情绪）。而根据辜鸿铭文后的解读来看，核心答案应是第2项。此项涉及到"善""恶"的本质性认识。而对"善""恶"的认识状况，则反映了一个人自身的道德品质状况。

在这方面，辜鸿铭拿莎士比亚、歌德、爱默生的思想来予以类比。他认为，他们与舜是同样的智者。因为，他们对"善""恶"有着同样的认知——在他们眼中，世上并无真正的、绝对的"恶"，所谓"恶"仅仅是"一种有缺陷或不充分的发展，一种丑陋或畸形——欠缺或过度地拥有某种道德特性"。在翻译中，"隐恶"译为"looked upon evil merely as something negative"（将恶仅仅视为某些消极的事情），"扬善"译为"recognised only what was good as having a positive existence"（将善仅仅视为具有一种积极的存在），也是这个意思。也就是说，此段重点说的是对"善""恶"的认知问题。

Ⅶ.
第七章

Confucius remarked: "Men all say 'we are wise'; but when driven forward and taken in a net, a trap or a pit-fall, there is not one who knows how to find a way of escape. Men all say, 'we are wise'; but in finding the true central clue and balance in their moral being (*i.e.*, their normal, ordinary, true self) and following the line of conduct which is in accordance with it, they are not able to keep it for a round month."

[As in the preceding chapter the writer of this book, seeing that the anarchy and want of moral social order in the world is due to defect and unsoundness of intellect in men, quotes a saying of Confucius showing the true characteristic of a great whole and sound intellect; so in the present chapter he quotes another saying of Confucius showing the conceit and uselessness of the half intellect of so-called wise men in dealing with the deadlock in private or public affairs — deadlock as if caught in a net, a trap or a pit — fall into which the ill-regulated passions of men sometimes drive their own life or the world.

Thus when the affairs of an individual get into and are in a mess or deadlock, the first thought which will naturally come into the man's head or mind is how to escape, to get out of the mess, out of the deadlock; and in the eagerness and excitement to get out of the mess, out of the momentary deadlock, the man is often, and naturally, tempted, especially if he is a clever man, to think of this or that or some clever dodge or contrivance which, instead of getting him out of the mess and deadlock, will only bring him into a greater mess and deadlock. It is for this reason that we often see at the present day that when the affairs of a nation or of the world are in a mess and deadlock there are always men who say

子曰："人皆曰予知,驱而纳诸罟攫陷阱之中,而莫之知辟也。人皆曰予知,择乎中庸而不能期月守也。"

孔子说："人们都说'我们是聪明的';但当被驱赶而落入一副罗网、一个陷阱或一种圈套,没人知道怎样找到一条逃脱的路。人们都说'我们是聪明的';但在找到他们道德本性(即他们平常的、普通的、真正的自我)中真正的中心线索与平衡,并遵从与之相一致的行为方式时,他们连完整的一个月时间都不能保持。"

[正如在前面的章节中,本书作者看到,由于人们智力的缺陷与不健全,世界上存在着无政府状态与道德秩序的缺失,于是他引用了孔子的话来表现一种伟大、完整、健全的智力的真正特性。同样的,在本章中他引用了孔子的另一句话,来表现那些所谓聪明人的愚笨:那些"聪明人"在处理私人生活或公共事务中的僵局时,是如此自以为是和百无一用,犹如困于一副罗网、一个陷阱或一种圈套。有时,正是他们病态式的激情致使自己的生活或整个世界深陷这样的僵局中。

因此,当一个人陷入困境或僵局时,自然的反应,就是怎样逃脱,摆脱混乱、摆脱僵局。而在摆脱混乱、摆脱暂时僵局的渴望与骚动中,他通常会自然而然地胡思乱想,或去想些聪明的诡计或计谋——尤其当他是那样的聪明人时。然而,这不仅不会让他摆脱混乱与僵局,还会更糟。正因如此,我们经常看到,今天当一个民族或整个世界陷入混乱或僵局时,总会有些自诩聪明的人,自告奋勇地提出改革方案,提出诸如立法机构的建制、征税,以及采纳金本位制等博学、繁琐、复杂、聪明的计策。或更有野心,提出教育上的形而上学与数学的办法、宪法的几何结构,以及比这些都迷人精彩的,去教给人们在不欺骗他人的情况下如何利用邻居的新算法,即政治经济学理论。但是所有这些聪明博学的聪明人都是无知的,

they are wise men, who come forward with schemes of reform, learned, laborious, complicated, clever contrivances in the shape of machinery of legislation, taxation, adoption of the gold standard; or more ambitious still, metaphysical and mathematical methods of education, geometrical forms of constitution and, most amazingly wonderful of all, new rules of arithmetic to teach men how to take advantage of their neighbour without cheating him, called systems of political economy. But ignorant all such wise men are with all their cleverness and learning; ignorant and blind to the plain and simple fact that if you want a man to succeed in the reform of his affairs which are in a deadlock and mess, you must self-evidently first of all tell him how to reform the instrument with which he has to carry out that reform—the instrument, viz, the man himself. If the condition of the man's being, *i.e.*, his character as well as his conduct, his way of feeling and thinking as well as his way of living and acting, is not in a state requiring reform, his affairs would not be in a state of mess and deadlock. But if the condition of the man's being is in a state really requiring reform, as is evident from the state of his affairs, it is surely of no earthly use for you to teach him complicated methods or *any* method how to deal with his affairs; in fact until the man whose affairs are in mess and deadlock, has put to right and reformed himself — his being — it is very self-evident that the poor man is not in a fit state, not to say, to carry out your fine and clever scheme for the reforms of his affairs, but even to see and understand the true and exact state of his affairs which are in a mess and deadlock so as to apply to it any sheme of reform whatever in such a way as to produce any effective or good result.

In other words, before a man or men in a nation undertake to carry out any scheme of reform in the state of his affairs or the affairs of a nation, he must first of all take in hand the reform of his or their own being and person. In short, moral

他们对这一普通而简单的事实盲目无知：如果你想要一个人能通过改革成功地摆脱困境，不言而喻，你必须首先告诉他如何去改革"改革者"，即他自己。如果那人的本质，即他的性格、言行，他的情感及思想的方式，以及他的生活与行为之道，并未亟需改革，那么，他也不会身处混乱与僵局。但如果那人的本质确实亟需改革，他的处境也表现为如此，那么，你教给他复杂的办法抑或任何办法去对付，都无济于事；其实，除非身处混乱与僵局的那个人，调适自己并改革自身——他的本质——那么，显而易见那个可怜人的境况才会改善，否则，不用说推行那些美妙聪明的改革计划，即便是了解其身处困局之真实境况，以便能够运用改革计划产生任何好的效果也不可能。

换言之，在一个人或一个民族的民众开始着手实施任何改革方案之前，他必须首先要自我改革。简言之，道德改革必须先于其他所有的改革。

因此，对于个体、民族以及整个世界来说，当身处僵局与混乱时，只有一种可以逃脱的真正途径，此途径如此简单，正如孔子所说的，多么惊讶那些所谓的聪明人用他们的聪明竟没看到；简单来说，途径就是，去找回你性情的平和与判断的冷静；去找回你真实的自我，或用孔子的话来说，去找回你道德本性中的中心线索与平衡。

道德改革，因此就意味着去找回我们真正的自我。当身处混乱与僵局的一个人或一个民族的民众，一旦重新找回性情的平和与判断的冷静———旦找回真实的自我——这样，也只有这样，才会看到并懂得其当下的真实境况。当一个人或一个民族理解了当下的真实境况，就将懂得采取何种合适的指导方法，以便促进秩序的建立——进入真正的秩序与宇宙万物的体系；其实，这就是去做我们所说的道德上正义与公平的事。当一个人掌握了他真实的自我，就能够看到并去做道德上公平与正义之

reform must precede all and every other reform.

Therefore it is true that for individuals, for nations and for the world, when affairs are in a deadlock and mess there is only one true way of escape, and that way is so simple that, as Confucius says, how astonishing it is that so-called wise men with all their cleverness do not see it; in fact, the way is, in simple language, to get back the evenness of your temper and your calm judgement; to get back your true self, or in the words of Confucius, to find the central clue and balance in your moral being.

Moral reform therefore means simply to get back our true self. When a man or a nation of men whose affairs are in a mess and deadlock once recovers evenness of temper and calmness of judgement—once get back the true self— then and only then he or it will see and understand the true and exact state of his or its affairs. When a man or nation understands the true and exact state of his or its affairs he or it will then know what line of conduct to take which will fit with the present state of those affairs in order to bring them into order — into the true order and system of things in the universe; in fact to do what is called morally right and just. When a man has got hold of his true self, which enables him to see and do what is morally just and right, then not only men and things, but the whole universe, governed as it is by the same moral order, by the same order and system of things, will respond and obey; and whatever things are about and around such a man will at once again arrange themselves into a harmonius and cosmic order. *See Appendix B.]

122

事，那时，被同样的道德秩序、万物的秩序与体系支配着的天地万物都将响应并遵从他；只要围绕着这样一个人，无论什么事情就立刻会进入到一种和谐的秩序中。*见附录B］

【评述】

本章实则是对"人皆曰予知"现象的一种批判。"人皆曰予知",辜鸿铭译为"men all say 'we are wise'"（"人们都说'我们是聪明的'"）。这里的"知",意思是"wise"（明智、聪明）的意思。那么,实际情况如何呢? "驱而纳诸罟擭陷阱之中,而莫之知辟也",按辜鸿铭的说法,即出现问题的人们普遍无法摆脱"a mess or deadlock"（混乱与困境）。辜鸿铭引申认为,不仅仅是个人,即使是一个民族,当他们陷入混乱与困境中时,那些给出各种改革方案的"聪明人",往往是无知的,他在解读中说:"在本章中他（《中庸》作者）引用了孔子的另一句话,来表现那些所谓聪明人的愚笨:那些'聪明人'在处理私人生活或公共事务中的僵局时,是如此自以为是和百无一用。"那么,改革（或说摆脱困境）应该怎样做才能成功呢? 辜鸿铭认为,不在于方案设计得多么精细与复杂,而在于首先要改革"改革者"自身。即,改革的对象首先是改革者"那人的本质,即他的性格、言行,他的情感及思想的方式,以及他的生活与行为之道"。"道德改革必须先于其他任何改革",这是辜鸿铭认为唯一"可以逃脱的真正途径",即唯一的改革途径。这条途径,他的解释就是"去找回你性情的平和与判断的冷静;去找回你真实的自我,或用孔子的话来说,去找回你道德本性中的中心线索与平衡"。在文中,这也是他对"中庸"的翻译,"the true central clue and balance in their moral being（i.e., their normal, ordinary, true self）","道德本性（即他们平常的、普通的、真正的自我）中真正的中心线索与平衡"。所以,可以说,改革的唯一途径是"改革者"首先要达到"中庸"的状态。而改革者通过改革自我达到这一状态的过程,辜鸿铭称之为"道德改革"。在这样的改革之下,"被同样的道德秩序、万物的秩序与体系支配着的天地万物都将响应并遵从他;只要围绕着这样一个人,无论什么事情就立刻会进入到一种和谐的秩序中"。在此,我们可以回忆一下第三章中我们对辜鸿铭"中庸"概念的总结:心中真正的平衡,即处于真正的、道德的普通自我的一种状态,而达到这种平衡,即合乎了普遍的道德秩序。这是一切改革根本的哲学前提。引申一步来说,"改革"首先并非是一个实际或专业的概念,而是个哲学概念——无论是对个人,还是对一个国家、一个民族来说。

Ⅷ.
第八章

Confucius remarked of his favourite disciple, Yen Hui: "Hui was a man who all his life sought the central clue in his moral being and when he got hold of one thing that was good he embraced it with all his might and never lost it again."

[As the Emperor Shun in the text above is the type of the intellectual nature, true representative of what Mr. Matthew Arnold calls Hellenism, so Yen Hui here is the type of the moral, emotional or religious nature, true representative of what Mr. Arnold calls Hebraism. Mr. Arnold says, "We may regard this paramount sense of duty, self control and work, this going forward manfully with the best light we have, as one force. And we may regard the intelligence driving at true ideas, which are after all the basis of all right practice, the ardent sense for all the new and changing combinations of these ideas which man's development brings with it, the indomitable impulse to know and adjust them perfectly—as another force. Now to give to these forces names from the two races of men who have supplied the most signal and splendid manifestations of them—we may call them respectively the forces of Hebraism and Hellenism."]

子曰:"回之为人也,择乎中庸,得一善,则拳拳服膺而弗失之矣。"

孔子谈论他最喜爱的学生颜回:"回是一个用一生来寻求他道德本性中的中心线索的人,当他把握住一件美好的事物时,他会用全部的力量拥抱它,永不再失去。"

[正如在上一段中,帝舜是位具有才智天性的典型人物,即马修·阿诺德先生所称作的"希腊精神"的代表人物,此处的颜回是道德的、情感的或宗教式的典型人物,是阿诺德先生所称作的"希伯来精神"的代表人物。阿诺德先生说:"至高无上的责任感、自我克制和勤奋、得到了最亮的光就勇往直前的热忱——所有这些我们都可看成为一种力。另外,那种作为正确行动之基础、指领着人们走向真理的智慧,那种对于随着人的发展而形成的、新的变化着的思想组合的敏感,欲彻底弄懂这些思想并作出完美调适的不可遏制的冲动——所有这些我们可看成为另一种力。……最显著、最辉煌地展示了这两种力的两个民族可以用来为之命名,我们可分别称之为希伯来精神和希腊精神。"①]

---

① 此处译文参考了相应段落已有中译,见[英]马修·阿诺德,《文化与无政府状态:政治与社会批评》,韩敏中译,读书·生活·新知三联书店,2002,第110—111页。

【评述】

上一章刚刚引用了孔子"择乎中庸,而不能期月守也"的感叹,并且在前几章反复提到"道之不行",而此处则称赞颜回"择乎中庸,得一善,则拳拳服膺而弗失之矣"。显然,这是对颜回修养的高度肯定。我们在第二章已经分析了"君子""小人"两个概念在哲学意义上的本质区别,就在于能否守持"中庸"之道。从这个意义上来讲,颜回是典型的哲学意义上的君子,因为他能守持"中庸"之道(all his life sought the central clue in his moral being[用一生来寻求他道德本性中的中心线索],这也是辜鸿铭在第七章中对"中庸"的翻译)。一般人"不能期月守也",而颜回则以终生追求。

文末,辜鸿铭也进行了有趣的解读。他引用英国19世纪著名批评家马修·阿诺德的《文化与无政府状态》一书中的观点,将舜比喻为"希腊精神"的代表人物,颜回则是"希伯来精神"的代表人物。对于两者的差别,阿诺德在书中说:"希腊精神最为重视的理念是如实看清事物之本相;希伯来精神中最重要的则是行为和服从。……希腊精神的主导思想是意识的自发性,希伯来精神的主导思想则是严正的良知。"但阿诺德还强调:"和一切伟大的精神传统一样,希腊精神和希伯来精神无疑有着同样的终极目标,那就是人类的完美或曰救赎。"(此处数句见[英]马修·阿诺德,《文化与无政府状态:政治与社会批评》,第110—111页)

无疑,此处辜鸿铭给我们提供了一个中西文化对比的独特视角,其实不仅仅是"对比"的问题,更是一种对两者本质意义上异同的再认识。他在《张文襄幕府纪闻》中说"中西固无二道",而且,他一贯主张中西文化在本质上是相同的,如他在《中国人的精神(在北京东方学会上所宣读的论文)》中对"道"的解释,即认为是"所有伟人,所有富有智慧的人们"都信仰的"上帝",即"对神圣的宇宙秩序的信仰"(见夏丹等选编,《辜鸿铭作品精选·中国人的精神》,第49页)。当然,这些人包括孔子、斯宾诺莎、费希特等不同文化之下的伟人。换言之,这些伟人所理解的终极真理是一致的,虽然所处文化不同。他在《约翰·史密斯在中国》中也说:"在东西方之间,对a+b=c式方程的解答是非常复杂和困难的问题。因为其中存在着许多未知数。不仅东方的孔子、康有为先生和端方总督之间有着不同的理解,而且在西方的莎士比亚、歌德和约翰·史密斯之间也存在着差别。实际的情况是,当你专门解答a+b=c的方程时,你将发现在东方的孔子与西方的莎士比亚和歌德之间,只存有微乎其微的差别;而倒是在西方的理雅各博士和西方的阿瑟·史密斯牧师之间,反而存在着大量的不同。"(同上,第97页)从中可以看出,辜鸿铭认为,孔子、莎士比亚、歌德等东西方文化伟人所体现出来的思想差别是"微乎其微"的。事实上,往往看到东西方之间的不同很易,看到它们的同则很难。借助此处对颜回"中庸"精神的称赞,辜鸿铭又一次强调了东西方间的相同之处。

128

IX.
第九章

Confucius remarked: "A man may be able to renounce the possession of Kingdoms and Empire, be able to spurn the honours and emoluments of office, be able to trample upon bare, naked weapons, with all that he shall not be able to find the central clue in his moral being."

[The word (均) in the text above, literally "even, equally divided" , is here used as a verb meaning "to be indifferent to" (平视), hence to renounce. As in the chapter immediately following that in which he describes the characteristics of the great intellect, the writer of this book shows the conceit and uselessness of the half intellect, the characteristics of false Hellenism; so in the present chapter following the above in which he gives the true type of Hebraism, he here again quotes another saying of Confucius showing the characteristics of false Hebraism, the evils and abuses resulting from the loss of balance on the moral, emotional or religious side. The religious history of the world with its manifestation of asceticism and fanaticism proves how truly Confucius has here seized the characteristics of false Hebraism or loss of balance, on the moral emotional or religious side of man's nature.

Goethe says, "Religious piety (Frommigkeit) is not an end, but only means wherewith through the most complete calmness of temper and state of mind (Gemuthsruhe) to attain the highest state of culture or human perfection." What Goethe here says of religious piety, the highest inculcated virtue of Christianity and Buddhism, is also true of the virtues insisted upon by the Japanese *Bushido*, viz., — self-denial, self-sacrifice and valour or fearlessness in presence of pain or death. These virtues insisted on by the Japanese *Bushido* are also not an end, but only a means to an end.Indeed, as Mr. Matthew Arnold truly says, — "Christianity is

子曰："天下国家可均也,爵禄可辞也,白刃可蹈也,中庸不可能也。"

孔子说:"一个人,或许能够宣布放弃他对王国或帝国的拥有,能够摈弃其职位所带来的荣誉与酬劳,能够脚踏在裸露的武器上,然而,尽管如此,他却不能够找到他道德本性中的中心线索。"

[上文中的"均"字,字面意思是"平均、平分",此处被用作动词,意思是"漠不关心、不在乎"(平视),因此而去放弃。正如在前面章节中,此书作者描述了伟大智者的特性,也展示了"半智者"的狂妄自大与百无一用,以及那些"伪希腊精神"的特征。那么,在此章中,他指出了真正的"希伯来精神"的类型。他再次引用孔子的话来展现那"伪希伯来精神"之特征,即在失去了道德、情感、宗教的平衡之后的邪恶与陋习之结果。表现为禁欲主义与狂热精神的世界宗教之历史,证明了孔子此处指出的伪希伯来精神,或人们本性中在道德情感及宗教方面平衡的失去,是多么的真实。

歌德说:"宗教的虔诚(Frommigkeit)并非终点,只是通过它,以性情与思想状态的彻底平静(Gemuthsruhe),达致文化或人类的完美状态。"歌德此处所言之宗教虔诚,即基督教与佛教所教诲的最高美德,也是日本的武士道所强调的真实美德,即自我节制、自我牺牲,以及面对痛苦与死亡时的勇猛与无畏。而这些日本武士道所强调的美德,也并非终点,而仅仅是达到终点的途径。确实,如马修·阿诺德所言,"基督教并非一套关于言行的公平正直的死规则,而是一种性情、一种思想的状态"。它或许比说基督教、佛教以及武士道仅仅是种戒律、是关于人类性情与精神的教育方法更为正确。此种戒律存在于某些美德的践行之中:基督教、佛教的虔诚,以及武士道的自我牺牲与勇猛精神之中。就如歌

not a dead set of square rules of conduct, but a temper, a certain state of mind." It is perhaps more correct to say that Christianity, Buddhism as well as *Bushido*, is really only a discipline, a method for the education of the temper and spirit of mankind. This discipline consists in the exercise of certain virtues: of piety in the case of Christianity and Buddhism, and in the case of *Bushido*, of self-sacrifice and valour. The exercise of these virtues is, as Goethe says, not an end, but only the means to enable a man or a nation of men to educate their temper and state of mind into a perfect condition, and through that perfect condition of temper and mind to attain the highest state of human perfection, or, as in the case of a nation, what is called the highest state of civilization.

But the disciplinary exercise of these virtues may be carried to excess or carried out in a way which is contrary to and destructive of the end which the exercise of these virtues is meant to serve; in fact, carried out in a spirit which, instead of promoting, injures and destroys the perfect state of temper and mind which the exercise of these virtues is intended to promote and bring about. In such a case the exercise becomes not a good but a harmful discipline. Thus for example, the exercise of self-denial when carried to excess and in a spirit of hatred and defiance as it was with the ancient Stoics; in a spirit of militant vain-glory as it was with the early Christians and is now with the modern Salvation Army: such exercise of the virtue of self-denial becomes, when judged from the point of the universal order, not a virtue, but a vice — a sin; because it does not promote but injures and destroys the sweetness and harmony of temper and mind and thereby does real harm to the cause of human perfection, of true civilization in the world. In the same way the exercise of the virtue of valour or fearlessness in presence of pain and death insisted upon by the Japanese *Bushido*, when carried to excess or exercised in a spirit of hatred and defiance, becomes fanaticism or moral madness which is not a virtue but a vice, a sin, and ceases to be an exercise of true *Bushido*. *See Appendix C.]

132

德所言，这些美德的践行并非终点，而仅仅是使一个人或民族能够教化他们的性情与思想状态以达完美状态的途径。而通过彼种性情与思想的完美状态达到人类完美的最高境界，抑或，当一个民族达到此种境界，这就是文明的最高状态。

但这些美德的训练可能导致过度，或者走上与其本来目的相违或消极的道路。事实上，在精神上贯彻这些美德，不仅不能促进，反而会有害甚至毁掉践行这些美德本来想要达到的性情与思想的完美状态。在此种情况下，那些践行就变成了一个有害而不是有益的戒律。例如，对自我节制的训练，当实施过度以及像古代斯多哥学派那样存在于憎恨、蔑视的精神之中，当像早期基督徒及当代救世军（Salvation Army）① 那样存在于好战的极端自负的精神之中；诸如此类的对自我节制的美德的践行，从普遍秩序的观点来看，不再是种美德，而是种恶行——一种罪恶。因为它不仅不促进反而有害，甚至能毁掉性情与思想的美好与和谐，因此，对人类完美的事业、对世界的真正文明是确然有害的。同样，当强调面对痛苦与死亡时勇猛、无畏的美德的日本武士道，过度贯彻或者存在于憎恨与蔑视的精神之中时，就会变为狂热或道德疯狂，这就不是种美德，而是种恶行，是种罪恶，并等于终止了对真正武士道的践行。＊见附录 C.］

---

① 辜鸿铭曾在《文明与无政府状态或远东问题的道德困境》中对"救世军"作过批评。他说："现在，即便欧洲人想恢复过去的真正的中世纪精神，他们也无法做到。欧洲人在试图恢复中世纪精神时要么像救世军那样胡作非为，要么像耶稣会会士的教皇极权主义那样招摇撞骗。如果有人想了解欧洲救世军的胡作非为总有一天会成为摧毁文明和所有真正的道德修养的多么可怕的力量，他最好读一读中国的太平天国的历史。参加那场起义的中国基督徒们丢掉他们本民族的诉诸理性的道德修养，而转向欧洲中世纪的道德修养，这种道德修养诉诸大多数人心中的希望与恐惧这类激情。其结果是，许多省份大局糜烂，上百万人惨遭杀戮。"（汪堂家编译，《乱世奇文·尊王篇》，上海人民出版社，2002，第130页）

133

【评述】

　　辜鸿铭认为,此章是在区分"伪希伯来精神"与"真希伯来精神"。他将文中"天下国家可均也,爵禄可辞也,白刃可蹈也"这样的行为视为"伪希伯来精神",即"人们本质中道德情感及宗教平衡的失去"。怎么来理解呢? 辜鸿铭认为,既然能做到上述三种牺牲,那么就表现了一种"自我节制"的精神,恰如"禁欲主义与狂热精神的世界宗教之历史"。然而,这种"自我节制"的精神,却未必有益,反而通常是有害的,甚至是毁灭性的。他列举了基督教、佛教及日本武士道的例子,认为,这些"宗教"都强调人的美德,然而,仅仅虔诚于这些美德,则往往会有害,甚至毁掉"性情与思想的完美状态",对于一个民族来说,则能毁掉其文明。比如古代斯多哥学派、早期基督徒、当代救世军等例子中的极端表现,他们虽然虔诚于自己的信仰,实则是种"狂热或道德疯狂",对于日本武士道来说,当"过度贯彻或者存在于憎恨与蔑视的精神之中时"同样如此。归根到底,正如辜鸿铭在解读中引用的歌德的话:"宗教的虔诚并非终点,只是通过它,以性情与思想状态的彻底平静,达致文化或人类的完美状态。"此章批判了伪希伯来精神,而"中庸"(the central clue in his moral being[道德本性中的中心线索])则自然是真希伯来精神。

X.
第十章

Tzu-lu asked what constituted force of character.

Confucius said: "Do you mean force of character of the people of the southern countries or force of character of the people of the northern countries; or do you mean force of character in an absolute sense? To be patient and gentle, ready to teach, returning not evil for evil: that is the force of character of the people of the southern countries. It is the ideal of the moral man.

["Gentle unto all men, apt to teach, patient, in meekness instructing those that oppose themselves." —2 *Timothy* Ⅲ ., 24–25.]

"To lie under arms and meet death without regret; that is the force of character of the people of the northern countries. It is the ideal of the brave man.

"But force of character in an absolute sense is another thing. Wherefore the man with the true force of moral character is one who is easy and accommodating and yet without weakness or indiscrimination. How unflinchingly firm he is in his strength! He is independent without any bias. How unflinchingly firm he is in his strength! When there is moral social order in the country, if he enters public life, he does not change from what he was when in retirement. When there is no moral social order in the country he holds on his way without changing even unto death. How unflinchingly firm he is in his strength!"

子路问强。

子曰:"南方之强与? 北方之强与? 抑而强与? 宽柔以教,不报无道,南方之强也,君子居之。

子路问什么才是品格的力量。

孔子说:"你是问南方国家人民的品格力量呢,还是问北方国家人民的品格力量? 或者你是问绝对意义上的品格的力量? 宽容、温和,甘愿实施教化,不以邪恶应对邪恶:这就是南方国家人民的品格的力量。这是道德之人的理想。

["温温和和地待众人,善于教导,存心忍耐,用温柔劝戒那些抵挡的人。"(提后3:24—25)]

"衽金革,死而不厌,北方之强也,而强者居之。

"故君子和而不流,强哉矫! 中立而不倚,强哉矫! 国有道,不变塞焉,强哉矫! 国无道,至死不变,强哉矫! "

"躺卧时全副武装,死亡面前毫不后悔:这是北方国家人民的品格的力量。它是勇敢之人的理想。

"但绝对意义上的品格的力量就是另外一回事了。因此,具有真正的道德品格力量的人,是个从容随和然而没有弱点的人,他也不会缺乏鉴别力。他的力量是多么彻底坚定! 他独立而没有任何偏见。他的力量是多么彻底坚定! 当国家拥有道德的社会秩序时,如果他入仕,他不会改变退隐时的自己。当国家失去了道德的社会秩序,他会坚守自己的方式,至死方休。他的力量是多么彻底坚定! "

【 评述 】

本章围绕"强"的概念而展开论述。按辜鸿铭的翻译,此章从两个层面阐释了"强"的含义:第一个是现实层面,即"南方之强"与"北方之强";第二个是"绝对意义"(in an absolute sense) 的层面。"强",译为"force of character"(品格的力量)。

从现实层面看,孔子讲了在"品格的力量"方面的不同性格特征。"君子居之"译为"It is the ideal of the moral man"(道德之人的理想)。"强者居之"译为"It is the ideal of the brave man"(勇敢之人的理想)。辜鸿铭在《中国人的精神(在北京东方学会上所宣讲的论文)》开头也讲到:"当我们谈及中国人的性格或特征时,也很难给予简单的概括和归纳。因为众所周知,中国北方人的性格是与南方人不同的,正如德国人不同于意大利人一样。"(夏丹等选编,《辜鸿铭作品精选·中国人的精神》,第24页)

然而,本章的重点则在于第二个层面。如辜鸿铭的译文中说:"force of character in an absolute sense is another thing."(绝对意义上的品格的力量就是另外一回事了)如果说,南方人的"品格的力量"(强)表现为"宽容、温和、教化",北方人的"品格的力量"(强)表现为"尚武、无畏",那么,绝对意义上的"品格的力量"(强)则表现为:1. "和而不流",译为"easy and accommodating and yet without weakness or indiscrimination"(从容随和然而没有弱点,也不会缺乏鉴别力);2. "中立而不倚",译为"independent without any bias"(独立而没有任何偏见);3. "国有道,不变塞焉",译为"When there is moral social order in the country, if he enters public life, he does not change from what he was when in retirement"(当国家拥有道德的社会秩序时,如果他入仕,他不会改变退隐时的自己);4. "国无道,至死不变",译为"When there is no moral social order in the country he holds on his way without changing even unto death"(当国家失去了道德的社会秩序,他会坚守自己的方式,至死方休)。其中,后两项可以视为是对前两项在各种环境中的坚持。所以,这四项中重点又在于"和而不流"与"中立而不倚"。

在辜鸿铭看来,上述的"强"本身就是一种德性,它的本质是对"和而不流"与"中立而不倚"品质的坚守,而"和而不流"与"中立而不倚"这两项,又可以说是坚持"道德品格"的一种表现,因为君子即"具有真正的道德品格力量的人"。那么,此处的关系是:[人对"道德品格"也即对"道德法则"的坚持即]君子—[君子对"和而不流"与"中立而不倚"的坚持即]强。那么,我们通过参考在第一章所总结出的从"神圣的宇宙秩序"到人间"道德秩序"的逻辑链条可以看到,"强"作为遵循"中庸"之道的君子的一种德性,也即坚守"中庸"之道的一种德性,而上述四项实则是坚守"中庸"之道的一种外在方法。

XI.

第十一章

Confucius remarked: "There are men who seek for some abstruse meaning in religion and philosophy and who live a life of singularity in order that they may leave a name to posterity. That is what I never would do.

[There were in Confucius' time men with speculative intellects like Laotzu who believed that the salvation of mankind depended upon some abstruse "ism" which they had discovered. There were also practical philanthropists like Metzu who believed that all the social evils of the world could be cured if men would take to some singular way of living: clout their own shoes or leave off wearing trousers.

In modern days the Christian Missionaries say that Confucianism is not a religion because it has no abstruse theory such as the Christian dogma of the Trinity, or the Godhead of the Eternal Son. "But surely," says Mr. Matthew Arnold, "if there be anything with which metaphysics have nothing to do, and where a plain man without skill to walk in the arduous paths of abstruse reasoning may find himself at home, it is religion. For the object of religion is *conduct*; and conduct is really, however men may overlay it with philosophical disquisitions, the simplest thing in the world." Indeed, the greatness of Confucius as a *true* religious teacher lies even in this: that his teaching contains no abstruse "ism" and it insists not upon any singular theory of living, but upon the simple doing of plain ordinary duties of every day life. Confucius, we are told in another place, taught four things: letters, conduct, honesty and truthfulness.

The late Mr. J. A. Froude says: "Many a hundred sermons have I heard in England, many a dissertation on the mysteries of the faith, on the divine mission

子曰："素隐行怪，后世有述焉，吾弗为之矣。

孔子说："有些人在宗教与哲学中寻求深奥难懂的意义，并且过一种怪异奇特的生活，以让子孙后代记住他们的名字。那是我永不会去做的。

[在孔子的时代，有一些玄思的智者，像老子，他相信人类的拯救依赖于他们已经发现的一些深奥难懂的"主义"。也有一些实用的博爱主义者，像墨子，他相信所有的社会上的邪恶都能治愈，只要人们开始过一些非凡的生活：给鞋子打补丁或不再穿长裤。

在今天，基督教的传教士们说儒学并非宗教，因为它没有深奥的理论，如基督教的三位一体的教理，或者上帝的永恒之子。"但可以确信的是，"马修·阿诺德说："如果有任何东西，形而上学对它毫无办法；以及如果任何一个地方，一个没有任何技巧的普通人，能走在深奥推理的艰难之路上而自我感觉舒适，那么，它就是宗教。因为宗教的目标是行为，而行为是世界上最简单的事情，尽管人们经常用哲学专论包装它。"确实，孔子作为一位真正的宗教导师的伟大之处在于：他的教义中并不包含深奥难懂的"主义"，而且，它不强调任何非凡的生活理论，而是强调日常生活中的普通而简单的责任。在其他地方我们了解到，孔子教人以四物：文学、行为、正直与坦率。

已故的J.A.弗劳德先生说："我曾在英国的教堂听过上百次布道，但所听到的要么是教中的圣迹，要么是教士们的传教和使徒的传承，要么是关于主教、正义、好好工作的理论、字句默示和圣餐效力等，但是我从没听到过对基督教最古老的戒律的宣讲，即教人做一个诚实的人，如

of the clergy, on apostolic succession, on bishops, and justification and the theory of good works, and verbal inspiration, and the efficacy of the sacraments; but never one that I can recollect on common honesty, on these primitive commandments, 'Thou shalt not lie' and 'Thou shalt not steal' ."]

"There are again good men who try to live in conformity with the moral law, but who, when they have gone half way, throw it up. I never could give it up.

[Mr. Matthew Arnold says: "Conduct is the simplest thing in the world as far as *understanding* is concerned; as regards *doing*, it is the hardest thing in the world." Hence the saying of the Latin poet, "Video meliora proboque deteriora sequ ar."]

"Lastly there are truly moral men who unconsciously live a life in entire harmony with the universal moral order and who live unknown to the world and unnoticed of men without any concern. It is only men of holy, divine natures who are capable of this."

'不要说谎','不要偷窃'。"①]

　　"君子遵道而行,半涂而废,吾弗能已矣。

　　"还有一些良善之人想过一种符合道德法则的生活,但他们走了一半路时就放弃了。我永不会放弃。

　　[马修·阿诺德先生说:"就理解而言,行为是世上最简单的事情;至于实干,它是世上最难的事情。"因此,那首拉丁文诗说:"我看到什么是善,也赞同善,但我却在作恶。"②]

　　"君子依乎中庸,遁世不见知而不悔,唯圣者能之。"

　　"最后,也有真正的有道德的人,他们无意识地过着与普遍道德秩序完全相一致的生活,他们在世界上默默无闻,不被人们所注意,然而,他们并不在意。只有本性圣洁、神圣的人才能做到如此。"

①　本段引文辜鸿铭在《中国人的精神(在北京东方学会上所宣讲的论文)》一篇中也曾引用过(见夏丹等选编,《辜鸿铭作品精选·中国人的精神》,第55—56页)。该书在注释中对弗劳德的解释是:"1818—1894,英国历史学家和作家。卡莱尔的友人和思想的信徒,也是卡莱尔遗嘱指定的处理其文学遗著者之一。曾发表卡莱尔的《回忆》,著有《信仰的因果》《托马斯·卡莱尔——他的一生的前四十年》等。"
②　此诗句的翻译转引自《自然法典》中对奥维德诗句的翻译(见[法]莫莱里,《自然法典》,黄建华、姜亚洲译,商务印书馆,1982,第85页)。

【评述】

通过对比"素隐行怪"与"遵道而行"(及后面的"依乎中庸"),本章实则是再次对儒家哲学"世俗性"的再次强调。同时,也表达了行道之难。

"素隐行怪",辜鸿铭译为"seek for some abstruse meaning in religion and philosophy and who live a life of singularity"(在宗教与哲学中寻求深奥难懂的意义,并且过一种怪异奇特的生活)。其中,"素"即"seek for"(寻找),"隐"即"abstruse meaning in religion and philosophy"(宗教与哲学中深奥难懂的意义),"行"即"live a life of"(过……的生活),"怪"即"singularity"(怪异、奇特的)。换言之,这句话表达的是刻意过一种迥异于日常生活的生活方式,以期留名于后世。而在辜鸿铭看来,这与孔子之道恰相违背。

在第四章的解读中,辜鸿铭曾有过这样的论述:"道德本性,我们所称作的道德存在,不是别的,正是我们真正的、道德上的普通自我。去过一种道德的生活,因此就意味着去生活;去生活,既不作为天使也不作为禽兽,而是作为本性的、普通的、理性的人类存在。"接着,在对本章第一段的解读中,辜鸿铭又进一步强调:"孔子作为一位真正的宗教导师的伟大之处在于:他的教义中并不包含深奥难懂的'主义',而且,它不强调任何非凡的生活理论,而是强调日常生活中的普通而简单的责任。"我们在此还可以引述他在《中国人的精神(在北京东方学会上所宣讲的论文)》中的一句话来说明:"欧洲人心目中的宗教,企图使每一个人都变成一个完人、一个圣者、一个佛陀和一个天使。相反,儒教却仅仅限于使人成为一个好的百姓,一个孝子良民而已。"(夏丹等选编,《辜鸿铭作品精选·中国人的精神》,第39页)概言之,儒学是教给人如何过好普通的日子,而非别的。为留名后世而"素隐行怪"的人,恰恰背离了孔子的学说——此处所说的"道",也即"中庸"。

后面,孔子强调了"遵道而行"与"依乎中庸"的困难。"遵道而行"易致"半涂而废",但孔子发誓"吾弗能已矣"(I never could give it up,我永不放弃)。而"依乎中庸",并且"遁世不见,知而不悔",恐怕只有"圣者"才能做得到了。其中,"道"译为"the moral law"(道德法则),"中庸"译为"the universal moral order"(普遍道德秩序)。可以说,在"中庸"的哲学逻辑中,"道德法则"是核心,"普遍道德秩序"则是其本体面目。

XII.
第十二章

The moral law is to be found everywhere and yet it is a secret.

[Goethe calls it the "open secret" .]

The simple intelligence of ordinary men and women of the people may understand something of the moral law; but in its utmost reaches there is something which even the wisest and holiest of men cannot understand. The ignoble natures of ordinary men and women of the people may be able to carry out the moral law; but in its utmost reaches even the wisest and holiest of men cannot live up to it.

Great as the Universe is, man with the infinite moral nature in him is never satisfied. For there is nothing so great but the mind of the moral man can conceive of something still greater which nothing in the world can hold. There is nothing so small but the mind of moral man can conceive of something still smaller which nothing in the world can split.

[Carlyle says: "Man's unhappiness comes of his greatness; it is because there is an infinite in him, which with all his cunning he cannot quite bury under the finite.Will the whole finance ministers and upholsterers and confectioners of modern Europe undertake, in joint stock company, to make one shoeblack *happy*? They cannot accomplish it; for the shoeblack also has a soul quite other than his stomach, and would require, if you consider it, for his permanent satisfaction and saturation, simply this allotment, no more and no less: God's infinite Universe altogether to himself."]

君子之道费而隐。

道德法则随处可见，然而，它仍是个秘密。

［歌德称它为"公开的秘密"。］

夫妇之愚，可以与知焉，及其至也，虽圣人亦有所不知焉；夫妇之不肖，可以能行焉，及其至也，虽圣人亦有所不能焉。

天地之大也，人犹有所憾。故君子语大，天下莫能载焉；语小，天下莫能破焉。

智力简单的普通男女也能懂得一些道德法则；但在它的最高程度上，即使是最聪明、最神圣的人也会有所不懂。品性卑贱的普通男女也能够践行一些道德法则；然而，在它的最高程度上，即使是最聪明、最神圣的人，也无法实践它。

即使大如宇宙，具有无限道德本性的人们也永不满足。因为，除了有道德的人的思想，无法设想还有什么能比世界承载的更多；除了有道德的人的思想，也无法设想还有什么能比世界分割得更小。

［卡莱尔说："人的不幸源于他的伟大；这是因为在他身上有一种无限，不管他行事多么巧妙，都不能把无限完全埋在有限之下。现在欧洲所有的财政部长、家具商、糕点商愿合伙开公司，以便使一个擦鞋匠生活幸福吗？他们完不成这个任务，因为擦鞋匠也有着一个与他的胃非常不同的灵魂；如果你考虑到这一点，为了能使他永远快乐满足，只为他要求得到这一份额，既不多也不少：上帝无限的世界都属于他个人。"①］

----

① 译文引自［英］托马斯·卡莱尔，《拼凑的裁缝》，马秋武、冯卉等译，2004，第176—177页。其译文中"一两个小时他们也不能完成这个任务"与辜鸿铭引述的英文"They cannot accomplish it"有出人，因此，我们在选引时做了改动。

The *Book of Songs* says: "The hawk soars to the heavens above and fishes dive to the depths below."

That is to say, there is no place in the highest heavens above nor in the deepest waters below where the moral law does not reign.

["If I take the wings of the morning and dwell in the uttermost parts of the universe, God is there." Emerson says: "The moral law lies at the centre of Nature and radiates to the circumference. It is the pith and marrow of every substance, every relation and every process."]

The moral law takes its rise in the relation between man and woman; but in its utmost reaches it reigns supreme over heaven and earth.

[Morality begins with Sex. Students of German literature may remember Faust's confession of faith to Margaret:

Lifts not the Heaven its dome above?
    Doth not the firm set Earth beneath us lie?
And beaming tenderly with looks of love,
    Climb not the everlasting stars on high?
Do we got gaze into each other's eyes?
    Nature's impenetrable agencies,

《诗》云："鸢飞戾天，鱼跃于渊。"

言其上下察也。

《诗经》[①]上说："鹰向上高翔，鱼向下深潜。"

那是说，无论是最高的天上，还是最深的水下，无处不在道德法则的支配之中。

["我若展开早晨的翅膀，飞到宇宙之极居住，那么，上帝就在那儿。"爱默生说："道德法则位于大自然的中心，并向周围辐射。它是每个物质、每个关系及每个过程的核心与精华。"]

君子之道，造端乎夫妇；及其至也，察乎天地。

道德法则始于男人与女人的关系之中，但它的最高状态，则是支配天地的最高原则。

[道德源自性（sex）。学德国文学的学生们，可能还记得浮士德向马嘉丽特如此表白忠心：

天不是在上形成穹顶？

地不是在下浑厚坚凝？

永恒的星辰

不是和蔼地闪灼而上升？

我不是用眼睛看着你的眼睛？

万物不是逼近

---

① 直译应为"诗之典籍"。

Are they not thronging on thy heart and brain,

Viewless, invisible to mortal ken,

Around thee weaving their mysterious chain?

Fill thence thy heart, how large soe'r it be,

And in the filling, when thou utterly art blest,

Then call it what thou wilt —

Call it Bliss! Heart! Love! God!]

你的头脑和胸心?

他们不是在永恒的神秘中

有形无形地在你身旁纷纭?

不论你的心胸多么广大也可充盈,

如果你在这种感觉中完全欣幸,

那你就可以随意将它命名,

叫它是幸福! 是心! 是爱! 是神! ①]

① 译文引自歌德,《浮士德》,董问樵译,复旦大学出版社,1983,第200页。

【评述】

除第一章外，可以说此章再次直接解释了"道"。因为在第二至十一章中，虽然作者表达了"道"的特征及行"道"之难，然而，都是借助"圣人"、"君子"及"小人"们的不同表现而侧面展现的。此章则直接解释了"道"的来源、内涵及存在形态，正式回应了"道"本身含义的问题。

首先让我们看一下"道"的来源及内涵。"道"，辜鸿铭译为"the moral law"（道德法则）。按照我们在第一章总结出的逻辑链条，道德法则从根本上讲即对"神圣的宇宙秩序"（天命）的遵循。换言之，也可以说此处要解决的是"天命"为何物的根本问题。辜鸿铭在《中国人的精神（在北京东方学会上所宣讲的论文）》中也说："孔子整个的教育思想体系或许可以被归纳为一句话：君子之道。"（夏丹等选编，《辜鸿铭作品精选·中国人的精神》，第50页）事实上，他在该书中对"道"的阐述已经相当详细，现录于下，无须赘言：

> 孔子称君子之道是个秘密。孔子说："君子之道无处不在，但它仍然是一个秘密。"（君子之道费而隐）然而，孔子还说过："甚至愚夫愚妇亦能够对这个秘密有所了解，他们也能够奉行君子之道。"（夫妇之愚，可以与知焉）同样知道这一秘密的歌德，就把它——君子之道，成为"公开的秘密"。那么，人类是在何处、又是怎样发现了这一秘密的呢？诸位想必还记得，我曾说过，对君子之道的认识始于对夫妻关系的认识。歌德所谓的"公开的秘密"，孔子所说的"君子之道"，首先是被夫妇们所发现的。……（同上，第50—51页）

> 换言之，宗教教我们服从的人之性，是我们必须服从的人之真性。这种本性既不是圣·保罗所说的世俗或肉体之性，亦非奥古斯特·孔德的著名弟子利特（Littre）先生所说的人类自我保护和繁衍的本性。这种人之真性是圣·保罗所说的灵魂之性，也就是孔子所言的君子之道。简言之，宗教告诉我们必须服从自己的真正本性，这个本性就是基督所说的我们心中的上帝。……（同上，第52页）

> 宗教的生命与灵魂是君子之道，君子之道由爱而生。人类首先自男女之间学到了爱，但人类之爱并不仅限于男女之爱，它包括了人类所有纯真的感情，这里既有父母与孩子之间的那种亲情，也含有人类对于万事万物所抱有的慈爱、怜悯、同情和仁义之心。事实上，人类所有纯真的情感均可以容纳在一个中国字中，这就是"仁"。在欧洲语言中，古老的基督教术语中的神性（godliness）一词与"仁"的

意义最接近。因为"仁"是人所具有的一种神圣的、超凡的品质。在现代术语中，"仁"相当于仁慈、人类之爱，或简称爱。简言之，宗教的灵魂、宗教的感化力的源泉便来自于这个中国字——"仁"，来自爱——不管你如何称呼它，在这个世界上，这种爱最初是起自夫妇。宗教的感化力就在于此，这也是宗教中的至上之德。正如我曾说过的那样，宗教正是据此使人服从道德规范或者说是服从"道"（它构成神圣的宇宙秩序的一部分）。孔子说："君子之道始于夫妻关系，将其推到极致，君子之道就支配了天地万物——即整个宇宙。"（君子之道，造端乎夫妇；及其至也，察乎天地。）（同上，第53—54页）

在此也应指出，在辜鸿铭的思想中所一以贯之的，也恰恰就是这种"道"的思想。他曾在《张文襄幕府纪闻》中总结说"中西固无二道"，指的也是这里的"道"（他又称之为歌德所说的"公开的秘密"）。这是辜鸿铭的思想的根基，在此基础之上，他对中西文化及现实进行了一系列的对比。

值得注意的是，"夫妇"只是发现了"道"的存在，但"道"本身却并非等于人间之爱，即辜鸿铭所说的"仁"。因为"道"所支配的并非仅仅是人间，而且是宇宙万物。正如文中所说：《诗》云：'鸢飞戾天，鱼跃于渊。'言其上下察也。君子之道，造端乎夫妇；及其至也，察乎天地。辜鸿铭的翻译是："That is to say, there is no place in the highest heavens above nor in the deepest waters below where the moral law does not reign. The moral law takes its rise in the relation between man and woman; but in its utmost reaches it reigns supreme over heaven and earth."（无论是最高的天上，还是最深的水下，无处不在道德法则的支配之中。道德法则始于男人与女人的关系之中，但它的最高状态，则是支配天地的最高原则。）也就是说，所谓"神圣的宇宙秩序"，即被"男女"发现的这一道德法则。这也是第一章所说的"天命之谓性，率性之谓道"的根本内涵。（也可以参考我们在第一章中所总结出的逻辑链条。）

可以说此章与第一章遥相呼应，极其重要。

XIII.

第十三章

Confucius remarked: "The moral law is not something away from the actuality of human life. When men take up something away from the actuality of human life as the moral law, that is not the moral law.

["The Kingdom of God is within you." Goethe says: " 'The Ideal' — our America, as one of the characters in *Wilhelm Meister* says, — is here in the present *actual* and not far away."]

"The *Book of Songs* says: 'In hewing an axe handle, the *pattern* is not far off.'

"Thus when we take an axe handle in our hand to hew the other and glance from one to the other there is still some distance between them as compared with the relation between the moral law and the man himself. Wherefore the moral man in dealing with men appeals to the common human nature and changes the manner of their lives and nothing more.

"When a man carries out the principles of conscientiousness and reciprocity he is not far from the moral law. What you do not wish others should do unto you, do not do unto them.

"There are four things in the moral life of a man, not one of which have I been able to carry out in my life. To serve my father as I would expect my son to serve me: that I have not been able to do. To serve my sovereign as I would expect a minister under me to serve me: that I have not been able to do. To act towards my elder brother as I would expect my younger brother to act towards me: that I have not

子曰："道不远人。人之为道而远人，不可以为道。

孔子说："道德法则是不可以脱离人类现实生活的。当人们将脱离人类现实生活的东西当作道德法则时，那并非道德法则。

["上帝的王国在你内心，"歌德说，"'理想'——我们的美国，就像《威廉·麦斯特》中的一个人物所说的——就在当下的现实中，并不遥远。"]

"《诗》云：'伐柯伐柯，其则不远。'

"执柯以伐柯，睨而视之，犹以为远。故君子以人治人，改而止。

"忠恕违道不远，施诸己而不愿，亦勿施于人。

"君子之道四，丘未能一焉：所求乎子，以事父未能也；所求乎臣，以事君未能也；所求乎弟，以事兄未能也；所求乎朋友，先施之未能也。

"《诗经》上说：'砍啊砍斧柄，样式并不远。'

"因此，当我们手持一把斧头去砍制另一把时，以及从一个而观察另一个时，它们之间仍有差距，如同拿道德法则同人本身作比较一样。因此，有道德的人在对待大众时，会按照普通的人类本质而转变他们的生活方式，仅此而已。

"当一个人践行尽责及互惠原则时，他就离道德法则不远了。你不希望别人对你做的事情，也不要对别人做。

"人的道德生活中有四件事，我在生活中一件都没能践行。像希望我自己的儿子照顾我一样去照顾我的父亲：我没能做到。像希望我自己的下属为我服务一样去为我的君主服务：我没能做到。像希望我的弟弟对待我一样去对待我的兄长：我没能做到。就像

been able to do. To be the first to behave towards friends as I would expect them to behave towards me: that I have not been able to do.

"In the discharge of the ordinary duties of life and in the exercise of care in ordinary conversation, whenever there is shortcoming never fail to strive for improvement, and when there is much to be said, always say less than what is necessary; words having respect to actions and actions having respect to words. Is it not just this thorough genuineness and absence of pretence which characterises the moral man?"

[Emerson says: "I look upon the simple and childish virtues of veracity and honesty as the root of all that is sublime in character. Speak as you think, be what you are, pay your debts of all kinds. I prefer to be owned as sound and solvent, — to all the *eclat* in the universe."]

我希望朋友对待我那样首先去对待朋友：我没能做到。

"庸德之行，庸言之谨，有所不足，不敢不勉，有余不敢尽；言顾行，行顾言，君子胡不慥慥尔！"

"在履行日常生活中的责任以及在日常谈话中小心谨慎时，每当有缺点但不至于阻止你前进，以及有很多话你要说时，说话要少于非说不可的。说话要顾及到行为，行为也要顾及到说话。难道不正是这样的完全真诚及毫不虚伪而刻画了有道德的人的性格吗？"

［爱默生说："我将老实诚恳这种简朴及孩童般的美德，视为品格中所有的高尚品质之根。所言如你所想，表现真实的自己，偿还一切债务。与宇宙中所有的荣誉相比，我更愿被承认是可靠与有偿还能力的。"］

【评述】

上一章讲述的是"道"的内涵，此章则重点讲，在日常生活中，一位君子应该如何遵"道"而行。

首先，在开头仍然强调的是那个老问题："道"离不开现实生活。文中说："道不远人。人之为道而远人，不可以为道"，辜鸿铭译为"The moral law is not something away from the actuality of human life. When men take up something away from the actuality of human life as the moral law, that is not the moral law"（道德法则不是可以脱离人类现实生活的。当人们将脱离人类现实生活的东西当作道德法则时，那并非道德法则）。"道"依然指"道德法则"。"人"指的是"the actuality of human life"（人类的现实生活）。

那么，该如何在现实生活中践行"道德法则"呢？文中指出四点：1."所求乎子，以事父"译为"To serve my father as I would expect my son to serve me"（像希望我自己的儿子照顾我一样去照顾我的父亲）; 2."所求乎臣，以事君"译为"To serve my sovereign as I would expect a minister under me to serve me"（像希望我自己的下属为我服务一样去为我的君主服务）; 3."所求乎弟，以事兄"译为"To act towards my elder brother as I would expect my younger brother to act towards me"（像希望我的弟弟对待我一样去对待我的兄长）; 4."所求乎朋友，先施之"译为"To be the first to behave towards friends as I would expect them to behave towards me"（就像我希望朋友对待我那样首先去对待朋友）。这四点，可以视为践行"道德法则"的四条"行为准则"。难度之大，孔子认为自己一条也"未能也"。然而，这里表面是强调的行为方式，其实是强调的人的内心（或曰思维方式），即文中所说的"忠恕违道不远"，即"When a man carries out the principles of conscientiousness and reciprocity he is not far from the moral law"（当一个人践行尽责及互惠原则，他就离道德法则不远了）。换言之，重点是要人有"尽责"与"互惠"之心——这是辜鸿铭对"忠恕"的解释。有了这样的心理去行事，就离"道"（道德法则）不远了。

下文又总结、强调说："庸德之行，庸言之谨，有所不足，不敢不勉，有余不敢尽；言顾行，行顾言，君子胡不慥慥尔！"这句话译为："In the discharge of the ordinary duties of life and in the exercise of care in ordinary conversation, whenever there is shortcoming never fail to strive for improvement, and when there is much to be said, always say less than what is necessary; words having respect to actions and actions having respect to words. Is it not just this thorough genuineness and absence of pretence which characterises the moral man?"（在履行日常生活中的责任以及在日常谈话中小心谨慎

时，每当有缺点但不至于阻止你前进，以及有很多话你要说时，说话要少于非说不可的。说话要顾及到行为，行为也要顾及到说话。难道不正是这样的完全真诚及毫不虚伪而刻画了有道德的人的性格吗？）强调的其实是心中要保持谨慎。如果说遵循"道德法则"是"中庸"之道的核心，以上四种行为方式是外在表现，"忠恕"是内心要求，那么，谨慎小心即其态度了。

XIV.
第十四章

The moral man conforms himself to his life circumstances; he does not desire anything outside of his position.

Finding himself in a position of wealth and honour, he lives as becomes one living in a position of wealth and honour. Finding himself in a position of poverty and humble circumstances, he lives as becomes one living in a position of poverty and humble circumstances. Finding himself in uncivilized countries, he lives as becomes one living in uncivilized countries. Finding himself in circumstances of danger and difficulty, he acts according to what is required of a man under such circumstances. In one word, the moral man can find himself in no situation in life in which he is not master of himself.

In a high position he does not domineer over his subordinates. In a subordinate position he does not court the favours of his superiors. He puts in order his own personal conduct and seeks nothing from others; hence he has no complaint to make. He complains not against God nor rails against men.

Thus it is that the moral man lives out the even tenor of his life calmly waiting for the appointment of God, whereas the vulgar person takes to dangerous courses, expecting the uncertain chances of luck.

Confucius remarked: "In the practice of archery we have something resembling the principle in a moral man's life. When the archer misses the centre of the target he turns round and seeks for the cause of his failure within himself."

君子素其位而行，不愿乎其外。

素富贵，行乎富贵；素贫贱，行乎贫贱；素夷狄，行乎夷狄；素患难，行乎患难；君子无入而不自得焉。

在上位不陵下，在下位不援上，正己而不求于人则无怨。上不怨天，下不尤人。

故君子居易以俟命，小人行险以徼幸。

子曰："射有似乎君子；失诸正鹄，反求诸其身。"

有道德的人总是让自己与他的生活环境相协调。他从不欲求超出他处境的任何东西。

发现自己身处财富与荣誉的环境之中，他就作为一个生活于财富与荣誉环境中的人去生活。发现自己身处贫穷与卑微的环境中，他就作为一个生活于贫穷与卑微环境中的人去生活。发现自己身处不开化的国家中，他就作为一个生活于不开化国家的人去生活。发现自己身处危险与艰难的环境中，他就按照此环境下所要求的那样去做。一句话，有道德的人在任何环境下都是自己的主人。

身处较高的职位，他不会欺凌下属。身处下级职位，他不会向上级献媚以获帮助。他规范自己的言行而不依求别人，因此，他没有抱怨，既不抱怨上帝，也不抱怨世人。

因此，有道德的人过着一种安稳平静的生活，等待上帝的安排。然而，粗俗之人则喜欢走危险路线，期待不确定的好运。

孔子说："在箭术练习中，有类似于有道德的人的生活的原则。当射手没射中靶心时，他会反思并寻找他自己的不足。"

【评述】

辜鸿铭认为，此章重在强调人在世俗生活中所应有的心理状态。什么样的状态呢？即"君子无入而不自得焉"的状态，辜鸿铭译为"the moral man can find himself in no situation in life in which he is not master of himself"（有道德的人在任何环境下都是自己的主人）。意思是，在任何环境下，一个君子（有道德的人），总会是自己的主人，而非被环境所奴役。这就是此章的核心意思，也是对"君子素其位而行，不愿乎其外"（The moral man conforms himself to his life circumstances; he does not desire anything outside of his position[有道德的人总是让自己与他的生活环境相协调。他从不欲求超出他处境的任何东西]）的一种解释。段中所举的例子是说明这个道理的，后面的论述则仍然在阐明这个道理。

"正己而不求于人则无怨。上不怨天，下不尤人"，辜鸿铭译为"He puts in order his own personal conduct and seeks nothing from others; hence he has no complaint to make. He complains not against God nor rails against men"（他规范自己的言行而不依求别人，因此，他没有抱怨，既不抱怨上帝也不抱怨世人），是这一道理的另一种表现。正因为在任何环境之下，自己都会做自己的主人，让自己的生活与环境相协调，那么，他就会遇事寻求自己之心，而非在心理上依傍于他人，从而不会怨天尤人。而寻求自己之心，也即依傍于自己内心的力量，善于反思自己、改进自己，从而促进自己的真正发展。这也是最后一段孔子之语的含义，"失诸正鹄，反求诸其身"，辜鸿铭译为"When the archer misses the centre of the target he turns round and seeks for the cause of his failure within himself"（当射手没射中靶心时，他会反思并寻找他自己的不足）。

换言之，前几章中他用以解释"中庸"的"道德存在的中心线索"，也即人的内心力量之所在，也即力量之源。坚持这样的"中心线索"，则外在表现为"君子无入而不自得焉"（在任何环境之下都做自己的主人）。并且，"正己而不求于人则无怨"（规范自己的言行而不依求别人，因此，他没有抱怨）。反过来，这样的"安稳平静"的心理状态，又是对"道德存在的中心线索"的护卫。最后应该强调的是，此处所说的"做自己的主人"，并非教人变得性格固执，其要害还在于寻找"道德存在的中心线索"，是对这一"道"的坚守，而非对"己见"的坚守。"在上位不陵下；在下位不援上"是这一"道"在日常生活中的一个表现，它蕴含着"自主"或"独立"的思想。——并且，在相当程度上，也是"己所不欲，勿施于人"、"己欲立而立人，己欲达而达人"被视为"忠恕"的思想的表现。因为它们都讲的是对自己的"道"的坚守，以及对他人的尊重与爱护。

XV.
第十五章

The moral life of man may be likened to travelling to a distant place; one must start from the nearest stage. It may also be likened to ascending a height; one must begin from the lowest step.

The *Book of Songs* says:

When wife and children dwell in unison,

'Tis like to harp and lute well played in tune;

When brothers live in concord and at peace

The strain of harmony shall never cease.

Make then your home thus always gay and bright,

Your wife and dear ones shall be your delight.

Confucius, commenting on the above, remarked: "In such a state of things what more satisfaction can parents have?"

[In what follows, I have ventured to transfer the sequence of the sections as they stand in the original text. The following section stands in the original as section XX.]

君子之道,辟如行远必自迩,辟如登高必自卑。

《诗》曰:"妻子好合,如鼓瑟琴;兄弟既翕,和乐且耽;宜尔室家,乐尔妻帑。"

子曰:"父母其顺矣乎!"

人的道德生活可以比作走向远方的长途旅行,必须从最近的地方开始出发。它同样可以比作向高处攀爬,必须从最低的一阶开始。

《诗经》上说:

> 当妻儿协调一致,
> 恰如琴瑟优美地合奏;
> 当兄弟和睦相处,
> 和谐旋律将永不终止。
> 让家中充满欢愉吧,
> 妻子家人将带来乐趣。

孔子评论上面的诗句说:"在这样的状态下,还有什么是能使父母更顺心的呢?"

[在下文中,我冒险地改动了原文的排序。下一章在原文中本是第二十章。]

【评述】

如果说第十三章是讲了"道"的行为准则,那么,此章则重点讲,在践行"道"时应遵循怎样的哲学思路。怎样的思路呢? 文中说是"辟如行远必自迩,辟如登高必自卑"。"君子之道",此处辜鸿铭译为"the moral life of man"(人的道德生活),即讲人怎样才能"实现"道德的生活。

下面所引的《诗经》的话,其实就是对这一道德生活的基本状态的描述,即所谓的"迩"与"卑"的指代意义——即对妻子、孩子、兄弟等家庭成员的关系状态的期待或要求。也可以说,此章是对道德生活下家庭应然状态的描述。

XVI.
第十六章①

Duke Ai (ruler of Confucius' native state) asked what constituted good government.

Confucius replied: "The principles of good government of the Emperors Wen and Wu are abundantly illustrated in the records preserved. When the men are there, good government will flourish, but when the men are gone, good government decays and becomes extinct.

"With the right men the growth of good government is as rapid as the growth of vegetation is in the right soil. Indeed, good government is like a fast growing plant.

"The conduct of government, therefore, depends upon the men. The right men are obtained by the ruler's personal character. To put in order his personal character, the ruler must use the moral law. To put in order the moral law, the ruler must use the moral sense.

"The moral sense is the characteristic attribute of man. To feel natural affection for those nearly related to us is the highest expression of the moral sense. The sense of justice is the recognition of what is right and proper. To honour those who are worthier than ourselves is the highest expression of the sense of justice. The relative degrees of natural affection we ought to feel for those who are nearly related to us and the relative grades of honour we ought to show to those worthier than ourselves: these are that which gives rise to the forms and distinctions in social life. For unless social inequalities have a true and moral basis, government of the people is an impossibility.

哀公问政。

子曰:"文武之政,布在方策。其人存,则其政举;其人亡,则其政息。

"人道敏政,地道敏树。夫政也者,蒲卢也。

"故为政在人,取人以身,修身以道,修道以仁。

哀公(孔子故国的统治者)询问什么才算是好的统治。

孔子回答说:"文王与武王的优良统治的原则,在那现存的记录中有丰富的阐释。人在时,优良的统治就非常繁荣;人不在了,优良的统治就衰退并最终绝迹了。

"当有合适的人时,优良统治的增长速度,就像长于肥沃土地的植物。事实上,好的统治恰如生长迅速的植物。

"因此,统治的表现,取决于人。合适的人,是通过统治者的个人品德而获得的。要规范他的个人品德,一位统治者必须运用道德法则。而规范道德法则,那统治者就必须运用道德情感。

"仁者人也,亲亲为大;义者宜也,尊贤为大;亲亲之杀,尊贤之等,礼所生也。在下位不获乎上,民不可得而治矣!

"道德情感是人的典型属性。去感受对那些与我们关系密切的人的天然情感,就是道德情感的最高表达。正义感就意味着识别正确与恰当。去尊敬那些比我们自己更有品德的人,就是正义感的最高表现。对那些与我们关系密切的人们,我们应感知对他们的关系的程度,对那些比我们自己更有品德的人们,我们应表现出对他们尊敬的等级:这些就构成了社会生活的形态与特性①。除

---

① 这句话是对"亲亲之杀,尊贤之等,礼所生也"的辜译之翻译,正如后面辜鸿铭对这段的解读所提及,他认为"礼所生"应为"礼所以生",故有此译。

[礼所生 in the text should be 礼所以生. The last sentence supposed by Chinese commentators to be an interpolation is really not so. I have freely translated it. Literally it means: "unless the lower orders are satisfied with those above them, government of the people is an impossibility."

According to Confucius, here, the basis of social inequalities rests upon two moral foundations, viz., the moral sense, the highest expression of which is natural affection — the feeling of love which all men feel for those nearly related to them — and the sense of justice, the highest expression of which is hero-worship — the feeling of respect and submission which all men feel for those worthier than themselves. In the family, natural affection makes submission easy, and in the state, hero-worship makes subordination natural and proper.

But in Europe, the plea for the justification of social inequalities is interests.The people are told to submit to the constituted authorities and to put up with social inequalities because it is to their interest to do so; for if they allow the anarchists to have their way and destroy social inequalities, the evils which will result from this will be worse than the evils of social inequalities. *See Appendix D.

In China, the peasant and coolie readily submit to the mandarins, because they have been taught to recognise the true moral basis of privilege: worthiness. *Noblesse oblige*. But woe to the mandarins when the peasants and coolies of China find out that they (the mandarins) are not worthier than the peasants and coolies over whom they are set to govern.]

非社会的不平等具有一个真实而道德的基础，否则，对人民的统治是不可能的。

[文中的"礼所生"应为"礼所以生"。中国的注释家们认为最后一句遭到了篡改，但我认为不是。我已经自由地翻译了此句[1]。它的字面意思是："除非较低职位的人满意在他们之上的人，否则对人民的统治是不可能的。"

通过此处孔子的阐述，社会的不平等依靠两种道德基础，即，道德情感，天然情感的最高表达——所有人对与他们关系密切的人们的爱；以及正义感，最高表达是英雄崇拜——所有人对比自己更有品德的人们的尊敬与恭顺。在家庭中，天然情感使得恭顺非常容易，在一个国家中，英雄崇拜则使从属变得自然与恰当。

但在欧洲，为社会不平等辩解的理由是利益。人们被告知，服从于设立的权威以及忍受社会不平等，是因为他们的利益使然。因为，如果他们允许无政府主义者大行其道并破坏掉社会不平等，那么，由此而产生的不幸将甚于社会不平等而产生的不幸。*见附录D。

在中国，农民与苦力对满清官员的服从，是因为他们能通过教育而认识到特权的道德基础：品性。位高则任重。但当中国的农民与苦力们发现他们（满清官员）并不比自己更加有品性，然而却统治他们时，那些满清官员就要遭殃了[2]。]

---

① 指"在下位不获乎上，民不可得而治矣！"《四书章句集注·中庸》引郑玄注："此句在下，误重在此。"辜鸿铭不同意郑玄的看法，并意译这句话为"For unless social inequalities have a ture and moral basis, sovernment of the people is an impossibility"（除非社会的不平等具有一个真实而道德的基础，否则，对人民的统治是不可能的）。

② 在《宪政主义与中国》中，辜鸿铭系统地论述了国家统治到底应该依靠什么，并批驳了从亚里士多德到霍布斯的"利害"理论（见黄兴涛主编，《辜鸿铭文集·下卷》，第175—191页）。

"Therefore it is necessary for a man of the governing class to set about regulating his personal conduct and character. In considering how to regulate his personal conduct and character it is necessary for him to do his duties towards those nearly related to him. In considering how to do his duties towards those nearly related to him it is necessary for him to understand the nature and organisation of human society. In considering the nature and organisation of human society it is necessary for him to understand the laws of God.

[君子 in the text above means a gentleman by his social position. And the phrase 知人 does not mean "man", but human society and institutions as opposed to 天, divine appointments.]

"The duties of universal obligation are five, and the moral qualities by which they are carried out are three. The duties are those between ruler and subject; between father and son; between husband and wife; between elder brother and younger; and those in the intercourse between friends. These are the five duties of universal obligation. Intelligence, moral character and courage: these are the three universally recognised moral qualities of man. It matters not in what way men come to the exercise of these moral qualities, the result is one and the same.

"Some men are born with the knowledge of these moral qualities; some acquire it as the result of education; some acquire it as the result of hard experience. But when the knowledge is acquired, it comes to one and the same thing. Some exercise these moral qualities naturally

"故君子不可以不修身；思修身，不可以不事亲；思事亲，不可以不知人；思知人，不可以不知天。

"因此，一个人作为统治阶层的一员，有必要调整他的个人言行与品德。"而考虑到如何去调整个人言行与品德，他有必要向那些与他关系亲密的人履行义务。而考虑到如何去向那些与他关系亲密的人履行义务，他有必要懂得人类社会的本质与构成。而考虑到如何了解人类社会的本质与构成，他有必要懂得上帝的律法。

［上文中的"君子"意指一位绅士的社会地位而言。而"知人"一词也并非指"人"而言，而是指与"天"——天职——相对的人类社会与组织。］

"天下之达道五，所以行之者三：曰君臣也，父子也，夫妇也，昆弟也，朋友之交也：五者天下之达道也。知、仁、勇三者，天下之达德也，所以行之者一也。

"或生而知之，或学而知之，或困而知之，及其知之一也；或安而行之，或利而行之，或勉强而行之，及其成功一也。"

子曰："好学近乎知，力行近乎仁，知耻近乎勇。

"知斯三者，则知所以修身；知所以修身，则知所以治人；知所以治人，则知所以治天下国家矣。

"凡为天下国家有九经，曰：修身也，尊贤也，亲亲也，敬大臣也，体群臣也，子庶民也，来百工也，柔远人也，怀诸侯也。

"修身则道立，尊贤则不惑，亲亲则诸父昆弟不怨，敬大臣则不眩，体群臣则士之报礼重，子庶民则百姓劝，来百工则财用足，柔远人则四方归之，怀诸侯则天下畏之。

and easily; some because they find it advantageous to do so; some with effort and difficulty. But when the achievement is made it comes to one and the same thing."

Confucius went on to say: "Love of knowledge is the characteristic of men of intellectual character. Strenuous attention to conduct is the characteristic of men of moral character. Sensitiveness to shame is the characteristic of men of courage or heroic character. *See note on section VIII., P.14.

"When a man understands the nature and use of these three moral qualities, he will then understand how to put in order his personal conduct and character. When a man understands how to put in order his personal conduct and character, he will understand how to govern men. When a man understands how to govern men, he will then understand how to govern nations and empires.

"For every one called to the government of nations and empires, there are nine cardinal directions to be attended to: —

1. — Putting in order his personal conduct.

2. — Honouring worthy men.

3. — Cherishing affection for, and doing his duty towards his kindred.

4. — Showing respect to the high ministers of state.

5. — Identifying himself with the interests and welfare of the whole body of public officers.

6. — Showing himself as a father to the common people.

7. — Encouraging the introduction of all useful arts.

8. — Showing tenderness to strangers from far countries.

"齐明盛服,非礼不动,所以修身也;去谗远色,贱货而贵德,所以劝贤也;尊其位,重其禄,同其好恶,所以劝亲亲也;官盛任使,所以劝大臣也;忠信重禄,所以劝士也;时使薄敛,所以劝百姓也;日省月试,既廪称事,所以劝百工也;送往迎来,嘉善而矜不能,所以柔远人也;继绝世,举废国,治乱持危,朝聘以时,厚往而薄来,所以怀诸侯也。

"凡为天下国家有九经,所以行之者一也。凡事豫则立,不豫则废。言前定则不跲,事前定则不困,行前定则不疚,道前定则不穷。

"在下位不获乎上,民不可得而治矣;获乎上有道:不信乎朋友,不获乎上矣;信乎朋友有道:不顺乎亲,不信乎朋友矣;顺乎亲有道:反诸身不诚,不顺乎亲矣;诚身有道:不明乎善,不诚乎身矣。

"有五种普遍义务,相应的有三种赖以实行的道德品质。那些义务存在于君臣、父子、夫妻、兄弟,以及朋友的交往之间,这就是五种普遍义务。才智、道德品质及勇气:这些是普世公认的三种道德品质。人们无论通过什么方式践行这些道德品质,结果只是一个,或曰相同。

"有些人生来就拥有关于这些道德品质的知识;有些人是通过教育获得的;有些人是通过艰难的经历而获得的。但当人们获得了这些知识,就会产生同样的结果。有些人践行这些道德品质是自然而容易的;有些人是因为对自己有利才去做;有些人则是通过努力而艰难地去做。但当它达成时,会产生同一个或曰同样的结果。"

孔子继续说:"对知识的爱,就是有才智的人的特性。不辞艰

179

9. — Taking interest in the welfare of the princes of the Empire.

"When the ruler pays attention to putting in order his personal conduct, there will be respect for the moral law. When the ruler honours worthy men, he will not be deceived. When the ruler cherishes affection for his kindred, there will be no disaffection among the members of his family. When the ruler shows respect to the high ministers of state, he will not make mistakes. When the ruler identifies himself with the interests and welfare of the body of public officers, there will be a strong spirit of loyalty among the gentlemen of the country. When the ruler becomes a father to the common people, the mass of the people will exert themselves for the good of the state. When the ruler encourages the introduction of all useful arts, there will be sufficiency of wealth and revenue in the country. When the ruler shows tenderness to the strangers from far countries, people from all quarters of the world will flock to the country. When the ruler takes interest in the condition and welfare of the princes of the empire, he will inspire awe and respect for his authority throughout the whole world.

"By attending to the cleanliness and purity of his person and to the propriety and dignity of his dress, and in every word and act permitting nothing which is contrary to good taste and decency, that is how the ruler puts in order his personal conduct. By banishing all flatterers and keeping away from the society of women; holding in low estimation possession of worldly goods, but valuing moral qualities in men: that is how the ruler gives encouragement to worthy men. By raising them

辛地致力于言行举止，就是有道德的人的特性。对羞耻的敏感，就是有勇气或英勇的人的特性。*见第八章解读，第14页①。

"当一个人懂得这三种道德品质的本质与运用，他就会懂得如何规范自己的言行与性格。当他懂得如何规范自己的言行与性格，他就会懂得如何去管理别人。而当一个人懂得如何去管理别人，他就会懂得如何去统治一个民族与帝国。

"对每一个要去参与统治国家与帝国的人来说，有九项基本原则需要注意：

1. 规范他自己的言行举止；

2. 尊崇品德高尚的人；

3. 珍视对亲人的情感，并对他们履行义务；

4. 向身居高位的朝廷公卿表现出敬意；

5. 让自己与全体公务人员的利益与福利相一致；

6. 对待普通民众犹如父亲对待儿子；

7. 鼓励所有实用技艺的引进；

8. 亲切、仁慈地对待从远方国度来的陌生人；

9. 关心帝国诸侯们的福利。

"当统治者留意规范自己的言行举止，那么，道德法则就会得到尊重。当统治者尊崇品德高尚的人，他就不会受到欺骗。当统治者珍视对他亲人的情感，在他的家庭成员中就不会存在不满。当统治者表现出对身居高位的公卿大臣们的尊敬，他就不会犯错。当统治者让自己与全体公务人员的利益和福利相一致，那么，在绅

---

① 星号后文字为辜鸿铭提示读者参见第八章他的解读。在那段解读中，辜鸿铭指出了希伯来精神和希腊精神的含义。

to high places of honour and bestowing ample emoluments for their maintenance; sharing and sympathising with their tastes and opinions: that is how the ruler inspires love for his person among the members of his family. By extending the powers of their functions and allowing them discretion in the employment of their subordinates: that is how the ruler gives encouragement to the high ministers of state. By dealing loyally and punctually with them in all engagements which he makes with them and allowing a liberal scale of pay: that is how the ruler gives encouragement to men in the public service. By strictly limiting the time of their service and making all imposts as light as possible: that is how the ruler gives encouragement to the mass of the people. By ordering daily inspection and monthly examination and rewarding each according to the degree of his workmanship: that is how the ruler encourages the artisan class. By welcoming them when they come and giving them protection when they go, commending what is good in them and making allowance for their ignorance: that is how the ruler shows tenderness to strangers from far countries. By restoring lines of broken succession and reviving extinguished states, putting down anarchy and disorder wherever they are found, and giving support to the weak against the strong, fixing stated times for their attendance and the attendance of their envoys at court, loading them with presents when they leave while exacting little from them in the way of contribution when they come: that is how the ruler takes interest in the welfare of the princes of the Empire.

"For everyone who is called to the government of nations and

士之间，就会产生一种强烈的忠诚的精神。当统治者成为普通人民的父亲，人民大众就会为国家的利益而竭尽全力。当统治者鼓励引进各种实用技艺，国家的财富与税收就会充足。当统治者向从远方国度而来的陌生人表示出亲切、仁慈，世界上四面八方的人民都会结伴涌入这个国家。当统治者关心帝国诸侯们的福利，他就会激起全世界对其权威的敬畏与尊重。

"留意他的身体的清洁与纯净，以及服装的规范与尊贵，每一句话、每个行为，都不允许违背好的品味与体面，这就是统治者规范个人言行的方法。赶走奉承谄媚者，远离女性群体；保持对世俗财物的占有的轻视，并重视人内在的道德品质：这就是统治者对品德高尚之人的勉励。通过给予他们崇高的地位和荣誉，并给他们提供丰厚的报酬；分享并赞同他们的趣味与观点：这就是统治者激发对其家人的爱的方式。通过延伸他们的职责，并允许他们在选用下属时有自己的判断：这就是统治者给身居高位的朝廷公卿的勉励。通过忠诚、准时地履行对他们的承诺，并给予慷慨的酬劳：这就是统治者给公务人员以勉励的方式。通过严格限制他们的役使时间，尽量少地向他们征税：这就是统治者给人民大众以勉励的方式。通过命令每天检查、每月考核，并根据每个人的手艺水平给予报酬：这是统治者勉励工匠阶层的方式。他们来时表示欢迎，他们离开时提供保护，称赞他们性格中好的方面而体谅他们的无知：这就是统治者向从远方国度来的陌生人显示亲切仁慈的方式。修复已断裂的传承，并复兴灭绝的国家，制止所发现的任何地方的无政府混乱状态，支持弱者以对抗强者，确定好他们出席或他们在朝廷的使者定期出席的时间；他们离开时使他们载满礼物回去，而当他们前来进贡时，只向他们要求很少的奉献：这是统治者

empire, these are the nine cardinal directions to be attended to; and there is only one way by which they can be carried out. In all matters, success depends on preparation; without preparation there will always be failure. When what is to be said is previously determined, there will be no breakdown. When what is to be done is previously determined, there will be no difficulty in carrying it out. When a line of conduct is previously determined, there will be no occasion for vexation. When general principles are previously determined, there will be no perplexity to know what to do.

"If those in authority have not the confidence of those under them, government of the people is an impossibility. There is only one way to gain confidence for one's authority. If a man is not trusted by his friends, he will not gain the confidence for his authority. There is only way to be trusted by one's friends. If a man does not command the obedience of the members of his family, he will not be trusted by his friends. There is only one way to command the obedience of the members of one's family. If a man, looking into his own heart, is not true to himself, he will not command the obedience of the members of his family. There is only one way for a man to be true to himself. If he does not know what is good, a man cannot be true to himself.

["To thine own self be true, / And it must follow, as the night the day, / Thou canst not then be false to any man."]

"Truth (诚) is the law of God. Acquired truth is the law of man.

保护帝国诸侯们利益的方式①。

"对于每个要去参与统治国家与帝国的人来说，上面是应予注意的九项基本原则，而要践行它们只有一种方式。在任何情况下，成功取决于事先准备；没有事先准备，总会导致失败。如果要说的话是事先确定好的，就不会出现口误。如果要做的事情是事先确定好的，实施起来就不会出现困难。如果你的行为是事先确定好的，你将不会有苦恼。如果普遍原则是事先确定好的，那么，对于应该做些什么就不会感到困惑。

"如果当权者得不到他们下属的信任，就不可能统治人民。只有这一种方法让自己的权威获得信任。如果一个人不被他的朋友信任，他将无法让自己的权威获得信任。只有这一种方法获取朋友的信任。如果一个人得不到家人的顺从，他将不被朋友信任。只有这一种方法可以获得家人的顺从。如果一个人反观自己的内心，他对自己并不真实，那么，他将无法获得家人的顺从。一个人要对自己真实，只有这一种方法。如果他不懂得什么是善，他就不能够对自己真实。

［"你必须对你自己忠实，/正像有了白昼才有黑夜一样，/对自己忠实，才不会对别人欺诈。"②］

"诚者，天之道也；诚之者，人之道也。
"真实（诚）是上帝的律法。被获得的真实，就是人的法则。

---

① 以上是统治者用以践行那九项原则的方法。
② 诗句出自莎士比亚戏剧《哈姆莱特》第一幕第三场（译文引自《莎士比亚全集》（第四册），朱生豪译，中国画报出版社，2012，第307页）。

[The truth that comes from intuition is the law implanted in man by God. The truth that is acquired is a law arrived at by human effort.]

"He who intuitively apprehends truth, is one who, with effort, hits what is right and without thinking, understands what he wants to know; whose life easily and naturally is in harmony with the moral law. Such a one is what we call a saint or a man of divine nature. He who acquires truth is one who finds out what is good and holds fast to it.

"In order to acquire truth, it is necessary to obtain a wide and extensive knowledge of what has been said and done in the world; to critically inquire into it; to carefully ponder over it; to clearly sift it; and earnestly carry it out.

"It matters not what you learn, but when you once learn a thing you must never give it up until you have mastered it. It matters not what you inquire into, but when you inquire into a thing you must never give it up until you have thoroughly understood it. It matters not what you try to think out, but when you once try to think out a thing you must never give it up until you have got what you want. It matters not what you try to sift out, but when you once try to sift out a thing, you must never give it up until you have sifted it out clearly and distinctly. It matters not what you try to carry out, but when you once try to carry out a thing you must never give it up until you have done it thoroughly and well. If another man succeed by one effort, you will use a hundred efforts. If another man succeed by ten efforts, you will

［源于直觉的真实，是上帝植入人内心的律法。被获得的真实，就是人类通过努力而达到的法则。］

"诚者不勉而中，不思而得，从容中道，圣人也。诚之者，择善而固执之者也。

"博学之，审问之，慎思之，明辨之，笃行之。

"有弗学，学之弗能弗措也；有弗问，问之弗知弗措也；有弗思，思之弗得弗措也；有弗辨，辨之弗明弗措也；有弗行，行之弗笃弗措也；人一能之己百之，人十能之己千之。

"果能此道矣，虽愚必明，虽柔必强。"

"一个直觉地理解真实的人，就是一个通过努力而偶然发现正确、无须思索就知道自己想要了解些什么的人；他的生活就会容易地、自然地处于道德法则的和谐之中。这样一个人，就是我们所说的圣人或具有神圣天性的人。他获得了真实，他就寻找到了什么是善，并牢牢地抓住了它。

"为了获取真实，有必要去获得关于在这个世界上所说所做的最广泛与全面的知识，去批判性地探询它，去仔细地考量它，去明确地筛选它，去认真地实施它。

"无论你学习什么，你一旦开始学习一件事情，你就不能放弃，直到你精通它。无论你探询什么，一旦你开始探询一件事，你就不能放弃，直到你彻底理解它。无论你试着思索什么，一旦你开始试着思索一件事，你就不能放弃，直到你获得了你想要的。无论你试着辨别什么，一旦你开始试着辨别一件事，你就不能放弃，直到你清楚明白地辨别了它。无论你试着实施什么，一旦你开始试着实施一件事，就不能放弃，直到你完全并很好地完成了它。如果另一

use a thousand efforts.

"Let a man really proceed in this manner, and though dull, he will surely become intelligent; though weak, he will surely become strong."

个人通过一份努力成功了，你就要用一百份努力。如果另一个人通过十份努力成功了，你就要用一千份努力。

"让一个人真正开始这样的习惯吧，果真如此，即使他愚钝，也必然变得聪慧；尽管柔弱，他也必然变得坚强。"

【评述】

本章通篇论述政治的根本哲理,这一论述与整部书所阐述的"道"息息相关。文章开头,孔子即将统治方式归结到"人"的因素。孔子指出"为政在人",辜鸿铭译为"The conduct of government, therefore, depends upon the men"(统治的表现取决于人)。

进而,孔子谈及对"人"(辜鸿铭认为此处指"统治者"而言)的具体要求。即,统治者要获取合适的人才来管理国家,他必须运用"道德法则"(the moral law)。

再进一步,论述深入到"道德情感"(仁,the moral sense)及"正义感"(义,the sense of justice)对社会形态及特征构成的影响。从辜鸿铭的翻译及文中的解读中我们可以看出,他认为,社会的最本质的基础是"道德"。其实,他在《宪政主义与中国》一文中有着较详细的阐释,在此引述如下,算作补充:

> 我想在这里指出的是,从亚里士多德到霍布斯、洛克,再到现代的卢梭和赫伯特·斯宾塞,所有欧洲政治科学的基本错误,就在于他们关于国家起源和存在理由的全部理论基于这样一个假设,即认为它是基于对物质利益的渴望——渴望人身和财产得到保护,或像卡莱尔所说的,保护人类第一次由自身构成的社会、那种被称之为国家的东西的"猪与猪槽"。但是我重申一遍,这种假设是错误的。的确,正像某些人所指出的,甚至人类的穿衣,最初也不是出于御寒的物质需要,而是激于内在的追求美观的道德意识,即追求体面。……
>
> 如同人们穿衣最初并非出于物质或功利目的,而是出于道德需要一样,被称之为国家的人类社会,也同样有其道德根源。孔子说:"君子之道,造端乎夫妇。"在原始社会早期,一个男人遇到了一个女人,他们相互吸引,不是激于动物的性冲动,而是第一次激于人类的情感,激于天然的爱的情感,从而结成夫妻;由于夫妻关系激于天然情感,那种被称为"婚姻"的关系就成了神圣的关系、一种天伦关系——即欧洲人所谓的"圣礼"。这样,婚姻的庄严与神圣就成为道德准则,即孔子所说的君子之道。一旦男女关系置于道德准则的统治之下,那么家庭就产生了。由家庭继而形成封建国家,那种封建时代早期的宗族国(Family-state)。
>
> 因此,我们看到所有人类社会,无论是家族还是国家,它的起源、存在的理由和根基,不是利益,而是爱,即人类的亲情。由这种爱与人类的亲情,生出一种道德准则、一种君子之道。事实上,如果没有爱、人类亲情和同情之心,你甚至不可能使男女在家庭生活中和睦相处,更不必说在社团、民族国家和国际联盟中保持和平了。因为,正如法国人茹伯所说的:"一个不自爱的人,也不可能公正合理地对待他的邻居。"("Les hommes ne sont justes qu-envers ceux qu' ils aiment.")

然而，一个国家为什么必须要有政府？换句话说，政府的起源和存在的理由是什么？正如我们所知道的，在人类社会产生之前，一个家庭或一个国家能够存在，他们必须首先具备某种道德准则，而这个道德准则就是我们所谓的文明。因此，政府存在的理由和真正的功能，不是去保护人身和财产，不是去保护"猪与猪槽"，而是为了保护这种称之为文明的道德准则。……

黄兴涛主编，《辜鸿铭文集·下卷》，第184—185页

　　论述回到统治者自身，他就必须要调整自己的言行与品德，以符合规范。符合怎样的规范呢？文中说："仁者人也，亲亲为大；义者宜也，尊贤为大。"辜鸿铭将这句话译为"The moral sense is the characteristic attribute of man. To feel natural affection for those nearly related to us is the highest expression of the moral sense. The sense of justice is the recognition of what is right and proper. To honour those who are worthier than ourselves is the highest expression of the sense of justice"（道德情感是人的典型属性。去感受对那些与我们关系密切的人的天然情感，就是道德情感的最高表达。正义感就意味着识别正确与恰当。去尊敬那些比我们自己更有品德的人，就是正义感的最高表达）。其中，"仁"即"道德情感"（the moral sense），"义"即"正义感"（the sense of justice）。这两者深刻地影响了国家与社会的构成——前者正如我们所引述的辜鸿铭的话，或如他在针对上述这句话的解读中所说的，即社会存在的基础；后者，则是体现文明社会的一个重要指标，即"英雄崇拜"。这两者的存在，用辜鸿铭的话说，就使得"在家庭中，天然情感使得恭顺非常容易，在一个国家中，英雄崇拜则使从属变得自然与恰当"。

　　我们知道，辜鸿铭的老师、英国思想家托马斯·卡莱尔曾有一部著作《论英雄与英雄崇拜及历史上的英雄业绩》。辜鸿铭与卡莱尔都是"英雄崇拜"哲学的推崇者。在此，辜鸿铭明确地指出，如果一个社会中具备了"道德情感"与"正义感"（仁与义），那么，"英雄崇拜"就变得"自然与恰当"。换言之，"英雄崇拜"是文明社会的一个重要表现。那么，什么是"英雄崇拜"呢？我们再次从辜鸿铭的其他著作中找到他的确切答案："中国人在选择他们的皇帝时，并不像美国人选择他们的总统那样，认为这个人将促进他们的利益，会为他们做'好事'；中国人选择皇帝，是由于在他们的内心深处，在他们的灵魂中，认为他是一个绝对比他们自身更优秀更高贵的人。这种对于一个人的高贵品质所产生的感情或赞赏，就是卡莱尔所谓的'英雄崇拜'。孔子说：'仁者人也，亲亲为大；义者宜也，尊贤为大。'因此，并非是什么成文宪法，而是孔子在此所谓的'尊贤为大'和卡莱尔所谓的'英雄崇拜'，即我们称之为天然情感的东西，将我们对于过去、家庭、国家和故土的记忆缠绕在一起——并赋予旧式中国的皇帝那种甘露德先生称之为'光环'的'神圣之权'，使得他的臣民不仅遵从他，而且当他有召唤的时候，去

为他而死。"（黄兴涛主编，《辜鸿铭文集·下卷》，第179—180页）

其实，"英雄崇拜"也是"道德情感"与"正义感"（仁与义）的一种表现形式。换言之，前后两者是可以相互指代的。在这个意义上，"英雄崇拜"也即文明社会的基础。

然而，统治者为了达成这样的标准，就必须懂得社会构成的本质为"道德"，而非"利益"，正如上文所说的。而了解这个，又必须"不可以不知天"，辜鸿铭译为"In considering the nature and organisation of human society it is necessary for him to understand the laws of God"（考虑到如何了解人类社会的本质与构成，他有必要懂得上帝的律法）。"天"，此处指"上帝的律法"（the laws of God）。

在此也需要指出的是，"上帝的律法"，实则也即《中庸》开头所说的"天命之谓性，率性之谓道"（上帝的法令，就是我们所说的我们本性的法则［性］。服从我们本性的法则，就是我们所说的道德法则［道］）的意思，换言之，"上帝的律法"与"道德法则"（道）是同义的。我们还可以说，在辜鸿铭的语境下，"道""道德""道德法则""上帝""上帝的律法""宇宙规律"等含义实质上是相同的，只是在不同的话语中，表述不同而已。

那么，在辜鸿铭看来，文中接下来是孔子对这一"上帝的律法"的阐述。孔子说："天下之达道五，所以行之者三。"辜鸿铭译为"the duties of universal obligation are five"（五种普遍义务），分别是君臣、父子、夫妇、昆弟、朋友之间的义务。"行之者三"即"the three universally recognised moral qualities of man"（普世公认的三种道德品质），这三种道德品质即知、仁、勇。此处也需要强调的是，辜鸿铭在论述儒学或中国文化时，从未认为这是中国独有的，而是具有普世的意义。

孔子进而阐述了治理国家的"九经"，辜鸿铭译为"nine cardinal directions"（九项主要原则），实则也是围绕"道德情感"或"上帝的律法"来谈的，是对其在实际生活表现的细分。

进而，从"齐明盛服"到"所以怀诸侯也"，则是统治者所以践行"九经"的方法。接下来，孔子论述的是践行"九经"的方法的注意事项，即必须做到"豫"与"前定"，辜鸿铭译为"preparation"（事先准备）与"previously determined"（事先确定好）。

然后，孔子的论述又回到了统治者的行为本身，即"道德法则"在其生活实践中实现的前提。在此，他提出了两个概念："善"与"诚"。孔子说："反诸身不诚，不顺乎亲矣；……不明乎善，不诚乎身矣。"在此，孔子将"诚"视为"天之道"，即"上帝的律法"的另一种说法。而"善"则是比"诚"更进一步的一个概念。"诚者，天之道也。诚之者，人之道也。"辜鸿铭译为"Truth is the law of God. Acquired truth is the law of man"（真实是上帝的律法。被获得的真实，就是人的法则）。那么"善"呢？"不明乎善，不诚乎身矣"一句，辜鸿铭译为"If he does not know what is good, a man cannot be true to himself"

（如果他不懂得什么是善，他就不能够对自己真实）。换言之，懂得"善"（good），是达到"诚"的前提。

最后，孔子论述了获得"诚"的注意事项，即对学问、思索及言行的执着与坚韧。其实，这也是捕获"善"的概念、洞悉"诚"（"天之道"或"上帝的律法"）的应有或曰必需的态度。

XVII.

第十七章

Confucius remarked: "The Emperor Shun might perhaps be considered, in the highest sense of the word, a pious man. In moral qualities he was a saint. In dignity of office he was the ruler of the Empire. In wealth all that the wide world contained belonged to him. After his death his spirit was sacrificed to in the ancestral temple, and his children and grandchildren preserved the sacrifice for long generations.

[The word 孝 in the text above does not mean merely a filial son, but has the meaning of the Latin "pius" — pious in its full sense, reverential to God, dutiful to parents, good faithful and orderly in all the relations of life.]

"Thus it is that he who possesses great moral qualities will certainly attain to corresponding high position; to corresponding great prosperity; to corresponding great name; to corresponding great age.

"For God in giving life to all created things, is surely bountiful to them according to their qualities. Hence the tree that is full of life, he fosters and sustains; while that which is ready to fall, he cuts off and destroys.

[The law of the survival of the fittest is here announced two thousand years ago. But Confucius' interpretation of this law is different from the modern interpretation. The survival of the fittest means, not the survival of the most brutally strong, but the survival of the morally fittest.]

子曰："舜其大孝也与！德为圣人，尊为天子，富有四海之内。宗庙飨之，子孙保之。

孔子说："帝王舜或许被视为最高意义上的虔诚的人了。在道德品质上，他是位圣人。在官职上，他贵为帝国的统治者。在财富上，世界万物都属于他。死后，他的灵魂被供奉在祖庙里，这种供奉，他的子孙保持了数代。

[上文中的"孝"字，并不仅仅指他是位孝顺的儿子，并且含有拉丁文"*pius*"的意思——完全意义上来说指虔诚，对上帝充满崇敬，对父母尽义务，在生活所有的关系中都是忠实、规矩的。]

"故大德必得其位，必得其禄，必得其名，必得其寿。

"故天之生物，必因其材而笃焉。故栽者培之，倾者覆之。

"因此，正是由于拥有伟大的道德品质，他必然会获得相应的崇高地位、相应的杰出成就、相应的美好声誉、相应的长寿延年。

"上帝在赋予所有被造之物以生命时，必然是根据它们的特性而慷慨给予。因此，充满生命力的树，他就会培养并维护它们。而那些即将朽坏的树，他就会砍倒并毁掉它们。

[这是两千年前对"适者生存"规律的揭示。但孔子对这个规律的阐释与当今的阐释不同。"适者生存"的意思，并非指那些最残暴、最强大者的生存，而是指那些道德意义上的最适者的生存。]

"The *Book of Songs* says:

> He is our good and noble King
>
> And oh!How charming in all his way!
>
> The land and people all do sing
>
> The praise of his impartial sway.
>
> Heaven to his sires the Kingdom gave
>
> And him with equal favour views;
>
> Heaven's strength and aid will ever save
>
> The throne whose grant it oft renews.

"It is therefore true that he who possesses exceedingly great moral qualities will certainly receive the divine call to the Imperial throne."

"《诗》曰：'嘉乐君子，宪宪令德！宜民宜人，受禄于天；保佑命之，自天申之！'

"故大德者必受命。"

"《诗经》上说：

> 良善与高贵的王
> 喔！他怎样做都迷人！
> 一国百姓齐声歌唱
> 公平的统治要颂扬。
> 王国给予祖先和他的
> 是上天一视同仁；
> 上天的力量与扶助永在
> 对君王再三重申。

"因此，由于他拥有非常伟大的道德品质，他必然会受到帝国王位的神圣召唤。"

【评述】

本章是在前一章对统治者的品德要求的基础之上，所举的帝舜的一个例证。并且通过此例证进而指出，作为一位统治者，如果拥有了应有的道德品质，那么，他的地位、成就、名誉、长寿等就会如期而至，这是因为存在"栽者培之，倾者覆之"的规律。这是一条什么规律呢？辜鸿铭在对这段的解读中指出，用现代的话来讲，就是"适者生存"。然而，辜鸿铭对"适者生存"的解释，与现代意义上的解释不同。他在《费解》中谈道："严复译《天演论》，言优胜劣败之理，人人以为中国数千年来所未发明之新理，其实即《中庸》所谓'栽者培之，倾者覆之'之义云尔。"（夏丹等选编，《辜鸿铭作品精选·张文襄幕府纪闻》，第180页）在此，他又进一步做了说明："'适者生存'的意思，并非指那些最残暴、最强大者的生存，而是指那些道德意义上的最适者的生存。"

这是他自己对"适者生存"或"优胜劣汰"所做出的解释，也是他再次对"道德"的意义的强调。正如我们在第一章及前几章所揭示的，辜鸿铭认为，"道"或"神圣的宇宙规律"或"上帝的律法"（the laws of God），以及人类社会得以存在的最根本的基础，其实是道德或曰道德法则（the moral law），或曰"爱"。（见第十二章）换言之，这是人类一切文明的基础。而上天要扶持并维护的，即那些符合这一"道"的事物，即"道德意义上的最适者的生存"。所打击的，也即违背这一"道"的事物。

此外还有一点需要注意的是，辜鸿铭此处对"孝"的理解。他认为，此处的"孝"并非单指对父母的"孝敬"，而是"完全意义上来说指虔诚"，是指一种虔诚的心灵状态与生活态度。

XVIII.
第十八章

Confucius remarked: "The man perhaps who enjoyed the most perfect happiness was the Emperor Wen. For father he had a remarkable man, the Emperor Chi, and for son also a remarkable man, the Emperor Wu. His father laid the foundation of his House and his son carried it on. The Emperor Wu, continuing the great work begun by his ancestor the great Emperor, his grandfather Chi and his father the Emperor Wen, had only to buckle on his armour and the Empire at once came to his possession.

"The Emperor Wen was a no less distinguished man. In dignity of office, he was the ruler of the Empire; in wealth all that the wide world contained belonged to him. After his death his spirit was sacrificed to in the ancestral temple and his children and grandchildren preserved the sacrifice for long generations.

"The Emperor Wen never actually ascended the throne. But his son, the Duke of Chow, ascribed the achievement of founding the Imperial House equally to the moral qualities of the Emperors Wen and Wu. He carried the Imperial title up to the Great Emperor (Wen's grandfather) and the Emperor Chi (Wen's father). He sacrificed to all the past reigning dukes of the House with imperial honours."

[武王未受命 in the text here, I think, should be 文王未受命. The subject of this section is 文王 the Emperor Wen and not 武王 the Emperor Wu.]

This rule is now universally observed from the reigning princes

子曰：“无忧者其惟文王乎！以王季为父，以武王为子，父作之，子述之。武王缵大王、王季、文王之绪。壹戎衣而有天下，身不失天下之显名。尊为天子，富有四海之内。宗庙飨之，子孙保之。武王末受命，周公成文武之德，追王大王、王季，上祀先公以天子之礼。”

孔子说：“或许享受最完全的快乐的那个人，就是文王吧。他的父亲是一位非凡的人物，是王季。他的儿子也是一位非凡的人物，是武王。他的父亲为他的王朝打下了基础，而他的儿子继承了下去。武王继承的伟大的工作，始于他伟大的先辈，他的祖父王季与父亲文王。他只需穿上甲胄，就立刻拥有帝国了。

“文王同样是位卓越的人物。在职务上，他贵为帝国统治者；在财富上，全世界的一切都属于他。死后，他的灵魂被供奉在祖庙中，并且这一供奉由他的子孙保持了数代。

“文王从未实际地登上王位①。但他的儿子，周公，将建立帝国的成就归功于文王与武王的道德品质。他将帝王的头衔追加给伟大帝王（文王的祖父）和王季（文王的父亲）。他以帝王的荣誉供奉所有以往的王朝的君王们。”②

[我认为，上文中“武王末受命”应为“文王未受命”。因为此部分的主题是谈论“文王”（the Emperor Wen），而非“武王”（the Emperor Wu）。]

斯礼也，达乎诸侯大夫，及士庶人。父为大夫，子为士；葬以大

---

① 原文为“武王末受命”，辜鸿铭认为有误，故有是译，理由见下面辜鸿铭的解读。

② 辜鸿铭认为，孔子的话到“上祀先公以天子之礼”一句为止，下文是《中庸》作者的阐述。

and nobles to the gentlemen and common people. In the case where the father is a noble and the son is a simple gentleman, the father when he dies, is buried with the honours of a noble, but sacrificed to as a simple gentleman. In the case where the father is a simple gentleman and the son a noble, the father, when he dies, is buried as a simple gentleman, but sacrificed to with the honours of a nobleman. The rule for one year of mourning for relatives is binding up to the rank of a noble. But the rule for three years of mourning for parents is binding for all up to the Emperor. In mourning for parents there is only one rule, and no distinction is made between noble and plebeian.

夫,祭以士。父为士,子为大夫;葬以士,祭以大夫。期之丧达乎大夫,三年之丧达乎天子,父母之丧无贵贱一也。

上至诸侯、贵族,下至绅士与普通民众,这一规则现在被普遍奉行着。如果父亲是一位贵族,而儿子是一位普通的绅士,在父亲去世后,就会以贵族的荣誉埋葬,然而,被作为一位普通的绅士供奉。如果父亲是一位普通的绅士,而儿子是一位贵族,那么,在父亲去世后,就会被作为一位普通的绅士埋葬,但被以贵族的荣誉供奉。为亲戚守丧一年,这样的规则在贵族诸侯这一级别还是必须遵守的。但为父母守丧三年,则是所有人直到帝王都必须遵守的。为父母服丧,贵族与平民没有区别,只有一种规则。

【评述】

上一章中，有"宗庙飨之，子孙保之"一句，指子孙后代对有德先人的供奉。而此章则就此而重点展开了论证。文中首先举了"文王"的例证，阐述了"父作之，子述之"是一个人最"无忧"（最完全的快乐）的状态。他父亲所创的事业，他进行了继承，而且，他的子孙又对他们进行了继承，并且最终也实现了"宗庙飨之，子孙保之"。

辜鸿铭认为，孔子的话到"上祀先公以天子之礼"一句为止，后面是《中庸》作者的阐述。进而，作者又根据孔子的话（主要指"上祀先公以天子之礼"）一句，总结出了关于"丧礼"的规则。他认为，"斯礼也，达乎诸侯大夫，及士庶人"，辜鸿铭译为"This rule is now universally observed from the reigning princes and nobles to the gentlemen and common people"（上至诸侯、贵族，下至绅士与普通民众，这一规则现在被普遍奉行着）。

为了便于读者的理解，我们可以这样归纳本书到目前为止所体现的一个重要逻辑：［神圣的宇宙秩序在人间的反映即］道德法则，遵循道德法则即君子（第一、二章）—道德的生活，意味着作为普通的、理性的人类去生活（第四、十一章）—道德之人生活中的行为准则（第十三、十四章）—道德之人的家庭秩序（第十五章）—统治者的道德要求及政治社会秩序（第十六章）—统治者的德行例证及一个重要表现："父作子述"（第十七、十八章）。

XIX.

第十九章

Confucius remarked: "The Emperor Wu and his brother, the Duke of Chow, were indeed eminently pious men. Now true filial piety consists in successful carrying out the unfinished work of our forefathers and transmitting their achievements to posterity.

"In Spring and Autumn they repaired and put in order the ancestral temple; arranged the sacrificial vessels, exhibited the regalia and heirlooms of the family, and presented the appropriate offerings of the season.

"The principle in the order of precedence in the ceremonies of worship in the ancestral temple is, in the first place, to arrange the members of the family according to descent. Ranks are next considered, in order to give recognition to the principle of social distinction. Services rendered are next considered as a recognition of distinction in moral worth. In the general banquet those below take precedence of those above in pledging the company, in order to show that consideration is shown to the meanest. In conclusion, a separate feast is given to the elders, in order to recognise the principle of seniority according to age.

"To gather in the same places where our fathers before us have gathered; to perform the same ceremonies which they, before us, have performed; to play the same music which they before us have played; to pay respect to those whom they honoured; to love those who were dear to them — in fact, to serve them now dead as if they were living, and now departed as if they were still with us — this is highest achievement of true filial piety.

"The performance of sacrifices to Heaven and Earth is meant

子曰："武王、周公,其达孝矣乎! 夫孝者:善继人之志,善述人之事者也。

"春秋修其祖庙,陈其宗器,设其裳衣,荐其时食。

"宗庙之礼,所以序昭穆也;序爵,所以辨贵贱也;序事,所以辨贤也;旅酬下为上,所以逮贱也;燕毛,所以序齿也。

"践其位,行其礼,奏其乐,敬其所尊,爱其所亲,事死如事生,事亡如事存,孝之至也。

"郊社之礼,所以事上帝也,宗庙之礼,所以祀乎其先也。明乎郊社之礼、禘尝之义,治国其如示诸掌乎。"

孔子说:"武王和他的兄弟周公,的确是非同寻常的虔诚的人。现在,真正的孝道包括成功地继承祖先未竟的事业,以及将他们达成的事业传给子孙后代。

"在春季与秋季,他们会修葺并整理祖庙,安排祭器并陈列出象征家族的标志与物品,并且摆上与季节相符的祭品。

"在祖庙中,祭祀的顺序是,首先,根据世系安排好每个家庭成员。下一步考虑等级问题,以确认社会区别的原则。作为道德品性品第的确认,仪式表达的问题被进一步考虑。在普通宴会上,敬酒时,在下的人先于在上的人,是为了显示也考虑到了地位最低的人。最后,为了确认根据年龄而言的长辈原则,将为长者举行单独的宴会。

"在我们的父辈曾经先于我们而聚集的地方聚集;去举行他们先于我们而举行过的仪式;去演奏那些他们先于我们而演奏过的乐曲;去向那些他们曾尊敬过的人表示敬意;去爱那些爱过他们的人——实际上,对待那些已经过世的人,就像他们依然活着;对待那些离开我们的人,就像他们依然与我们在一起——这就是真

for the service of God. The performance of ceremonies in the ancestral temple, is meant for the worship of ancestors. If one only understood the meaning of the sacrifices to Heaven and Earth, and the signification of the services in ancestral worship, it would be the easiest thing to govern a nation."

[The above three sections give examples of men who have realised the moral law in their lives, in the different important relations of their lives.]

正孝道的最高境界。

"对天地的祭祀仪式就意味着服侍上帝。在祖庙举行的仪式，就意味着对祖先的崇拜。如果一个人哪怕仅仅懂得祭祀天地的意义，以及崇拜祖先的仪式的含义，那么，统治一个国家也将是最简单的事情。"

［以上三章[①]，举历史上的伟大人物为例，这些人在他们的生活，以及生活中各种重要的亲属关系里都实现了道德法则。］

---

① 指第十七、十八、十九三章。

【 评述 】

本章再次用“善继人之志，善述人之事者也”对“孝”进行了阐释，与前一章“父作之，子述之”，其实含义一致。然而，本章则又对此意进行了延伸，即，不仅仅要对自己的父辈表示出敬意，而且对与父辈们亲近的人也要表示出同样的亲近与敬意，不管他们是已过世还是健在，是已远离我们还是近在身边。实现这种对自己父辈的敬意的“延伸”，就是孝道的最高境界。

辜鸿铭在文末的解读中总结，上面三章（第十七、十八、十九章）列举了关于“孝”的现实例证。到此，我们可以体会出，辜鸿铭之所以将《中庸》原书的第二十章提前至此处的第十六章，是因为如此一来，第十六、十七、十八、十九四章构成了通顺的逻辑关系——第十六章讲的是对统治者的道德要求，而后三章则举了三个例证。

辜鸿铭认为，在生活中实现了“孝”，实则是认识到了道德法则的存在及真实含义的表现。而如果懂得“郊社之礼，禘尝之义”，那么，治理国家将变成最简单的事情——前者，辜鸿铭认为指服侍上帝，后者，则指对祖先的崇拜。根据本书前几章的叙述，我们知道，所谓“上帝”，实则代指“神圣的宇宙秩序”又或称作“道德法则”；而崇拜祖先，无疑是实现“道德法则”的一个表现。懂得这个道理，治理国家将变得最为简单。其实辜鸿铭也说过：“我们中国人认为孝——那种孩子对父母的爱亲之情，是一切道德的根基，即仁之本。”（夏丹等选编，《辜鸿铭作品精选·所有受过英语教育的中国人应读之文·中国人会变成布尔什维克吗》，第393页）

辜鸿铭将文中“宗庙之礼，所以祀乎其先也”译为“The performance of ceremonies in the ancestral temple, is meant for the worship of ancestors”（在祖庙举行的仪式，就意味着对祖先的崇拜）。换言之，他将中国人“祭祖”又称为“祖先崇拜”。如果说“孝”与“祭祖”是中国人日常生活中的行为表现，那么，“祖先崇拜”则是这些行为表现背后的文化内涵。这一点，辜鸿铭在《中国人的精神（在北京东方学会上所宣讲的论文）》一文中有所阐释，他说：“正如孔子所宣扬的绝对的神圣的忠君义务保证了国家的种族不朽一样，儒家学说所宣扬的祖先崇拜也保证了家庭绵延不绝。的确，中国的祖先崇拜者的迷信与其说是建立在对来生的信仰上，还不如说是建立在对种族不朽的信仰上。中国人死的时候并没有受到这种信仰的安慰，而是受到另外一种信仰的安慰——他的子孙、所有亲近的人会永远记得他、想到他、爱他。这样，在他的想象中，中国人的死就像一个漫长的旅程，如果没有重逢的希望至少可以做重逢的假定。因此，在儒家学说中，这种祖先崇拜的迷信和神圣的忠君义务给活着的中国人提供了不朽意识，提供了安慰，就像宗教中对来世的信仰给其他国家的广大民众提供了不朽意识和安慰一样。正因如此，中国人既强调祖先崇拜的迷信，又强调神圣的忠君义务的原则。”（汪堂家编译，《乱世奇文·春秋大义》，第314页）

XX.
第二十章①

Confucius remarked: "The power of spiritual forces in the Universe — how active it is everywhere! Invisible to the eyes, and impalpable to the senses, it is inherent in all things and nothing can escape its operation.

[Carlyle says: "Dost thou know any corner of the world where 'force' is not? The withered leaf is not dead and lost. There are forces in it and around it; else how could it rot?"]

"It is the fact that there are these forces which makes men in all countries to fast and purify themselves, and with solemnity of dress to institute services of sacrifice and religious worship. Like the rush of mighty waters the presence of unseen Powers is felt: sometimes above us, sometimes around us.

"In the *Book of Songs* it is said:

The presence of the Spirit:

It cannot be surmised,

Inspiring fear and awe.

"Such is the evidence of things invisible that it is impossible to doubt the spiritual nature of man."

子曰：“鬼神之为德，其盛矣乎！视之而弗见，听之而弗闻，体物而不可遗。

孔子说：“宇宙中神灵的力量——它无处不在，多么活跃呀！对于眼睛它是看不到的，对于感觉它是触不及的，它天然就存在于所有的事物之中，没有什么东西可以逃脱它的影响。

［卡莱尔说：“你知道世界上有什么角落不存在‘力量’的吗？干枯的树叶并未死去或消失。力量充满了它，环绕着它，不然，它怎么会腐朽呢？”］

“使天下之人齐明盛服，以成祭祀。洋洋乎！如在其上，如在其左右。

“《诗》曰：‘神之格思，不可度思！矧可射思！’夫微之显，诚之不可揜如此夫。”

“事实上确实存在一些力量，使得所有国家的人们都能够斋戒并纯净他们自己，并身着庄重的礼服去制定祭祀及宗教崇拜的仪式。不可见力量的存在，恰如巨大水流的汹涌冲击被感知着：有时它在我们之上，有时环绕着我们。

“《诗经》上说：

神灵的存在：

不可臆测，

它激励着敬畏之心。

“这就是不可见事物的证据，怀疑人的精神本质是不可想象的。”

【评述】

实际上，本书第四章到第十九章侧重的是对现实生活的描述，算是"中庸"思想的一个分支。现在，论述完生活方面的哲理之后，便开始了对抽象哲理的另一个分支的描述。这一论述是从无处不在的"神灵的力量"开始的。"鬼神"，辜鸿铭译为"spiritual forces in the Universe"（宇宙中神灵），"天下之人"译为"men in all countries"（所有国家的人们）。辜鸿铭认为，神灵之力的存在是普世的、普遍的，它让各国的人们能够保持对神的敬畏与崇拜，并由此净化心灵。他引用了他的苏格兰老师卡莱尔的话予以论证这一"力量"的无处不在。根据辜鸿铭的一贯思想，我们或许也可这样推断：此章中所说的"神灵之力"与前面所讲的"道"（即作为神圣的宇宙秩序的"上帝"或"道德法则"），实则是一回事，只是表述不同。它们同样都充盈在世界的每个角落。当然，此处辜鸿铭并未明说。

XXI.
第二十一章

The intelligence which comes from the direct apprehension of truth is intuition. The apprehension of truth which comes from the exercise of intelligence is the result of education. Where there is truth, there is intelligence; where there is intelligence, there is truth.

自诚明,谓之性;自明诚,谓之教。诚则明矣,明则诚矣。

来自对真实的直接洞悉的才智,就是直觉。而源于才智之实践对真实的洞悉,是教育的结果。哪里有真实,哪里就有才智;哪里有才智,哪里就有真实。

【评述】

辜鸿铭一贯将"诚"译为"truth"（真实），可见第十六章对"诚"的翻译。"真实"并非作形容词用，而是指"真实"这个概念本身。此处则对"性"与"教"进行了区别于前面的翻译。"性"译为"intuition"（直觉），"教"译为"education"（教育），"明"译为"intelligence"（才智）。按辜鸿铭的翻译，此处要表明的实则是人在微观层面体察"道"的一种内心素质或曰心理过程，即"人的才智—真实—人的直觉—教育"之间的关系：1."人的才智"对"真实"的直接洞悉即"人的直觉"；2.通过"实践（才智）"而获得"直觉"是"教育"的结果；3."才智"与"真实"相伴相随。

XXII.
第二十二章

It is only he, in the world, who possesses absolute truth, who can get to the bottom of the law of his being. He who is able to get to the bottom of the law of his being, will be able to get to the bottom of the law of being of other men. He who is able to get to the bottom of the law of being of men, will be able to get to the bottom of the laws of physical nature. He who is able to get to the bottom of the laws of physical nature, will be able to influence the forces of creation of the Universe. He who can influence the forces of creation of the Universe, is one with the Powers of the Universe.

唯天下至诚,为能尽其性;能尽其性,则能尽人之性;能尽人之性,则能尽物之性;能尽物之性,则可以赞天地之化育;可以赞天地之化育,则可以与天地参矣。

　　在世界上,一个人只有拥有绝对的真实,他才能洞悉他本性的法则的本质。他只要能洞悉他本性的法则的本质,就能够洞悉别人本性的法则的本质。他只要能洞悉人们本性的法则的本质,那么,他就能洞悉大自然法则的本质。他如果能洞悉大自然法则的本质,他将能影响宇宙的创造力。他如果能影响宇宙的创造力,他就是一个拥有宇宙力量的人。

【评述】

本章依然延续了对"诚"（truth，真实）的论述，并且论述了"至诚"（possesses absolute truth，拥有绝对的真实）的状态，以及对人生的意义。辜鸿铭描述了从"至诚"到"宇宙创造"的一个逻辑关系：［拥有绝对的真实即］至诚——达到至诚即可洞悉人性的（自己的与他人的）本质（尽人之性）——洞悉人性本质就能洞悉大自然的本质（尽物之性）——洞悉大自然的本质就能影响宇宙创造力（赞天地之化育）——影响宇宙的创造力就说明拥有了宇宙的力量（与天地参）。这段话描述的其实是当人达到"至诚"的最高境界之后，与宇宙的创造本身的关系。

其中，"尽"译为"get to the bottom of"（洞察到根本，洞悉），"性"译为"the law of being"（本性的法则），"物"译为"physical nature"（大自然），"天地"译为"the Universe"（宇宙），"赞"译为"influence"（影响），"化育"译为"the forces of creation"（创造力）。

XXIII.
第二十三章

The next order of the process of man's mind is to attain to the apprehension of a particular branch of knowledge. In every particular branch of knowledge there is truth. Where there is truth, there is substance. Where there is substance, there is reality. Where there is reality, there is intelligence. Where there is intelligence, there is power. Where there is power, there is influence. Where there is influence, there is creative power. It is only he who possesses absolute truth in the world who can create.

其次致曲,曲能有诚,诚则形,形则著,著则明,明则动,动则变,变则化,唯天下至诚为能化。

人类思想过程的次一个等级,是能够洞悉某一特定的知识领域。在每个特定的知识领域中,都存在真实。哪里存在真实,哪里就有实质。哪里有实质,哪里就有实在。哪里有实在,哪里就有才智。哪里有才智,哪里就有力量。哪里有力量,哪里就会产生影响。哪里会产生影响,哪里就有创造力。世界上只有拥有绝对真实的人,才能创造。

【评述】

第二十二章讲的是人在达到"至诚"(拥有绝对真实)的至高状态下的效应,而此章则降了一个等级,讲人在没有达到"至诚"(拥有绝对真实)状态,然而却达到"致曲"(洞悉某一特定的知识领域)状态时的效应。

本章中出现了一系列概念,我们分别看一下辜鸿铭的翻译:"致曲"译为"attain to the apprehension of a particular branch of knowledge"(能够洞悉某一特定的知识领域),"形"译为"substance"(实质),"著"译为"reality"(实在),"明"译为"intelligence"(才智),"动"译为"power"(力量),"变"译为"influence"(影响),"化"译为"creative power"(创造力)。

"曲能有诚"译为"In every particular branch of knowledge there is truth"(在每个特定的知识领域中,都存在真实)。可以说,从"形"到"化"实则是从特定知识领域的"诚"到"至诚"境界的一个逻辑变化过程。最后作者再次强调,只有"至诚"(拥有绝对真实)的人,才能创造,或曰拥有创造力。

这一翻译再次说明了辜鸿铭的这一思想:任何人类知识的领域都是相通的,它们都蕴藏着最本质的东西,此处称之为"诚"(真实)。而这,也正是人类一切创造与进步的源动力所在。他在《中国人的精神(在北京东方学会上所宣讲的论文)》一文中有详细的阐述。他说:

> 在我看来,人类需要宗教同需要科学和哲学的原因是一样的,都在于人是有心灵的。我们先以科学为例,这里我指的是自然科学。是什么原因促使人们去追求科学呢?多数人会认为是出于对铁路、飞机一类东西的需要导致了对科学的追求。实际并非如此。当前所谓进步的中国人为了铁路、飞机去追求科学,他们永远也无法懂得科学的真谛。在欧洲历史上,那些真正献身科学、为科学进步而努力的人们,那些使修筑铁路、制造飞机成为可能的人们,他们最初就根本没有想过铁路和飞机。他们献身科学并为科学进步做出贡献,是因为他们的心灵渴望探求这广袤宇宙那可怕的神秘。人们之所以需要宗教、科学、艺术乃至哲学,都是因为人有心灵。不像野兽仅留意眼前,人类还需要回忆历史、展望未来——这就使人感到有必要懂得大自然的奥秘。在弄清宇宙的性质和自然法则之前,人类就如同处在黑屋之中的孩子,感到危险和恐惧,对任何事情都难以把握。正如一个英国诗人所言,大自然的神秘啊,沉重地压迫着人们。因此,人们需要科学、艺术和哲学,出于同样的原因,也需要宗教,以便减轻神秘的大自然,这个难以理解的世界所带来的重压。
>
> 艺术和诗歌能够使艺术家和诗人发现大自然的美妙及宇宙的法则,从而减轻

了他们所承受的压力。因此诗人歌德曾这样说过："谁拥有了艺术，谁就拥有了宗教。"所以，艺术家们不需要宗教。哲学能够使哲学家懂得宇宙的法则和秩序，从而缓解了这种神秘所带来的压力。因此，对像斯宾诺莎那样的哲学家来说，智力生活的极致便是一种转移，正如对于圣徒来说宗教生活的极致是一种转移一样。所以他们不感到需要宗教。最后，科学也能够令科学家认识宇宙的奥秘和秩序，使来自神秘自然的压力得以减轻。因此，像达尔文和海克尔教授那样的科学家也不感到需要宗教。

夏丹等选编，《辜鸿铭作品精选·中国人的精神》，第34—35页

XXIV.
第二十四章

It is an attribute of the possession of absolute truth to be able to foreknow. When a nation or family is about to flourish there are sure to be lucky omens. When a nation or family is about to perish, there are sure to be signs and prodigies. These things manifest themselves in the instruments of divination and in the agitation of the human body. When happiness or calamity is about to come, it can be known beforehand. When it is good, it can be know beforehand. When it is evil, it can also be known beforehand. Therefore he who possesses absolute truth is like a spiritual being.

至诚之道，可以前知。国家将兴，必有祯祥；国家将亡，必有妖孽；见乎蓍龟，动乎四体。祸福将至：善，必先知之；不善，必先知之。故至诚如神。

人能够预知未来，是因为他拥有绝对的真实。如果一个国家或家族将要繁荣，必然会出现幸运的征兆。如果一个国家或家族将要灭亡，必然会出现相应的迹象及非常的事物。这些事物在占卜器具及人体的躁动中显现出来。当幸福或不幸将要来临时，它们都会被预知到。如果它是善的，它将被预知。如果它是恶的，它也将被预知。因此，拥有绝对真实的人，就像一个超自然的存在。

【评述】

从第二十二章开始讨论人达到"至诚"(拥有绝对的真实)状态时的问题。第二十二章认为,人若"至诚"则能"赞天地之化育"(将能够影响宇宙的创造力)。第二十三章认为,人若"至诚"即能"化"(能创造)。而此章则认为,人若"至诚",则能"前知"(foreknow,预知未来)。

为何能够预知未来呢?文中讲,因为"国家将兴,必有祯祥;国家将亡,必有妖孽;见乎蓍龟,动乎四体"。其中,"祯祥"译为"lucky omens"(幸运的征兆),"妖孽"译为"signs and prodigies"(相应的迹象及非常的事物),"见乎蓍龟,动乎四体"译为"These things manifest themselves in the instruments of divination and in the agitation of the human body"(这些事物在占卜器具及人体的躁动中显现出来)。换言之,因为未来会有相应的来自大自然的征兆,因此,是可以预知的。而第二十二章讲到,在"至诚"的状态下人是"能尽物之性""可以赞天地之化育"(能洞悉大自然法则的本质,能影响宇宙的创造力)的。因此,"至诚"的人能够理解自然并影响自然,于是能觉察征兆,预知未来。

XXV.
第二十五章

Truth means the realisation of our being; and moral law means the law of our being. Truth is the beginning and end (the substance) of existence. Without truth there is no existence. It is for this reason that the moral man values truth.

Truth is not only the realisation of our own being. It is that by which things outside of us have an existence. The realisation of our being is moral sense. The realisation of things outside of us is intellect. These, moral sense and intellect, are the powers or faculties of our being. They combine the inner or subjective and outer or objective use of the power of the mind. Therefore with truth, everything done is right.

诚者自成也，而道自道也。诚者物之终始，不诚无物。是故君子诚之为贵。

诚者非自成己而已也，所以成物也。成己，仁也；成物，知也。性之德也，合外内之道，故时措之宜也。

真实意味着我们本性的实现，而道德法则意味着我们本性的法则。真实就是存在的开始与结束（实质）。没有真实，就没有存在。正因如此，有道德的人重视真实。

真实并不仅仅指我们自己的本性的实现，而是能由此使我们之外的事物得以存在。我们本性的实现，就是道德情感。而使我们之外的事物得以存在，就是才智。道德情感与才智，就是我们本性的力量或能力。它们联合了内在或主观的，以及外在或客观的思想力量的运用。因此，拥有了真实，每件事物都将是恰当的。

【评述】

本章是对"诚"这个概念的一个剖析。我们可以试着这样来理解:"诚"(真实)是什么? 1."诚者自成也"; 2."诚者物之终始"; 3."诚者非自成己而已也,所以成物也"。这是"诚"(真实)这一概念的三个界定。

其中,"自成"译为"the realisation of our being"(我们本性的实现),这又叫作"仁"(moral sense,道德感)。"物之终始"译为"the beginning and end(the substance)of existence"(存在的开始与结束[实质])。"非自成己而已也,所以成物也"是对"自成"的进一步论述,译为"not only the realisation of our own being. It is that by which things outside of us have an existence"(并不仅仅指我们自己的本性的实现,而是能由此使我们之外的事物得以存在),这又叫作"知"(intellect,才智)。

由此,我们可以这样总结"诚":它意味着我们本性的实现,但不仅仅是我们本性的实现,还意味着通过"诚"能使我们之外的事物得以存在,即得以对象化("知"),使事物的本性得以实现。这就是"存在"的实质或本质。

同时,本章还讲了"诚"(真实)与"道"(道德法则)的关系:"诚者自成也。而道自道也"。"道自道也"译为"moral law means the law of our being"(道德法则意味着我们本性的法则)。因为"诚"(真实)指的是"本性的实现",而"道"(道德法则)又指"本性的法则"。于是,可见,"诚"(真实)是指"道"(道德法则)的实现。

我们可以再回顾一下,在本书第一章中,"天命之谓性,率性之谓道"一句译为"The ordinance of God is what we call the law of our being(性). To fulfill the law of our being is what we call the moral law(道)"(上帝的法令,就是我们所说的我们本性的法则[性]。服从我们本性的法则,就是我们所说的道德法则[道])。在这句话中,实则"天命"(the ordinance of God,上帝的法令,有时又直接用"上帝"来代指)、"性"(the law of our being,本性的法则)与"道"(the moral law,道德法则)是同义的,表述层面不同而已。那么,"诚"指的是"本性的实现",于是,我们可以得出结论:"诚"实则是指"天命"或"性"或"道"的实现。

本章还讲了"知"的概念,它是指"成物"(即事物的本性得以实现),实则是对"诚"的一种描述。"仁"(道德感)是它的另一种描述。"合外内之道,故时措之宜也","They combine the inner or subjective and outer or objective use of the power of the mind. Therefore with truth, everything done is right"(它们联合了内在或主观的以及外在或客观的思想力量的运用。因此,拥有了真实,每件事物都将是恰当的)。实际上,指的是"诚"的一种内外均实现的完全的状态。在这种状态之下,任何事物都是恰当的,

238

因为它们的本性都得到了实现。

　　根据以上描述，我们可以总结如下逻辑："天命（上帝的法令）/性（我们本性的法则）/道（道德法则）"的实现，即诚（真实）。其中，成己（自我的本性实现）即仁（道德感）；成物（使物的本性得以实现）即知（才智）。

XXVI.
第二十六章

Thus absolute truth is indestructible. Being indestructible, it is eternal. Being eternal, it is self-existent. Being self-existent, it is infinite. Being infinite, it is vast and deep. Being vast and deep, it is transcendental and intelligent. It is because it is vast and deep that it contains all existence. It is because it is transcendental and intelligent that it embraces all existence. It is because it is infinite and eternal that it fills all existence. In vastness and depth it is like the Earth. In transcendental intelligence it is like Heaven. Infinite and eternal, it is Infinitude itself.

Such being the nature of absolute truth, it manifests itself without being evident; it produces effects without action; it accomplishes its ends without being conscious.

The principle in the course and operation of nature may be summed up in one word: it exists for its own sake without any double or ulterior motive. Hence the way in which it produces things is unfathomable.

Nature is vast, deep, high, intelligent, infinite and eternal. The heaven appearing before us is only this bright, shining spot; but, when taken in its immeasurable extent, the sun, moon, stars and constellations are suspended in it, and all things are embraced under it. The earth, appearing before us, is but a handful of soil; but, taken in all its breadth and depth, it sustains mighty Himalayas without feeling their weight; rivers and seas dash against it without causing it to leak. The mountain appearing before us is only a mass of rock; but taken in all the vastness of its size, grass and vegetation grow upon it, birds and

故至诚无息。不息则久，久则征，征则悠远，悠远则博厚，博厚则高明。博厚，所以载物也；高明，所以覆物也；悠久，所以成物也。博厚配地，高明配天，悠久无疆。

如此者，不见而章，不动而变，无为而成。

天地之道，可一言而尽也：其为物不贰，则其生物不测。

天地之道：博也，厚也，高也，明也，悠也，久也。今夫天，斯昭昭之多，及其无穷也，日月星辰系焉，万物覆焉。今夫地，一撮土之多，及其广厚，载华岳而不重，振河海而不泄，万物载焉。今夫山，一卷石之多，及其广大，草木生之，禽兽居之，宝藏兴焉。今夫水，一勺之多，及其不测，鼋鼍、蛟龙、鱼鳖生焉，货财殖焉。

《诗》云："维天之命，於穆不已！"盖曰天之所以为天也。"於乎不显！文王之德之纯！"盖曰文王之所以为文也，纯亦不已。

绝对的真实是不可毁灭的。因为不可毁灭，所以是永恒的。因为是永恒的，所以它是自我存在的。因为是自我存在的，所以它是无限的。因为是无限的，所以它是广博而深厚的。因为广博而深厚，所以它是先验而智慧的。因为它广博而深厚，所以它包含了所有的存在。因为它先验而智慧，所以它容纳了所有的存在。因为它无限而永恒，所以它充满了所有的存在。在广博而深厚方面，它就像大地。在先验而智慧方面，它就像上天。无限而永恒，它自己就是无限的。

绝对真实有这样的本性，它虽不明显，却显示出了自己。它没有任何行为，却产生效果。它没有意识到，却达到了自己的结果。

大自然的发展及发生作用的常理，可以总结为一句话：它的存在只为了自己的目的，而没有可疑及隐藏的动机。因此，它创造万物的方式深不可测。

大自然是广博、深厚、高级、智慧、无限，及永恒的。上天表现

beasts dwell on it and treasures of precious stones are found in it. The water appearing before us is but a ladleful of liquid; but taken in all its unfathomable depths, the largest crustaceans, fishes and reptiles are produced in them, and all useful products abound in them.

In the *Book of Songs* it is said:

The ordinance of God,

How inscrutable it is and goes on for ever.

That is to say, this is the attribute of God. It is again said:

How excellent it is,

The moral perfection of King Wen.

That is to say, this is the characteristic of the nobleness of the Emperor Wen. Moral perfection also never dies.

[Tolstoi says: "In studying the men who have behind them a force which continues to act, we can see why these men in subjecting their individuality to season and in giving themselves up to a life of love, never could doubt and never have doubted the impossibility of the destruction of life."]

244

在我们面前的，往往只是明亮、华丽，但领悟到它的不可测度，太阳、月亮、群星悬浮其中，而万物都包含其内。大地表现在我们面前的，只是一把土，但领悟到它的全部宽度与厚度，它承受了巨大的喜马拉雅山，而感觉不到山的重量；河流与大海强烈地冲刷着它，却不会引起它的渗漏。高山表现在我们面前的，只是一堆岩石，但领悟到它规模的广度，草木植物生长在它之上，鸟类、野兽居住在它里面，宝石财物也可以在其中找到。水表现在我们面前的，只是一勺液体，但领悟到它无限的深度，贝类、鱼类、爬行类动物，以及其他大有用处的物类在其中繁衍生息。

《诗经》上说：

> 上帝的法令，
> 不可思议，并持续永恒。

那是说，那就是上帝的本性。它还说：

> 多么优秀，
> 文王的道德成就。

那是说，那就是文王的高尚的特性。道德成就永不消亡。

［托尔斯泰说："研究那些背后拥有持续发生效用的力量的人们，我们可以看到，为何这些人在征服他们的个性以趋于理性，并投身于爱的生活中时，从不感到疑惑，也从未怀疑生活之毁坏的不可能性。"］

【评述】

本章重点论述的是"至诚"(绝对的真实)的属性,即"不息""久""征""悠远""博厚""高明"。辜鸿铭分别译为:不息,"indestructible"(不可毁灭的);久,"eternal"(永恒的);征,"self-existent"(自我存在的);悠远,"infinite"(无限的);博厚,"vast and deep"(广博而深厚的);高明,"transcendental and intelligent"(先验而智慧的)。

"至诚"(绝对的真实)的这些属性特点,作者认为正好与"天地"的特点相"配"。"配",辜鸿铭认为指 like(像,似)的意思。其实,根据前面分析,我们已经知道,所谓"诚",指的是"天命"或"性"或"道"的实现。而"至诚"则是"诚"的最高状态,前几章认为,人若"至诚"则能"赞天地之化育"(将能够影响宇宙的创造力);人若"至诚"即"能化"(能创造);人若"至诚",则能"前知"(foreknow,预知未来)。换言之,"至诚"的境界已经是与"天地"(宇宙)一体的了。

那么,此处,文中"天地"实则与第二十二章"赞天地之化育"是相同的含义,而此处辜鸿铭的翻译则有所不同,"天地"译为"nature"(大自然),但与"宇宙"所包含的意思是一样的,都指客观存在的外部世界。因为后文都是讲的地球上的大自然景象,因此,辜鸿铭译为"nature"(大自然)。

"天地之道"一节,表现的其实是"不见而章,不动而变,无为而成"的含义。而《诗》云"一节,同样是对这一道理的概括。

"不见而章,不动而变,无为而成",辜鸿铭译为"it manifests itself without being evident; it produces effects without action; it accomplishes its ends without being conscious"(它虽不明显,却显示出了自己。它没有任何行为,却产生效果。它没有意识到,却达到了自己的结果)。这种"无为"的境界,实则与"可以赞天地之化育,则可以与天地参矣"的境界是相同的,如前几章所述,都是达到"至诚"境界后的一种与宇宙相称的创造性的表现。

文章最后落到文王的例证上,来体现这一道理。"文王之德之纯","How excellent it is,/The moral perfection of King Wen"(多么优秀,/文王的道德成就)。最后"纯亦不已"译为"Moral perfection also never dies"(道德成就永不消亡)。"至诚"的境界,就是最高的、永恒的"道德"的境界。它们在内在涵义上都是相同的。

XXVII.
第二十七章

Oh! How great is the divine moral law in man. Vast and illimitable, it gives birth and life to all created things. It towers high up to the very heavens. How wonderful and great it is! All the institutions of human society and civilisation — laws, customs and usages — have their origin there. All these institutions wait for the man before they can be put into practice. Hence it is said: Unless there be highest moral power, the highest moral law cannot be realised.

["Two things fill the soul with always renewed and increasing wondering admiration the oftener and more deeply our thought is occupied with them: the starry sky above me and the moral law within me." — Kant.]

Wherefore the moral man, while honouring the greatness and power of his moral nature, yet does not neglect inquiry and pursuit of knowledge. While widening the extent of his knowledge, he yet seeks to attain utmost accuracy in the minutest details. While seeking to understand the highest things, he yet lives a plain, ordinary life in accordance with the moral order. Going over what he has already acquired, he keeps adding to it new knowledge. Earnest and simple, he respects and obeys the laws and usages of social life.

Therefore, when in a position of authority, he is not proud; in a subordinate position, he is not insubordinate. When there is moral social order in the country, what he speaks will be of benefit to the nation; and when there is not moral social order in the country, his

大哉圣人之道！洋洋乎！发育万物，峻极于天。优优大哉！礼仪三百，威仪三千。待其人而后行。故曰苟不至德，至道不凝焉。

噢！人类的神圣道德法则多么伟大。它赋予所有创造物以起源与生命。它高耸入天，直达最高处。它是多么奇妙与伟大呀！人类所有的社会与文明的体系——法则、习俗与风俗——均源于此。除非有人能付诸实践，这些体系才得以确立。因此，俗话说：除非有最高的道德力量，否则，最高的道德法则不会实现。

［"有两样东西，我们愈经常愈持久地加以思索，它们就愈使心灵充满日新月异、有加无已的景仰和敬畏：在我之上的星空和居我心中的道德法则。"——康德[①]］

故君子尊德性而道问学，致广大而尽精微，极高明而道中庸。温故而知新，敦厚以崇礼。

是故居上不骄，为下不倍，国有道其言足以兴，国无道其默足以容。《诗》曰"既明且哲，以保其身"，其此之谓与！

因此，有道德的人在遵循其道德本性的伟大与力量之外，他也不忽视对知识的渴望与追求。当他在扩大知识范围的同时，也会寻求获取最微小的细节上的最可能的准确。当他在寻求理解最高深的事物时，他也会过一种简单、平常的合乎道德秩序的生活。复习已经获取的知识时，他会用新的知识去补充它。真诚而朴素地，他尊重并遵循社会生活的法则与风俗。

因此，当他身处当权的职位时，他不会自傲。当身处下级职位

[①] 译文引自［德］康德，《实践理性批判》，韩水法译，商务印书馆，1999。

silence will ensure forbearance for himself. In the *Book of Songs,* it is said:

> With wisdom and good sense,
>
> He guards his life from harm.

That is the description of the moral man.

时，他不会犯上。当国家存在道德的社会秩序时，他说的话将有益于国家。而当国家缺乏道德的社会秩序时，他的沉默足以保证他雍容地生活。《诗经》上说：

> 拥有智慧与良好理智，
> 他保卫生活远离危害。

这就是对有道德的人的描述。

【评述】

本章首先同样是对"道"（道德法则，也即本书前面所讲的神圣的宇宙规律）的赞叹。"礼仪三百，威仪三千"，辜鸿铭译为"All the institutions of human society and civilisation—laws, customs and usages—have their origin there"（人类所有的社会与文明的体系——法则、习俗与风俗——均源于此）。实则，辜鸿铭在此指出，"道德法则"即人类社会及文明的基础。实际上，辜鸿铭在《宪政主义与中国》一文中，对此也有过明确的描述。他在该文中指出了人们对社会存在的根基的一个普遍误解，并指出了社会、文明的真正基础："我们看到所有人类社会，无论是家族还是国家，它的起源、存在的理由和根基，不是利益，而是爱，即人类的亲情。由这种爱与人类的亲情，生出一种道德准则、一种君子之道。"（黄兴涛主编，《辜鸿铭文集·下卷》，第185页）

然而，文中进一步指出，"待其人而后行"，辜鸿铭译为"Unless there be highest moral power, the highest moral law cannot be realised"（除非有人能付诸实践，这些体系才得以确立）。意思是，尽管社会、文明的基础是道德法则，然而，它依赖有能力的人才得以实现。换言之，只有有能力的人，才能使社会符合或遵循道德的法则。这应与第十六章"其人存，则其政举；其人亡，则其政息"及"为政在人"表达的是同样的思想。都是强调"人"在实现社会道德方面的决定性意义。

那么，"有道德的人"应该怎么做呢？文中说："故君子尊德性而道问学，致广大而尽精微，极高明而道中庸。温故而知新，敦厚以崇礼。"这就是作为"有道德的人"的"君子"应该做的。换言之，即使社会实现"道德法则"，或曰实现建立于"道德法则"之上的人类文明体系的途径。

其中，"尊德性而道问学"译为"while honouring the greatness and power of his moral nature, yet does not neglect inquiry and pursuit of knowledge"（遵循其道德本性的伟大与力量之外，他也不忽视对知识的渴望与追求）。这其实是同时顾及到了"仁"与"智"的追求。

"致广大而尽精微"译为"While widening the extent of his knowledge, he yet seeks to attain utmost accuracy in the minutest details"（当他在扩大知识范围的同时，也会寻求获取最微小的细节上的最可能的准确）。这是在追求知识的时候，同时顾及到了"宏观"与"微观"的层面。忽视前者往往不能统筹把握，忽视后者则往往不够扎实。

"极高明而道中庸"译为"While seeking to understand the highest things, he yet lives a plain, ordinary life in accordance with the moral order"（他在寻求理解最高深的事物时，他也会过一种简单、平常的合乎道德秩序的生活）。这是同时顾及到了追求学问与现实生活两个层面。在第四章中，我们已经解释过，辜鸿铭认为，儒学所教给人的最主要的，其实就是如何懂得生活、好好生活。脱离现实生活，也就脱离了儒学的本意。所以，"君子"不可能只追求学问，而放弃现实生活。这也是辜鸿铭在论著中"一以贯之"的思想。

"温故而知新"译为"Going over what he has already acquired, he keeps adding to it new knowledge"（复习已经获取的知识时，他会用新的知识去补充它）。辜鸿铭这一句的翻译与他对《论语》为政第二中此句的翻译基本一致（在《论语》中辜鸿铭译为："a man will constantly go over what he has acquired and keep continually adding to it new acquirements."），都是指不断扩充学问的方式，也是同时顾及到了"旧"与"新"的学问。

"敦厚以崇礼"译为"Earnest and simple, he respects and obeys the laws and usages of social life"（真诚而朴素地，他尊重并遵循社会生活的法则与风俗）。前一句讲的是扩充学问，这一句则是讲现实生活的。"温故而知新，敦厚以崇礼"两句也可以理解为对"极高明而道中庸"一句的解释。"敦厚"指人的心态，真诚、朴素；"礼"指社会生活的法则与风俗。如果说前一句话讲的是人应如何"极高明"（扩充学问），那么这句话讲的是人应如何"道中庸"（遵循现实生活）。

再接下来，则是对"君子"本身与社会关系的描述。即，当社会实现了道德法则的情况下，君子该如何做；当社会现实没有实现道德法则，而这种现实又超出君子的实际能力的情况下，君子又该如何做。文中说"国有道其言足以兴，国无道其默足以容"，这就是君子面对这两种社会现实时应有的心态和作为。

"国有道其言足以兴"译为"When there is moral social order in the country, what he speaks will be of benefit to the nation"（当国家存在道德的社会秩序时，他说的话将有益于国家）。

"国无道其默足以容"译为"When there is not moral social order in the country, his silence will ensure forbearance for himself"（而当国家缺乏道德的社会秩序时，他的沉默足以保证他雍容地生活）。

这两句话所体现的"处世哲学"，作者认为体现在"既明且哲，以保其身"的诗句之中。后来又被概括为"明哲保身"一词。其含义就是：社会的基础是道德法则—道德法则的实现赖于君子的作为（文中讲了应该怎样作为）—当君子所处的社会实现了道德法则时，他将有益于社会/当他所处的社会脱离道德法则而又超出他的实际抵抗能力时，他将沉默，以自我保护。

或许有人说这与儒家著名的"知其不可为之"的精神相违。然而，"知其不可而为之"这句话是《论语》第十四章中"晨门"根据孔子的言行而描述他的话，而非孔子对自己思想的说明，因此，不可完全视为孔子的思想。实际上，孔子在多个地方阐述了这种"明哲保身"的思想。诸如，《论语》公冶长第五中讲孔子对南容的称赞："邦有道，不废；邦无道，免于刑戮。"述而第七中孔子称赞颜回说："用之则行，舍之则藏，唯我与尔有是夫！"泰伯第八中孔子说："笃信好学，守死善道。危邦不入，乱邦不居。天下有道则见，无道则隐。"宪问第十四中孔子说："邦有道，危言危行；邦无道，危行言孙。"卫灵公第十五中孔子又称赞蘧伯玉说："君子哉蘧伯玉！邦有道，则仕；邦无道，则可卷而怀之。"《中庸》的作者实则是对孔子"明哲保身"的思想进行了深度阐释。在《论语》述而第七中，孔子还说"暴虎冯河，死而无悔者，吾不与也"，他并不赞成对社会有勇无谋的冲动和抗争。当要将理想作用于社会现实时，他也并非完全是"知其不可而为之"的。

XXVIII.[①]
第二十八章

---

① 辜鸿铭英译《中庸》1906年的版本遗漏了第二十八章的编号，译者在此处做了补充。

Confucius remarked: "A man who is foolish and yet is fond of using his own judgment; who is in humble circumstances and yet is fond of assuming authority; who, while living in the present age, reverts to the ways of antiquity: such a man is one who will bring calamity upon himself."

To no one but the supreme head of the Empire does it belong to disturb the established religious and social institutions, to introduce new forms of government, to change the form and use of language. At the present day throughout the Empire, carriage wheels all have the same standard form and size; all writing is written with the same characters, and in all the relations of life, all recognise the same established principles.

Although a man may occupy the position of the Supreme Head of the Empire, yet unless he possesses the moral qualities fitting him for the task, he may not take upon himself to make changes in the established moral and religious institutions. Although one may possess the moral qualities fitting him for the task, yet unless occupies he the position of the Supreme Head of the Empire, he may not take upon himself to make changes in the established moral and religious institutions.

[The late Mr. J. A. Froude says: "Depend upon it, that in all long established practices or spiritual formulas there has been some living truth; and if you have not discovered and learned to respect it, you do not yet understand the questions which you are in a hurry to solve."]

子曰："愚而好自用，贱而好自专，生乎今之世，反古之道。如此者，栽（灾）及其身者也。"

非天子，不议礼，不制度，不考文。今天下车同轨，书同文，行同伦。

虽有其位，苟无其德，不敢作礼乐焉；虽有其德，苟无其位，亦不敢作礼乐焉。

孔子说："一个人，明明愚蠢，却特别喜爱坚持自己的判断；明明身份低下，却特别喜爱假装身居高位；明明生活在当前的时代，却要恢复古代的生活方式：这样一个人，将给自己招来灾难。"

除了帝国的最高首脑，任何人不能干扰已经建立的宗教与社会体系，不能引进新的政治模式，不能改变语言的模式及使用。今天，在整个帝国，所有的马车车轮在形制与尺码上都是同样的标准；所有的书写都是同样的字符写成；而且，在所有的生活关系中，都认可同样的已经确立起来的原则。

一个人，尽管处于帝国的最高元首的地位，然而，如果他没有与他工作相称的道德品质，他将无法承担修改已确立的道德与宗教体系的工作。尽管他或许拥有与那件工作相符的道德品质，然而，除非他处于帝国最高元首的地位，否则，他也不能承担修改已确立的道德与宗教体系的工作。

［已故的J.A.弗劳德先生说："依赖于它，在所有已经长久确立的习惯或精神性的规则中，存在了一些活生生的真理；如果你尚未发现或学着去尊重它，就不会明白那些你正急于解决的问题。"］

Confucius remarked: "I have tried to understand the moral and religious institutions of the Hsia dynasty, but what remains of those institutions in the present state of Chi are not sufficient to give me a clue. I have studied the moral and religious institutions of the Yin dynasty, the remains of them are still preserved in the present state of Sung. I have studied the moral and religious institutions of the present Chow dynasty, which are now in use. In practice, I follow the forms of the present Chow dynasty."

子曰："吾说夏礼,杞不足征也;吾学殷礼,有宋存焉;吾学周礼,今用之,吾从周。"

孔子说："我曾经试着去理解夏代的道德与宗教体系,但遗留在当今杞国的那些体系,不足以给我线索。我曾经研究过殷代的道德与宗教体系,那些体系依然保存于当今的宋国。我曾经研究过当今周代的道德与宗教体系,它们至今仍在沿用中。在实践中,我采用当今周代的模式。"

【评述】

本章第一段应该是承接上一章，对人的社会心态的描述。上一章，在"至道不凝"的洞察中，孔子讲到了君子"尊德性而道问学"及在国家处于"有道"及"无道"状态时应当遵守的原则。那么，此章则讲了与君子相反的，"愚"人在社会上的表现。一个"愚"人，他与"君子"的"尊德性而道问学，致广大而尽精微，极高明而道中庸。温故而知新，敦厚以崇礼"及"居上不骄，为下不倍。国有道其言足以兴，国无道其默足以容"截然相反，他会"愚而好自用，贱而好自专，生乎今之世，反古之道"。这句话辜鸿铭译为"A man who is foolish and yet is fond of using his own judgment; who is in humble circumstances and yet is fond of assuming authority; who, while living in the present age, reverts to the ways of antiquity"（一个人，明明愚蠢，却特别喜爱坚持自己的判断；明明身份低下，却特别喜爱假装身居高位；明明生活在当前的时代，却要恢复古代的生活方式）。他"自用""自专"，并且违反社会发展规律"生乎今之世，反古之道"，那么，这样一个故步自封、不求进步，且违背社会规律的人，结果只能是"菑（灾）及其身"了。

接下来，孔子讲了"人"与"制度"的关系。孔子认为，只有恰当的人，才能对制度的变革做出决策。而所谓"恰当的人"，指的是"有其位""有其德"的有德天子。孔子认为，缺少任何一个条件，都不能"议礼"（to disturb the established religious and social institutions，干扰已经建立的宗教与社会体系）、"制度"（to introduce new forms of government，引进新的政治模式）、"考文"（to change the form and use of language，改变语言的模式及使用）。

注意此处辜鸿铭对"礼"字的翻译，译为"religious and social institutions"（宗教与社会体系），文中"礼乐"译为"moral and religious institutions"（道德与宗教体系），下文中的"礼"也译为"moral and religious institutions"（道德与宗教体系）。可见，辜鸿铭是将"礼"及"礼乐"视为"道德、宗教的社会体系"的代称。在《论语》八佾第三，"夏礼吾能言之，杞不足征也；殷礼吾能言之，宋不足征也。文献不足故也，足则吾能征之矣"一句中，辜鸿铭将"礼"译为"the state of the arts and civilisation"（艺术与文明的情况），指的是整个朝代或社会的文明与艺术状态。与此处的翻译应是相同的含义、不同的表述，都是指社会文明方面的概况。

XXIX.

第二十九章

To attain to the sovereignty of the world, there are three important things necessary; they may perhaps be summed up in one: blamelessness of life.

However excellent a system of moral truths appealing to supernatural authority may be, it is not verifiable by experience; what is not verifiable by experience, cannot command credence; and what cannot command credence, the people will never obey. However excellent a system of moral truths appealing merely to worldly authority may be, it does not command respect; what does not command respect, cannot command credence; and what cannot command credence, the people will never obey.

Therefore every system of moral laws must be based upon the man's own consciousness. It must be verified by the common experience of men. Examined into by comparing it with the teachings of acknowledged great and wise men of the past, there must be no divergence. Applying it to the operations and processes of nature in the physical universe, there must be no contradiction. Confronted with the spiritual powers of the universe a man must be able to mantain it without any doubt. He must be prepared to wait, a hundred generations after him, for the coming of a man of perfect divine nature to confirm it without any misgiving. The fact that he is able to confront the spiritual powers of the universe without any doubt, shows that he understands the will of God. The fact that he is prepared to wait, a hundred generations after him, for the man of perfect divine nature without any misgiving, shows that he understands the nature of man.

王天下有三重焉,其寡过矣乎!

上焉者虽善无征,无征不信,不信民弗从;下焉者虽善不尊,不尊不信,不信民弗从。

故君子之道:本诸身,征诸庶民,考诸三王而不缪,建诸天地而不悖,质诸鬼神而无疑,百世以俟圣人而不惑。质诸鬼神而无疑,知天也;百世以俟圣人而不惑,知人也。

是故君子动而世为天下道,行而世为天下法,言而世为天下则。远之则有望,近之则不厌。

《诗》曰:"在彼无恶,在此无射;庶几夙夜,以永终誉!"

君子未有不如此而蚤有誉于天下者也。

要获取世界的统治权,有三种事情是必要的,它们或许可以总结为一句话:生活中无过错。

无论一种道德真理的理论多么杰出,如果它诉诸超自然的权威,那么,它就是无法用经验证实的。如果它无法用经验证实,那么,就不会博得信任。而不能博得信任,人们就永远不会遵从它。无论一种道德真理的理论多么杰出,如果它仅仅诉诸世俗世界的权威,它将不会赢得尊重。如果它不能赢得尊重,就不会赢得信任。如果它不能赢得信任,人们就永远不会遵从它。

因此,任何关于道德法则的体系,都必须基于人们自己的意识之上。它必须是人们的普通经验可以验证的。通过拿它与世所公认的过去那些伟大而明智的人们的学说相比较,你会发现,它们之间一定没有分歧。将它应用于物质宇宙中大自然的运作与过程之中,必然不会出现矛盾。面对宇宙中神灵的力量,一个人必然能够持守它而不感到困惑。他必然会没有任何疑虑地准备好去等待,等待在他一百代人之后一位拥有完全神圣的本性之人的到来。他

Wherefore it is that it is true of the really great moral man that every act of his life becomes an example for generations; every thing he does, becomes a statute for generations; and every word he utters, becomes a law for generations. Those who are far away and do not know him look up to him, while those who are near and know him do not reject him.

In the *Book of Songs* it is said:

There they found no fault in him;

Here they ever welcome him;

Thus from day to day and night to night,

They will perpetuate his praise!

Thus a moral man unless he realises this description of a man, can never obtain at once recognition of his moral qualities throughout the world.

能够在面对宇宙中神灵力量时毫不困惑这一事实，表现了他是理解上帝的意志的。他没有任何疑虑地准备好去等待，等待在他一百代人之后一位拥有完全神圣的本性之人的到来，这一事实表现了他懂得人的本性。

因此，真正伟大的有道德的人，他生活中的每个举动都成为了百世的榜样；他做的每件事，都成为了百世的标准；他说出的每句话，都成为了百世的法则。那些远离他并且不认识他的人，会尊敬他，而那些近在身边并认识他的人，则不会弃绝他。

《诗经》上说：

> 在那里，他们发现他毫无过错；
> 在这里，他们永远欢迎他。
> 日复日，夜复夜，
> 对他的赞颂，永不断绝。

因此，一个有道德的人，除非他认识到对人的这一描述，否则，在整个世界上，他都将无法立刻获得对他的道德品质的认可。

【评述】

本章从"统治哲学"再次返回到了人的"道德"本身。也可以说是对前面阐述的一个总结。作者认为，"王天下有三重焉，其寡过矣乎"（To attain to the sovereignty of the world, there are three important things necessary; they may perhaps be summed up in one: blamelessness of life；要获取世界的统治权，有三种事情是必要的，它们或许可以总结为一句话：生活中无过错）。下文中阐述的，即君子如何才能保证"寡过"（生活中无过错）。

文中指出，人的道德既不能"上"，也不能"下"。"上"，辜鸿铭译为"appealing to supernatural authority"（诉诸超自然的权威）。也就是说，建立于超自然权威之上，换言之，是种形而上学。这种道德"虽善无征"，"it is not verifiable by experience"（它是无法用经验证实的），并推导出"民弗从"。

"下"，辜鸿铭译为"appealing merely to worldly authority"（仅仅诉诸世俗世界的权威）。也就是说，这种道德完完全全是按照现实生活的逻辑的，没有一点高于日常生活之上的东西。如果以此为来源，这种道德同样"虽善不尊"，"it does not command respect"（它将不会赢得尊重），因为这将是种肤浅、粗俗的道德。最后的结果，同样是"民弗从"。

那么，合理的"道德"应该是怎样的呢？此处，辜鸿铭是将"君子之道"译为 system of moral laws，即关于道德法则的体系。从第一章中我们已经得知，所谓"道德"，其实是"天命"（神圣的宇宙秩序）或"性"（人类本性的法则）的一种表现。换言之，"道德"一词所代表的含义，既包含了宇宙中最根本的原理，也是指人性而言。而所谓"道德法则的体系"，则自然是指人类根据对宇宙及人性的观察研究而总结出的理论或学说。在上文中，作者说了，人的道德既不能"上"，也不能"下"。那么，此处，作者指出，"君子之道，本诸身"，辜鸿铭译为"every system of moral laws must be based upon the man's own consciousness"（任何关于道德法则的体系，都必须基于人们自己的意识之上）。其实，所谓"the man's own consciousness"（人们自己的意识），指的就是"人性"本身，也即第一章中所说的"the law of our being"（我们本性的法则），而这又是"神圣的宇宙秩序"在人心中的一种反映（也可以说是投射）。遵从这样的"道德法则体系"，才会使人"质诸鬼神而无疑，知天也；百世以俟圣人而不惑，知人也"，"The fact that he is able to confront the spiritual powers of the universe without any doubt, shows that he understands the will of God. The fact that he is prepared to wait, a hundred generations after him, for the man of perfect divine nature without any misgiving, shows that he understands the nature of man"（他能够在面对宇宙中神灵力量时毫不困惑这一事实，表现了他是理解上帝的意志的。他没有任何疑虑地准备好去等待，等待在他一百代人之后一位拥有完全神圣的本性之人的到来，这一事实表现了他懂得人的本性）。可以说，这段话再次印证了"天命"（神圣的宇宙秩序）—"性"（人类本性的法则）—"君子之道"（道德法则的体系）的内在关系：三者在本质上应是一致的。懂得这一规律的人，甚至不会因为当前的困局而产生疑惑，因为"百世以俟圣人而不惑"，他相信人类道德是以此为基本的，"圣人"终将产生。

XXX.
第三十章

Confucius taught the truth originally handed down by the ancient Emperors Yao and Shun; and he adopted and perfected the system of moral laws established by the Emperors Wen and Wu. He showed that they harmonise with the divine order which governs the revolutions of the seasons in the Heaven above and that they fit in with the moral design which is to be seen in the nature of water and land upon the Earth below.

These moral laws form one system with the laws by which Heaven and Earth, support and contain, overshadow and canopy all things. These moral laws form the same system with the laws by which the seasons succeed each other and the sun and moon appear with the alternations of day and night. It is this same system of laws by which all created things are produced and developed themselves each in its order and system without injuring one another; that the operations of Nature take their course without conflict or confusion; the lesser forces flowing everywhere like river currents while the great forces of Creation go silently and steadily on. It is this — one system running through all — that makes the Universe so impressively great.

仲尼祖述尧舜，宪章文武；上律天时，下袭水土。辟如天地之无不持载，无不覆帱，辟如四时之错行，如日月之代明。

万物并育而不相害，道并行而不相悖，小德川流，大德敦化，此天地之所以为大也。

孔子传授的真理，是古代的尧帝与舜帝传下来的。他也采用了古代文王与武王确立的道德法则的体系，并使之完美。他展现出，他们与上天掌控季节转变的神圣秩序相一致，他们也与在大地之上的大自然水土中所体现出来的道德目的相协调。

这些道德法则形成了一个体系，通过这些法则，天地支持并容纳，也遮蔽并笼罩了万物[①]。这些道德法则也形成了同样的体系，通过这些法则，季节更替，日月轮换。也正是通过这同样的法则体系，被创造的万物在其各自的秩序与系统中产生并发展了自己，而彼此并不相互伤害。大自然的运作顺其自然而不出现冲突与混乱。创造物的小些的力量恰如水流一般四处流动，而伟大的力量则无声、恒稳地运行着。正是这一运行于万物的体系，使宇宙的伟大如此醒目。

---

① 辜鸿铭在翻译时，略去了原文中的"辟如"二字。

【评述】

本章描绘了"道德法则"或曰"法则体系"在宇宙及大自然中的存在方式。而根据文中所述，这一体系是由孔子"祖述尧舜，宪章文武"而表现出来的。即，"Confucius taught the truth originally handed down by the ancient Emperors Yao and Shun; and he adopted and perfected the system of moral laws established by the Emperors Wen and Wu"（孔子传授的真理，是古代的尧帝与舜帝传下来的。他也采用了古代文王与武王确立的道德法则的体系，并使之完美）。而且，作者认为，孔子所传授的"尧舜"、"文武"的道德真理，是"上律天时，下袭水土"的，即，"they harmonise with the divine order which governs the revolutions of the seasons in the Heaven above and that they fit in with the moral design which is to be seen in the nature of water and land upon the Earth below"（他们与上天掌控季节转变的神圣秩序相一致，他们也与在大地之上的大自然水土中所体现出来的道德目的相协调）。

换言之，正如前几章所表现的，"神圣的宇宙秩序"或曰"道德法则"，是存在于宇宙及所有的大自然的事物及秩序之中的。而本章则是对这一观点的总结与描述。

辜鸿铭在翻译中略去了"辟如"二字。他不认为这是作者在打比喻，而是直接对"道德体系"的描述。这些描述，我们可以概括如下：

1. "天地之无不持载，无不覆帱"。这句话讲的是"法则体系"在宏观角度上与万物的关系。辜鸿铭译为"by which Heaven and Earth, support and contain, overshadow and canopy all things"（通过这些法则，天地支持并容纳，也遮蔽并罩住了万物）。即，整个宇宙是通过这些法则而与万物发生关系的。

2. "四时之错行""日月之代明"。由对宏观关系的描述进入到具体运作。作者认为，通过这一"法则体系"，四季、日夜才得以有序更替。辜鸿铭译为"by which the seasons succeed each other and the sun and moon appear with the alternations of day and night"（通过这些法则，季节更替，日月轮换）。即，这一"法则体系"实际上也是大自然的运行规律。

3. "万物并育而不相害，道并行而不相悖"。此句讲的是大自然在"法则体系"的规律运行之下，有怎样的效果。辜鸿铭译为"It is this same system of laws by which all created things are produced and developed themselves each in its order and system without injuring one another; that the operations of Nature take their course without conflict or confusion"（正是通过这同样的法则体系，被创造的万物在其各自的秩序与体系中产生并发展了自己，而彼此并不相互伤害。大自然的运作顺其自然而不出现冲突与混乱）。即，在这样的规律之下运行，万物是井然有序，互不冲突的。

4. "小德川流，大德敦化"。这句话最后强调了"法则体系"的存在方式：它处于被创造物之内，无处不在，并表现为它们的力量。辜鸿铭译为 "the lesser forces flowing everywhere like river currents while the great forces of Creation go silently and steadily on"（创造物的小些的力量恰如水流一般四处流动，而伟大的力量则无声、恒稳地运行着）。

XXXI.
第三十一章

It is only the man with the most perfect divine moral nature who is able to combine in himself quickness of apprehension, intelligence, insight and understanding: qualities necessary for the exercise of command; magnanimity, generosity, benignity and gentleness: qualities necessary for the exercise of patience; originality, energy, strength of character and determination: qualities necessary for the exercise of endurance; dignity, noble seriousness, order and regularity: qualities necessary for the exercise of critical judgement.

Thus all-embracing and vast is the nature of such a man. Profound it is and inexhaustible like a living spring of water, ever running out with life and vitality. All-embracing and vast, it is like Heaven. Profound and inexhaustible it is like the abyss.

As soon as such a man shall make his appearance in the world, all people will reverence him. Whatever he says, all people will believe it. Whatever he does, all people will be pleased with it. Thus his fame and name will spread and fill all the civilised world extending even to savage countries; wherever ships and carriages reach; wherever the labour and enterprise of man penetrate; wherever the heavens overshadow and the earth sustains; wherever sun and moon shine; wherever frost and dew fall: all who have life and breath will honour and love him. Therefore we may say: "He is the equal of God."

唯天下至圣，为能聪明睿知，足以有临也；宽裕温柔，足以有容也；发强刚毅，足以有执也；齐庄中正，足以有敬也；文理密察，足以有别也。

溥博渊泉，而时出之。溥博如天，渊泉如渊。

见而民莫不敬，言而民莫不信，行而民莫不说。是以声名洋溢乎中国，施及蛮貊；舟车所至，人力所通；天之所覆，地之所载，日月所照，霜露所队；凡有血气者，莫不尊亲，故曰配天。

只有拥有最完美的道德本性的人，才能够同时在内心具有敏捷的悟性、才智、洞察力，以及理解力——作为掌控局面的必要品质。宽宏大量、慷慨、仁慈，及友善——实行容忍的必要品质。创造力、活力、性格的力量，及决心——实行耐力的必要品质。威严、高贵的严肃、秩序感及规则感——实行批判性判断的必要品质[①]。

因此，包括一切与广阔，就是这样一个人的本性。它深邃渊博，而且像一眼活泉，充满生命与活力，永不枯竭。包含一切与广阔，它就像上天。深邃渊博与无穷无尽，它就像深渊。

这样一个人，一旦出现在世界上，所有人将会崇敬他。不管他说什么，所有人都会相信。不管他做什么，所有人都会感到愉悦。如此，他的名望将在所有的文明世界传播，甚至延伸到未开化的国度。无论哪里车船可以抵达，无论哪里人的劳作与事业可以到达，无论哪里在上天的覆盖之下、在大地的支撑之上，无论哪里在日月的照耀之下，无论哪里可以降下霜露——所有那些但凡有生命与呼吸的人们，都将尊敬并热爱他。因此，我们可以说："他就等同于上帝。"

---

① 此处辜鸿铭翻译似乎有误：漏掉了"足以有敬也"及"文理密察"，而是将"齐庄中正，足以有敬也。文理密察，足以有别也"一句误作"齐庄中正，足以有别也"翻译了。

【评述】

上一章总结的是"道德法则"本身在大自然中的存在方式，而此章则总结的是拥有"最完美道德"的人（至圣，即至诚）在社会环境中的存在方式。文中首先总结了这样的人的一些品质特征："聪明睿知""宽裕温柔""发强刚毅""齐庄中正""文理密察"。其中，前四项，辜鸿铭分别译为"quickness of apprehension, intelligence, insight and understanding"（在内心具有敏捷的悟性、才智、洞察力，以及理解力）、"magnanimity, generosity, benignity and gentleness"（宽宏大量、慷慨、仁慈，及友善）、"originality, energy, strength of character and determination"（创造力、活力、性格的力量，及决心）、"dignity, noble seriousness, order and regularity"（威严、高贵的严肃、秩序感及规则感）。

具有这些品质，才能够"有临""有容""有执""有敬""有别"。其中，"有临"译为"the exercise of command"（掌控局面）；"有容"译为"the exercise of patience"（实行容忍）；"有执"译为"the exercise of endurance"（实行耐力）；"有别"译为"the exercise of critical judgement"（实行批判性的判断）。

那么，这样的人在社会上是怎样的存在情况呢？文中指出："见而民莫不敬，言而民莫不信，行而民莫不说。是以声名洋溢乎中国，施及蛮貊；舟车所至，人力所通；天之所覆，地之所载，日月所照，霜露所队；凡有血气者，莫不尊亲。"即辜鸿铭所译的"As soon as such a man shall make his appearance in the world, all people will reverence him. Whatever he says, all people will believe it. Whatever he does, all people will be pleased with it. Thus his fame and name will spread and fill all the civilised world extending even to savage countries; wherever ships and carriages reach; wherever the labour and enterprise of man penetrate; wherever the heavens overshadow and the earth sustains; wherever sun and moon shine; wherever frost and dew fall: all who have life and breath will honour and love him"（这样一个人，一旦出现在世界上，所有人将会崇敬他。不管他说什么，所有人都会相信。不管他做什么，所有人都会感到愉快。如此，他的名望将在所有的文明世界传播，甚至延伸到未开化的国度。无论哪里车船可以抵达，无论哪里人的劳作与事业可以到达，无论哪里在上天的覆盖之下、在大地的支撑之上，无论哪里在日月的照耀之下，无论哪里可以降下霜露——所有那些但凡有生命与呼吸的人们，都将尊敬并热爱他）。

先讲这样一个人的品质特征，然后讲社会是怎样对待他的，这就是"拥有最完美道德的人"（至圣）的生存方式。

最后一句"配天"，辜鸿铭译为"He is the equal of God"（他就等同于上帝）。其实，根据辜鸿铭的翻译及思想，我们完全也可以推导出这样的结果。因为"道德"其实即"神圣的宇宙秩序"的反映，而"上帝"则是"神圣的宇宙秩序"的另一种说法。因此，拥有这种最完美道德的人，无疑懂得或者洞悉了"神圣的宇宙秩序"，因此，他等同于"上帝"。

XXXII.
第三十二章

It is only he in this world who is possessed of absolute truth that can order and adjust the great relations of human society, fix the fundamental principles of morality, and understand the laws of creation of the Universe.

Now where does such a man derive his power and knowledge except from himself? How all-absorbing his humanity! How unfathomable the depth of his mind! How infinitely grand and vast his divine nature! Who can understand such a nature except he who is gifted with the most perfect intelligence and endowed with the highest divine qualities of nature and mind?

唯天下至诚，为能经纶天下之大经，立天下之大本，知天地之化育。

　　夫焉有所倚？肫肫其仁！渊渊其渊！浩浩其天！苟不固聪明圣知达天德者，其孰能知之？

　　只有这个世界上拥有绝对真理的人，才能安排与调适人类社会的重大关系，确定道德的基础性原则，以及了解宇宙创造的法则。

　　这样一个人，他的力量与知识，除了他自身外，还可以源自哪里呢？他的仁慈是多么万众瞩目！他的思想是多么深不可测！他神圣的天性是多么无穷壮丽与广阔！除了被赋予最完美的才智以及最神圣的天性与思想之特性的人，谁能了解这样一种天性呢？

【评述】

此章实则也是在总结掌握"道德法则"或曰"上帝律法"的人的状态。因为，所谓"诚"，第十六章中说"诚者，天之道也"，辜鸿铭译为"Truth（诚）is the law of God"（真实［诚］是上帝的律法）。在第十六章中，我们同样总结过：在辜鸿铭的语境下，"道""道德""道德法则""上帝""上帝的律法""宇宙规律"等含义实质上是相同的。其实，这个词汇链条还应该加上"真理"（诚）和"绝对真理"（至诚），这些含义都是相同——起码是非常之接近的。

上一章总结的是这样一个人的社会状态，而且是外界对他的态度，而此章则总结他的内在心灵状态，以及他对外界的作用。文中说，只有这样的人，"为能经纶天下之大经，立天下之大本，知天地之化育"，辜鸿铭译为"can order and adjust the great relations of human society, fix the fundamental principles of morality, and understand the laws of creation of the Universe"（才能安排与调适人类社会的重大关系，确定道德的基础性原则，以及了解宇宙创造的法则）。在第十六章中，我们引述过辜鸿铭《宪政主义与中国》一文中的话，辜鸿铭认为，人类社会的最根本基础是道德。那么，在这里他则指出，只有"至诚"的人，才能确定人类"道德"的相关内容。这是"至诚"的人的能力，也是他的使命。

XXXIII.

第三十三章

In the *Book of Songs* it is said: "Over her brocaded robe, She wore a plain and simple dress." — in that way showing her dislike of the loudness of its colour and magnificence. Thus the life of the moral man is unobtrusive and yet it grows more and more in significance; whereas the life of the vulgar person is ostentatious but it loses more and more in significance until it becomes nothingness.

The life of the moral man is plain and yet not unattractive; it is simple and yet full of grace; it is easy and yet methodical. He knows that accomplishment of great things consists in doing little things well. He knows that great effects are produced by small causes. He knows the evidence and reality of what cannot be percived by the senses. Thus he is enabled to enter into the world of ideas and morals.

In the *Books of Songs* it is said:

How deep the fish may dive below,

And yet it is quite clearly seen.

Therefore the moral man must examine into his own heart and see that he has no cause for self-reproach, that he has no evil thought in his mind. Wherein the moral man is superior to other men consists even in that which is not seen by men.

《诗》曰"衣锦尚绢"，恶其文之著也。故君子之道，暗然而日章；小人之道，的然而日亡。

君子之道：淡而不厌，简而文，温而理，知远之近，知风之自，知微之显，可与入德矣。

《诗》云："潜虽伏矣，亦孔之昭！"

故君子内省不疚，无恶于志。君子之所不可及者，其唯人之所不见乎。

《诗》云："相在尔室，尚不愧于屋漏。"

《诗经》上说："她在锦袍之上，穿了一件朴素的衣裳。"这种方式表现了她对色彩与华丽之显露的厌恶。因此，有道德的人的生活是不显眼的，然而，它的意义却日益彰显。而粗俗之人的生活则是喜炫耀的，但它的意义则日益消亡，直至虚无。

有道德的人的生活是简单的，然而并不乏味。它是朴素的，然而却充满文雅。它是安适的，然而很有条理。他知道，要完成大事，在于做好小事。他知道，大的结果，是由小的原因促成的。他知道那些不能被感知的事物的证据与存在。因此，他能够进入到思想与道德的世界。

《诗经》上说：

　　　无论鱼潜水多深，
　　　它都会清晰可见。

因此，作为有道德的人，他必须审查自己的内心，并确定没有自责的理由，思想中没有邪恶的念头。有道德的人优于其他人的地方，甚至在人们所不可见之处。

In the *Book of Songs* it is said:

In your secret chamber even you are judged;

See you do nothing to blush for,

Though but the ceiling looks down upon you.

["All is, if I have the grace to use it so, /As ever in my great Task Master's eyes." — Milton.]

Therefore the moral man, even when he is not doing anything, is serious; and, even when he does not speak, is truthful.

In the *Book of Songs* it is said:

All through the solemn rite not a word was spoken,

And yet all strife was banished from their hearts.

Hence the moral man, without the inducement of rewards, is able to make the people good; and without the show of anger, to awe them into fear more than if he had used the most dreadful instruments of punishment.

In the *Book of Songs* it is said:

He makes no show of his moral worth,

Yet all the princes follow in his steps.

《诗经》上说：

> 在你的私室中，即使你受到审判，
>
> 也会看到你没做什么可以惭愧的，
>
> 哪怕只有天花板在俯视着你。

[只要我好自为之，一切都还是/在我的严厉主人监督的眼里。——弥尔顿①]

故君子不动而敬，不言而信。

《诗》曰："奏假无言，时靡有争。"

是故君子不赏而民劝，不怒而民威于铁钺。

《诗》曰："不显惟德！百辟其刑之。"

是故君子笃恭而天下平。

《诗》云："予怀明德，不大声以色。"子曰："声色之于以化民，末也。"《诗》曰"德辅如毛"，毛犹有伦。"上天之载，无声无臭"，至矣！

因此，有道德的人，即使他什么都不做，也是庄重的；即使他什么也不说，也是诚实的。

《诗经》上说：

> 整个庄严仪式悄然无声，
>
> 但他们在心中早已摈弃了纷争。

---

① 诗句译文引自殷宝书译，《弥尔顿诗选》，人民文学出版社，1958。

Hence the moral man by living a life of simple truth and earnestness alone can help to bring peace and order in the world.

In the *Book of Songs* it is said: "I keep in mind the fine moral qualities which make no great noise or show." Confucius remarked: "Among the means for the regeneration of mankind, those made with noise and show, are of the least importance." In another place in the *Book of Songs* it is said, "His virtue is light as hair." Still a hair is something material. "The workings of almighty God have neither sound nor smell." There is nothing higher than that.

因此，有道德的人，不用报酬引诱，就可以让人民变得善良；不用表现出愤怒，就可以使他们感到敬畏，比动用最可怕的刑具还有效。

《诗经》上说：

> 他并未彰显道德品质，
>
> 诸侯王们却都跟随他的脚步。

因此，有道德的人仅仅通过过一种朴素的真实而诚挚的生活，就能给世界带来和平与秩序。

《诗经》上说："我在内心保持良好的道德品质，它并不故作喧哗与炫耀。"孔子说："在革新人类的各种方法中，那些故作喧哗与炫耀的方法，是最不重要的。"《诗经》上的另一处说："他的美德，轻如毛发。"而毛发仍然是种物质。"全能上帝的工作，既无声响也无气味。"没有比它更高级的。

【评述】

本章是最后一章,通过引用《诗经》中的一些诗句,概括了"君子之道"(the life of the moral man,有道德的人的生活)或 "德"(moral worth,道德品质)应有的特征。按照文中的描述,"德"应有的特征可概括为这么几点:

1. "暗然而日章"、"简而文,温而理,知远之近,知风之自,知微之显"。辜鸿铭分别译为 "The life of the moral man is unobtrusive and yet it grows more and more in significance"(有道德的人的生活是不显眼的,然而,它的意义却日益彰显)、"The life of the moral man is plain and yet not unattractive; it is simple and yet full of grace; it is easy and yet methodical. He knows that accomplishment of great things consists in doing little things well. He knows that great effects are produced by small causes. He knows the evidence and reality of what cannot be percived by the senses"(有道德的人的生活是简单的,然而并不乏味。它是朴素的,然而却充满文雅。它是安适的,然而很有条理。他知道,要完成大事在于做好小事。他知道,大的结果是由小的原因促成的。他知道那些不能被感知的事物的证据与存在)。这一点讲的是,"有道德的人"在生活中应朴素、安静而不张扬,然而,他却能洞悉事物背后的因果原理。

2. "内省不疚,无恶于志"。辜鸿铭译为 "examine into his own heart and see that he has no cause for self-reproach, that he has no evil thought in his mind"(审查自己的内心,并确定没有自责的理由,思想中没有邪恶的念头)。比 "朴素、简单"的外在特征更进一层,指对人的内心的要求:审查自我,净化心灵。

3. "不动而敬,不言而信"。辜鸿铭译为 "even when he is not doing anything, is serious; and, even when he does not speak, is truthful"(即使他什么都不做,也是庄重的;即使他什么也不说,也是诚实的)。这一点讲的是达到以上的道德境界之后能形成的社会效应:形成一种鲜明的道德感染力。

4. "不赏而民劝,不怒而民威于铁钺"。辜鸿铭译为 "without the inducement of rewards, is able to make the people good; and without the show of anger, to awe them into fear more than if he had used the most dreadful instruments of punishment"(不用报酬引诱,就可以让人民变得善良;不用表现出愤怒,就可以使他们感到敬畏,比动用刑具还有效)。这一点讲的是如果统治阶层达到这样的道德状态之后所形成的政治效应:人民将深受统治阶层的道德感染力的影响而同样具有较高的道德水准。

5. "笃恭而天下平"。辜鸿铭译为 "the moral man by living a life of simple truth and earnestness alone can help to bring peace and order in the world"(有道德的人仅仅通过过一种朴素的真实而诚挚的生活,就能给世界带来和平与秩序)。这一点讲的是,如果统

治者本身达到这样的道德境界，将会达到的统治效应：整个世界都将处于符合道德的井然秩序之中。

最后，文中通过讲述"上天"（almighty God，全能的上帝）的状态，做一整体的总结，认为，"上天之载，无声无臭"（The workings of almighty God have neither sound nor smell；全能上帝的工作，既无声响也无气味）是至高的道德境界。"无声无臭"其实就是前文"暗然""不动""不言"等所描述的状态。我们在本书已经总结出，在辜鸿铭看来，"道德"与"上帝"实则是同源或同义的概念。因此，可以说，此处所描述的"君子"（有道德的人）与"上天"（上帝）的道德状态，实则是同义的，只不过是程度上的不同而已。"上帝"所体现出的境界是最高的。

APPENDIX[①]

附 录

---

① 这里的四篇附录为辜鸿铭所撰。

APPENDIX A

The prevalence of pessimism at the present day in the general thought and literature of Europe, I may point out here, is the natural result of the modern system of education — education for every body, encouraged and supported by the State, which aims at quantity rather than quality of education, quantity of indifferently educated men rather than quality of really educated men. In short, the inevitable result of a system of education which aims more at quantity than quality, is incomplete *half education*, and the product of half education is an incompletely developed nature. Now if it is true, as Goethe says, that the devil, incarnation of the spirit which does all the mischief in this world, is only an incompletely developed nature, then it follows that the average product of the modern system of half education in Europe at the present day, — is really an incarnate devil. The distinguishing traits of the devil's character, as we know from Milton, are in an active form, — pride, arrogance, conceit, ambition, presumption, insubordination, "having no regard or fear for the moral law " or for any thing ; and all these qualities you will find in the average product of the modern system of *half education*, when the man happens to be of a strong and coarse nature. The other distinguishing traits of the devil's character in a passive form are meanness, callousness of feeling, want of natural affection, envy, jealousy, suspicion and pessimistic views of men, men's nature and motives and of things in general ; and all these qualities you will also find in the average product of the modern system of half education when the man happens to be of a weak and

附录A

当前在欧洲思想与文学中普遍盛行的悲观主义，我要指出，它是现代教育体系的自然结果。在这一教育体系中，国家所鼓励和支持的目标在于，教育的数量要重于质量，即平庸的受教育者的数量重于真正的受教育者的质量。简言之，这种与教育质量相比更重视数量的教育体系，不可避免的结果，就是不完全的半教育，而半教育的结果自然就是天性的不充分发展。若诚如歌德所言，魔鬼，这种制造了世界上所有灾祸的幽灵的化身，仅仅是一种不充分发展的天性，那么，当今欧洲的半教育的现代教育体系的典型产物，就真的化身成了一种魔鬼。从弥尔顿那里，我们知道了魔鬼性格的显著特征，就积极形式而言，是傲慢、自大、自负、野心、放肆、犯上、"对道德法则缺少敬畏"或其他表现；而所有这些特质，你都会在半教育的现代体系的典型产物中找到，如果这个人恰好具有强烈且粗鄙的天性。魔鬼性格另一方面的显著特征，就消极形式而言，是吝啬、感情冷漠、天然情感的匮乏、嫉妒、猜忌、怀疑，以及对人们、人们的天性和动机，以及所有事情都持悲观态度；而所有这些特质，你也都可以在半教育的现代体系中找到，如果恰巧这个人具有软弱与温和的天性。那么，如果一个人牢记这样一个事实，那就是，人类的福祉以及世界的文明事业，实际上正被握在真正的魔鬼手中，即具有上述所有性格的半教育的现代体系的

soft nature. Now when one bears in mind the fact that the welfare of man-kind and the cause of civilisation in the world now are actually in the hands of really incarnate devils, unhappy products of the modern system of half education, with all the characteristics I have shown in the above, who form the greater part of the so called educated and governing class in Europe and America at the present day ; when one bears this fact steadily in mind, one ought not to be surprised, as Count Tolstoi seems to be, that the affairs of the world are in such a *mess* as can be seen in the "scientific butchery" called war for the cause of civilisation which is now going on in Manchuria. (This was written during the Russo-Japanese war.) The moral of all this is that the real cause of the anarchy or want of moral social order resulting in a big mess of all public affairs in the world at the present day, is when traced to its root, — decay, insufficiency, unsoundness of intellect; and this decay, insufficiency, unsoundness of intellect, is the result of the modern false system of State encouraged education or rather half education, which aims more at *quantity* than *quality* of education. Therefore, if there is ever to be again true moral social order and peace in the world, the present modern false system of education, of State supported education, must be thoroughly reformed; and the first step towards such a reform must be to strictly limit the quantity of education, of would-be educated men, and to improve the quality of the really educated men, this last by saving the money which is now spent in building colleges and universities, as Emerson says for fools and men who are really unfit for a thorough higher education, and spending that money for the encouragement and support of the few men who are found to be really fit for a higher education in order

不幸产物——而他们构成了今日欧美所谓受过教育的与统治阶层的较大部分；当一个人牢记这样的事实时，他就会像托尔斯泰伯爵那样，对于世界事务如此混乱并不感到吃惊了，正如我们看到的满洲正在发生的、因文明事业而导致的、被称为"科学杀戮"的战争。（本文写于日俄战争期间）所有这一切的教训就是，当我们追根溯源时，无政府状态或社会道德秩序的欠缺导致的今日世界巨大混乱的真实原因，就是才智的衰退、不足和不健全；而这种才智的衰退、不足和不健全，正是国家所鼓励的现代教育的虚伪体系，或更确切地说，是更重视数量而非质量的半教育的结果。因此，如果世界要重新拥有真正道德的社会秩序与和平，当前国家所支持的、虚伪的现代教育体系，就必须彻底改革；而走向这一改革的第一步，就是必须严格地限制受教育的以及自诩为受教育者的人数，并去提高真正的受教育者的质量，而对于后者，正如爱默生在谈及那些蠢人和那些确实不适合完全的高等教育的人时所说的，通过省下现在用于修建学院与大学的钱，把这些钱用来鼓励和支持少数被发现的、真正适合高等教育的人，让他们能够彻底地、完美地完成他们的教育。实际上，去采取中国在旧时代及日本在德川政体中所实行的国家教育体系，即"养士"以及"造士"，支持并培养绅士。正是对世界上数量不受限制的、自诩为受教育者的糟糕结果的思考，歌德在他的晚年倾向于认为，正是马丁·路德应该为欧洲的文明状态倒退了二百年而负责，因为他把《圣经》译

to enable them to thoroughly and perfectly complete their education; in fact, to adopt such a system of State education as the Chinese in old times and the Japanese in the days of the Tokugawa regime, called 養士 and 造士 support and making of *gentlemen*. It was the thought of the awful consequences of the unlimited quantity of would-be educated men in the world, which was in Goethe's mind when in his latter days he was inclined to think that Martin Luther was responsible for putting back the state of civilision in Europe for two hundred years, because Luther, by translating the Bible into vernacular German, prepared the way for the disuse and supercession of the Latin language among the really educated gentlemen in Europe and thus opened the door for easy education to the unlimited quantity of would-be educated men to take part in the affairs of the world, with the consequences which we now see.

为白话德文，从而为废弃欧洲真正受过教育的绅士所使用的拉丁文而铺平了路，由此，为那些在数量上不受限制、自诩为受教育者的人，打开了简易教育之门，让他们参与世界事务，结果，就是现在我们看到的样子。

APPENDIX B

To find the central clue in our moral being and to follow the line of conduct which is in accordance with it: all this means simply to do what is morally right. What is morally right again means what a man's whole being in a normal condition tells him to be right. In other words what is morally right means not that which a part only of a man's nature, merely the mechanical part of his intellect, tells him to be right; what is morally right is that which a man's whole being including feeling, the emotional as well as thinking, the intellectual part of his nature, fully developed, properly balanced, and in a well-ordered harmonious condition, — tells him to be right. Therefoie in order to think aright and find out what is morally right and true, we must first of all, put and keep the state of our whole nature and being in a proper and well ordered condition. The more fully our whole nature and being is developed and the more perfectly it is kept in proper, well ordered and well balanced condition the more exact, just and true will be the product of our thought; i. e. the nearer the idea in our mind or the product of our thought approaches that which the thing we think about really *is*, as it exists by the law of its nature; and in this way brings the action which we take nearer to that which is in unison with the universal order and system of things in the Universe ; in fact, what we think then is true and what we do is just. It is therefore evident from this that if a man wants to find out and see what is true in a thing or what is just in an action or line of conduct, he must, — before considering the truth or untruth of the thing, or the right or wrong of the action, first of all find out whether

附录 B

找出我们道德本性的中心线索，并遵循与之一致的指导原则：所有这些意味着只须去做道德上正确的事情。而道德上的正确，就是指一个人在正常条件下的整个本性所告诉他的正确。换句话说，道德上的正确并非一个人的本性的一部分，即仅仅他的呆板的智力部分告诉他的正确；道德上的正确，是指包括情感（含情感及思想）部分、本性中的智力部分在内的全部本性，在得到充分地发展、恰当地平衡，以及处于完美秩序的和谐状态时，告之于他的正确。因此，为了恰当地思考并找出道德上的正确和真实，我们首先必须要把我们的整个本性，置于恰当和良好秩序的状态之中。我们整个本性的发展越充分，它在保持恰当、有序方面越完美，以及保持平衡状态上越精确，作为结果，我们的思想就越正确和真实，即我们意识中的观念或者我们思想的结果，越接近于我们所认为的事物真实的所是，如它的本性那样存在。如此，我们就越接近于宇宙的普遍秩序及万物体系之间的和谐。实际上，这样的话，我们所思的就是真实而所做的就是正确。因此，这样就很明显了：如果一个人试图找出一件事物中的真实，或者一个行为或指导原则中的正确，在他考虑事物的真实与不真实或行为的对与错之前，他必须搞清楚，他自己的本性是处于对的还是错的状态之中；其实，在对待外在于他的事物之前，在对与错方面，一个人必须首先如此严

he himself, the state of his own being, is in a right or wrong condition ; in fact before dealing with the things outside of him, with the right and wrong of things, a man must first strictly deal with himself. It is for this reason then that all education without moral education, which means the education of a man's being and person; and all reform without moral reform which means the reform of man's being and character ; all such education and reform are equally useless.

It was General Gordon who, when he saw that the British policy guided by so-called wise and clever men, the policy of profit-and-loss calculation, had made a mess of things in Egypt, said: "Depend upon it when we grope in the dark as we must in the East, the best course is that which is just and right." Gordon should have gone farther and said, grope in the dark we all must, not only in the East but everywhere when we look at things only from the profit-and-loss point of view. For having to do, as we all have everywhere, with infinite multiplicity of things and forces outside of us and outside of our control, there is no man who can tell for certain how any line of action of his, profitable for the moment, may eventually affect the future of himself or others from the profit-and-loss point of view. No more can a statesman calculate and know how any line of national conduct or policy, advantageous for the moment, will ultimately affect the future of his nation, will affect the future of Manchuria, of China or of the yellow or white races. Confucius in the preceding chapter said: "Shun loved to inquire into 'near objects' , the ordinary facts of everyday life." Now this is another true characteristic of the great, whole and sound intellect, to which I have in the above omitted to call attention, the characteristic, namely, modesty, limiting and confining attention

格地对待他自己。正因如此，所有不包括对人的本性进行道德教育的教育，以及所有不包括对人的本性及品质进行改革的改革，所有这样的教育和改革，都是无用的。

正是戈登将军，当他看到被所谓聪明人操纵的、一种计算利益得失的不列颠政策，在埃及把事情搞得一团糟时，他说："当我们在东方不得不在黑暗中摸索前行时，最佳的做法是蹈义而行。"戈登应该进一步说，当我们仅仅从利益得失的角度来看待事物时，不仅在东方而且在任何地方，我们都必须在黑暗中摸索。在任何一个地方，由于我们都与事物的无限多样性及外在于我们的、无法控制的力量紧密相关，所以，从利益得失的观点来看，没有人可以确定地说，其行为在当下能够获益，就必然会对他自己及别人的未来也产生效果。没有一个政治家能够计算并清楚，如果国家的行为及政策对于当下是有利的，最终对未来也是有效的，对于中国，或者，对于黄色或白色种族，最终都是有效的。孔子在前面的章节中说："舜喜欢探求'近旁的目标'、日常生活的寻常事实。"[①] 那么，这就是我在前文忽略了的，伟大、完全而且彻底的智者的另一种真实特质，这种特质，即对近旁事实的谦逊的、克制的态度和探求。因此，这种谦逊、对自己的局限性有自知之明，就是全部和彻底的智者的特质。所以，去假设和相信，一个人不但能计算他自己和别人的近期行为的利益得失的效果及结果，而且还能计算满洲、整个国家、

---

① 即"舜好问而好察迩言"，语出《中庸》第六章。

and inquiry into near facts. Thus as modesty, self-knowledge of its own limitation, is the characteristic of the whole and sound intellect, so it is the conceit of the half intellect, the presumption of the devil's intellect, to suppose and believe that it can calculate the profit-and-loss effect and result of his own or other men's action and calculate that effect and result not only upon the near future, but upon the distant future of Manchuria, of nations, of races of men and of mankind. Confucius elsewhere speaking to one of his disciples, said: "Shall I tell you what is true intellect and real understanding ? To know what it is that you do and can know and to know what it is that you do not and can not know: that is true intellect and real understanding." Indeed, as the German philosopher Fichte in his *Wissenschaftslehre* has proved, the true aim and end of philosophy is to find out and know the limit of knowable knowledge, the limitation of man's intellect. It is said that this Fichte's famous book on metaphysics was intended by him to put an end to the study of metaphysics. At any rate it is when a man's education and study of philosophy have taught him the limitation of his intellect, taught him modesty in the use of his intellect, that he becomes really an educated man and true philosopher or lover of wisdom. But when a man's education and study of philosophy do not and can not teach him the limitation of his intellect, cannot teach modesty in the use of it, then that education and study is a useless, false, dangerous, perilous study. Confucius says: It is a dangerous and perilous thing for a man to give himself to the study of half truths (異端) i.e. half truths, products of the misuse of the intellect, deduced from abstract, abstruse, metaphysical and so-called scientific speculations on the origin and destiny of man, the why and wherefore

人类各种族及整个人类的近期未来的效果和结果，甚至能计算遥远未来的效果和结果，这其实是一种半智者的幻想、魔鬼智力的设想。在另一个地方，孔子跟他的一个学生说："让我来告诉你什么是真正的才智和真正的聪明吧。知道你所知道及能够知道的事情，也知道你所不知道及不能知道的事情：这就是真正的才智和真正的聪明。"① 实际上，就如德国哲学家费希特在他的《知识学》中已经证明的，哲学的真正目标和目的，在于找出并搞清楚可知知识的界线、人类才智的局限。也就是说，费希特的这一形而上学的名著，恰恰是为了终结形而上学的研究而作的。至少，如果一个人其哲学的教育与研究已经教给他关于他才智的局限，教给他在运用其才智时保持谦逊，他就会成为一个真正受过教育的人，以及一个真正的哲学家，或一位爱智者。但如果一个人的哲学教育与研究并没有、也不能教给他关于他的才智的局限，也不能教给他在运用时保持谦逊，那么，这种教育与研究就是无用的、虚伪的、危险的和冒险的。孔子说："如果一个人致力于研究半真理（异端），的确有害。"② 换言之，此即误用才智的结果——对人类的起源与命运、道德本性的原因与理由、个人及国家未来行为的利益得失的结果，以及所有类似的连智者都不可能知道的问题进行抽象、深奥、形而上学以及所谓科学推断似的演绎，是件危险且冒险的事情。因此，古话说得对：一天的难处一天当就够了！

---

① 即"知之为知之，不知为不知"，语出《论语·为政》。
② 即"攻乎异端，斯害也已"，语出《论语·为政》。

of his moral nature, the profit-and-loss results of man's or nations' actions upon the future, and all such questions which the intellect of man cannot know. Therefore it is truly said of old : Sufficient for the day is the evil thereof!

But although a man's intellect can not calculate the future profit-and-loss result of his actions, yet nevertheless his intellect can observe, apprehend and know the consequeuces, i.e. the past and accomplished result, of the actions of himself, of other men and things, which observation and knowledge is called experience. Now all experience — the experience of the individual man himself as well as the experience of masses of men called nations, the experience derived from the observation and study of inanimate as well as of animate objects in nature — all experience of mankind hitherto teaches, proves and confirms the fact that in the life and existence of all and every created thing in the universe, man, beast, bird, fish, reptile, plant, flower, grass, stone, fire, water, air, — when it follows the line of conduct or action which the law of its being, the normal God-ordained condition of its nature, directs and dictates, then that line of conduct or action produces the most effective, the greatest, most beneficent, best result. This knowledge, derived from exprience or inspired, is what Fichte calls the "divine idea" of the universe. Confucius also says that a man who does not know this divine idea (天命) of the universe can not be a moral man (君子). It is for this reason then that although we can not in the least calculate the future result of our actions, yet we can with confidence say with Gordon that the best course of action or line of conduct is that which is just and right, i.e. that which the law of our being, the whole of our nature and being in its pure and God- ordained normal state, tells us to be right.

但尽管一个人的才智并不能计算其行为未来的利益得失，然而，他的才智至少能够观察、理解并懂得事情的结果，即他自身的、其他人的行为与事物在过去造成的结果，这种观察和知识就是所谓的经验。那么，所有的经验——每个人自己的经验、民族的经验都源于对大自然中无生命的和有生命的目标的观察与研究。迄今为止，所有的人类经验都在教诲、证明并确认着所有及每一个在生活中和在宇宙中存在的被造物（人类、野兽、鸟类、鱼类、爬虫、植物、鲜花、青草、石头、火、水、空气），当它遵循其活动的路线，也即其本性的法则、上帝赋予的本性的寻常条件，以之为指导和命令，那么，这种活动的路线就会产生最有效、最伟大、最仁慈、最成功的结果。这种源自或被经验所激发的知识，就是费希特所说的宇宙的"神圣思想"（divine idea）。孔子也说，一个不知道宇宙的神圣思想（天命）的人，不会成为一个有道德的人①。也正因如此，尽管我们不能在哪怕最小程度上计算我们行为未来的结果，然而，我们能够自信地如戈登所说，行为最好的理由或指导路线，就是正义与正确，即依从我们本性的法则（我们的整个本质和本性处于一种纯粹状态以及上帝赋予的寻常状态）去正确行事。

---

① 即"不知命无以为君子"，语出《论语·尧曰》。

APPENDIX C

It is indeed true, as Ruskin says, that the trade of a true soldier is not the trade of slaying, but of being slain. But the soldier does not wantonly give away his life; he must give his life only for a purpose, for the true purpose for which he becomes a soldier. Now what is the purpose for which the moral man becomes a soldier? Moltke, ("Moltke regarded the battle of Koniggratz not as a victory for him, but as a defeat. He has only one notion of a battle and that is to capture, not to kill the enemy. A dead enemy does not count with him. He shoots only in order to capture and every man killed is a leaf taken from the victor's chaplet." *Von Bunsen's Memoirs.*) the greatest modern European, as well as Sun Wu-tzu, the greatest ancient Chinese strategist, both agree in saying that true strategy and tactics consist in winning a battle with the least number of men killed or injured not only on one's own side, but also on the side of the enemy; and that to win a battle by killing or injuring more of the enemy than is absolutely necessary, is bad tactics and bad strategy. We see now the true purpose for which the moral man becomes a soldier and goes to war. As the true object to be aimed at in a battle — the greatest masters of the art of war tell us — is to render the enemy harmless, *so the true purpose of war is to disarm*: to disarm savages; to disarm an unreasonable, violent, armed, dangerous madman, or a nation of such men who threaten to injure and destroy moral, civil or social order, the cause of true civilisation in the world. The honour and glory of the true soldier therefore does not lie in killing the enemy. The glory

附录 C

确实如罗斯金所说，士兵的天职并非杀戮，而是被杀。但士兵并不会轻易放弃他的生命，他必须仅仅为了一个目的而牺牲，那就是为了成为一名真正的士兵。那么，有道德的人成为一名士兵是为了什么呢？毛奇（"对于毛奇来说，克尼格雷茨战役并不是一场胜利，而是一次失败。他对于战争只有一个观念，那就是去俘获而非杀死敌人。一个死掉的敌人对他来讲并不作数。他只是为了去俘获敌人而开枪，而每一个被杀死的人，都是从胜利花环上被扯下的一个绿叶。"——《冯·本森回忆录》），最伟大的现代欧洲人，以及孙子，最伟大的古代中国战略家，都同意这种说法：真正的战略和策略存在于不仅我方而且敌方也伤亡最小的战斗中；而如果要通过杀伤超过绝对必要数量的敌人来赢得胜利，就是坏的策略和战略。现在，我们看到了一个有道德的人成为一名士兵，并开赴战场的真正目的。最伟大的战争艺术大师告诉我们，正如在战斗中的真实目的是使敌人变得无害一样，战争真正的目的就是解除武装：让野蛮人放下武器，让非理性的、暴力的、武装的、危险的疯子放下武器，让由诸如此类疯子所组成的，危害和破坏道德、公共秩序，乃至世界文明的国家，放下武器。因此，真正的士兵，他的荣誉和荣耀并非在于杀死敌人。真正士兵的荣誉和荣耀在于，当他试着让危险的疯子放下武器时，情愿被杀死。因此，当一名士兵奔

and honour of the true soldier lies in his being willing to be slain in trying to disarm the dangerous armed madman. The temper and state of mind, therefore, with which the true soldier goes to war, to the work of disarming the dangerous madman, is the spirit and temper not of anger, hatred, defiance or exultation, but of sadness, sorrow and infinite pity at the inevitability of having to do it. When the true soldier gets slain in trying to disarm the dangerous madman, he dies not with hatred, defiance thought of vengeance in his heart, but with the spirit and temper of peace and satisfaction for having done his duty, having done what his whole being tells him to be right to do. The true discipline of *Bushido* therefore does not lie in hardening of the mind and body to the sensibility ·of pain and fear of death, but in ordering the natural impulses and passion of anger, hatred, and vengeance and bringing these impulses and passions under control and not allowing them to disturb the calm and evenness of a man's temper and state of mind.

The spirit, temper and state of mind with which the true soldier becomes a soldier, goes to war and dies, can be best seen in the life and death of General Gordon. The life and death of General Gordon is the truest exercise of *Bushido* in modern times. I have said that *Bushido* is a discipline for the education of the temper and state of mind of a man in order to enable him to attain human perfection. I will add here that the life of the true soldier while he lives is a discipline which is confined more especially to himself, but the death of the true soldier in a right and necessary war is a discipline for his nation and for the world. The spirit, temper and state of mind with which General Gordon faced and met his death at Khartoum, as revealed in

赴战场去解除危险疯子的武装的时候，他的思想的性情与状态，并非愤怒、仇恨、蔑视或得意，而是忧伤、悲哀及对于无法避免的行为的无限怜悯。当真正的士兵在试图让危险的疯子放下武器而被杀时，他的心中也并非充满仇恨和复仇的思想，而是具有一种因已履行了职责，并完成了其全部本性所告之于他的、正确的事情，所产生的平静和满足。因此，真正的武士道训练，并不在于面对痛苦的感觉与死亡的恐惧时，让思想和身体变得坚强，而是在于控制愤怒、仇恨及复仇的天然的冲动和激情，并且，不让这些冲动和激情搅乱一个人性情与思想的平静与均衡。

　　让一名士兵之所以成为一名士兵，从而奔赴战场并赴死的精神、性情及思想状态，能够在戈登将军的生死中得以验证。戈登将军的生死是现代武士道的最真实的践行。我已经说过，武士道是为了让人能达到人类的完美而培养其性情与思想状态的一种风纪。在此，我想补充说，一名真正士兵的生活，当他活着时，尤其对他自己而言，是种约束人的风纪，而一名真正士兵在一场正义与必要的战争中的死亡，则是一种为了他的国家及整个世界的风纪。戈登将军在喀土穆面对死亡时，他的精神、性情及思想状态，正如在他最后的日志中所展现的，接近了这个世界上所知的、作为人类精神与性情教育的风纪之最高形态，即被歌德称为深切的"神圣悲痛"的殉道风纪。卡莱尔说："你可以轻蔑地对待大地的伤害，这是小事一桩；正像希腊古人芝诺训练你的那样：大地伤害你，甚至因为大地伤害，你也能热爱大地。世界需要有一个比芝诺更伟大

his last journals, approaches that highest form of discipline known in this world for the education of the spirit and temper of mankind, viz., — the discipline of martyrdom called by Goethe the depth of Divine Sorrow. Carlyle says, "Small is it that thou canst trample the Earth with its injuries under thy feet as Greek Zeno trained thee ; but thou canst love the Earth while it injures thee ; for this a greater than Zeno was needed and he, too, was sent."

Now that greater than Zeno whom Carlyle meant, is the Divine Man of Nazareth, whose life and death two thousand years ago gave to the then so-called civilised people in Europe who were then as now becoming or had become incarnate devils, a new civilisation or a renewal of civilisation : the civilisation known now as modern European civilisation which the Chinese are so much called upon to admire and which I am sometimes accused of not being able to admire, a civilisation which among other wonderful things, has produced a Dante, Renaissance with its art and artists, Chivalry, Bayard, Shakespeare, Elizabethan literature, Goethe, Moltke, German literature and philosophy, Carlyle, Ruskin, Gordon, Mayflower Puritanism, Emerson, the United States of America, with its largest population of the greatest good-natured fools and its recent biggest variety show at St. Louis, the great Russian Empire with its Count Tolstoi, its Kolonial Politik, its present war for the cause of civilization, and its *Moscow Gazette*, which calls the whole Japanese nation a viper and preaches the doctrine of no quarter and no prisoners in warfare; finally, last and not least of wonderful things which the civilisation originally created by the life and death of the Divine Man of Nazareth has produced, namely-Christian missionaries in China

的人,而这个人也被派来了。"①

那么,卡莱尔所指的比芝诺更伟大的人,就是那位神圣的拿撒勒人②,他在两千年前的生死,为那时正在或已经成为一种魔鬼化身的所谓欧洲文明人,带来一种新的文明或文明的重建:一种作为现代欧洲文明而被熟知的、中国人被大量号召去欣赏,而我有时被指责不够欣赏的文明,一种拥有其他许多美妙事物的文明,产生了但丁、文艺复兴、骑士品质、贝阿德、莎士比亚、伊丽莎白文学、歌德、毛奇、德国文学和哲学、卡莱尔、罗斯金、戈登、五月花清教主义、爱默生、美利坚合众国、拥有最多最大的性情温和的弄臣及近来圣路易斯发生的巨变、拥有托尔斯泰伯爵的伟大的俄罗斯帝国、它的殖民政治、它因文明事业而发生的当前的战争、它那称整个日本民族为毒蛇并鼓吹在战争中没有同情和俘虏的《莫斯科报》,而最后但同样重要的、由那位神圣的拿撒勒人的生死所创造出的文明所产生的美妙事物,也即在中国的基督教传教士们,因一位基督教主教被一场他自找的街头暴力所杀死,而向饥饿的中国人民要求赔偿六十万两白银。确实,正如托尔斯泰伯爵所说,人们在输出并把那种条款加诸中国、日本,而今远至西藏之前,需要反思并考虑到底什么才是真正的文明!

我在前文的说明中一直在试图强调的道德就是,道德教育的目标(在宗教的教诲上)并非对这样、那样或任何一种独特的美德

① 译文引自[英]托马斯·卡莱尔,《拼凑的裁缝》,马秋武、冯卉等译,第179页。
② 指耶稣。

who demand six hundred thousand taels from the starving people of China for the death of a Christian Bishop killed in a street brawl of his own seeking! Truly, as Count Tolstoi says, men should bethink them and consider what civilisation really is before they export and bring that article into China, into Japan, and now into far Tibet !

The moral of what I have been trying to say in illustration of the text above is that the object to be aimed at in moral education — in religious instruction — is not the practice of this or that or any particular virtue. The object in moral education is to promote and bring about a certain temper, spirit and state of mind. The essence and power of Christianity, as indeed it is with all great systems of religious teaching, does not lie in any particular precept such as even the golden rule, much less in the collection of theories, rules of conduct and discipline which men in after times have reduced to a system called Christianity. The essence and power of Christianity lies in the perfect state of temper, spirit and mind in which Christ lived and died.

Mencius, speaking of the two ancient worthies famous for the purity and saintliness of their lives and character, who, living in a world of anarchy, amidst militarism and wars for the cause of civilization, rather than give their consent and approval to that state of things, chose to starve themselves to death at the foot of a lonely mountain, said: "When people even after a thousand years heard of the spirit and temper of Pe-yi and Shuch'i, the covetous man became unselfish and the cowardly man strong."

In this connection I cannot help venturing to call the attention of educationalists in Japan and of all men who have the cause of moral culture at heart, to the set of moral text-books now in use in public

的实践。道德教育的目标，在于促进并实现某种性情、精神及思想状态。基督教的本质和力量，确如所有伟大宗教体系的学说一样，不在于任何特定的戒律，甚至诸如黄金律，更不用说各种理论的集成、行为的规则以及被称为基督教的、人们后来所简化的风纪体系了。基督教的本质和力量在于基督为之生死的性情、精神和思想的完美状态。

孟子在评价古代两位生活在无政府世界、被因文明事业而起的军国主义与战争所包围、却没有对那种状态妥协和苟同，而是选择在一座孤山的脚下绝食而死、终因生活和品性的纯粹与圣洁而著名的两位杰出人物时，他说："即使一千年之后的人们，在听说了伯夷和叔齐的精神和性情之后，贪婪的人会变得无私，而懦弱的人会变得坚强。"[1]

就此而言，我不得不冒险地提醒日本的及所有心怀道德教化事业的教育人士，要注意当前在日本的公立学校里正在使用的德育课本。在我浅陋的然而深思熟虑的观点看来，如果现代日本有什么东西会让日本人民不仅丢失他们原有的整个良好与高尚的道德文化，而且丢掉所有道德文化，那就是最近日本文部省发行的这套可怕的德育课本。我已经说过，道德教育的目标，并非这种、那种或任何一种特定美德的实践，而是促进并实现某种性情、精神及思想的状态。如今，唯一可以促进并实现那种性情、精神及思想的

---

① 即"圣人，百世之师也……故闻伯夷之风者，顽夫廉，懦夫有立志"，语出《孟子·尽心下》。

schools in Japan. It is my humble, but my very deliberate opinion, that if there is anything in modern Japan which will make the Japanese people lose entirely not only their original fine and high moral culture, but all moral culture, it is this terrible set of moral text books recently issued by the department of Education. I have said that the object to be aimed at in moral education is not the practice of this, that, or any particular virtue, but in promoting and bringing about a certain state of temper, spirit and mind. Now the only one way to promote and bring about that perfect state of temper, spirit and mind, is by coming under the influence of some great religious genius such as those who have given their names to great religious systems of the world, by studying and understanding not only his life, his conduct and his precepts, but his way of feeling and thinking: his temper, spirit and state of mind, in fact, what we Chinese call his tao (道) — his way or manner of being or living. I venture to say, therefore, that for the object to be aimed at in moral education such a sentence from the New Testament: *"Learn of me that I am mild and lowly in heart and ye shall find rest unto your souls;"* or, to take a sentence from the sayings of Confucius: "The master is gentle, simple, earnest, modest, humble." (夫子温良恭儉讓) Such sentences, when properly apprehended and taken in by a scholar, will do more for the education of his moral character, of his temper, spirit, and state of mind than the most exact and rigid set of square rules of conduct about public and private virtue which the most accomplished and erudite professor in Tokio or Berlin can ever hope to draw up. Mr. Matthew Arnold says: "It is a mistake to suppose that rules for conduct and recommendations of virtue, presented in correct scientific statement or in a new rhetorical statement from

完美状态的方法，就是将这一过程置于创建了世界上伟大宗教体系的宗教天才的影响之下，不仅要研究并理解他的生活、行为和戒律，更包括他的感知与思考的方式：他的性情、精神及思想状态，事实上，也就是我们中国人称之为"道"的东西——他的本性或生活的方式或方法。因此，我冒险地说，道德教育的目标存在于《新约》的这样一个句子中："我心里柔和谦卑，你们当负我的轭，学我的样式，这样，你们心里就必得享安息。"① 或者，我们从孔子的话中摘出一句："老师是和蔼、简朴、诚挚、谦逊而又恭敬有礼的。"（夫子温良恭俭让② ）这样的句子，如果被一位学者恰当地理解和领会，那么，对他的道德品质、性情、精神及思想状态的培养，将远胜于那一系列由东京或柏林的最有才华和博学的教授所希望拟定的、最精确和僵硬的公私美德行为方面的古板规则。马修·阿诺德先生说："设想一种排除了旧有谬误的、表现为以正确科学化的语言或新的雄辩陈述来表述的行为规则及对美德的劝诫，对于人类来讲，能够像我们长久以来已经习惯的、我们的情感为之缠绕的旧有规则和劝诫那样，产生同样的效果，是错误的。卖弄学问的人，总是假设我们能够做到，但是，这些错误已经司空见惯，它只是证明了我们有多少人也混合了这种卖弄习气。对于人类的大多数来讲，一种对于美德规则的正确科学化的陈述，没有产生任何效果。而如果他们的一种新的雄辩陈述，试图像熟悉的旧式基督教（或者，

① 语出《马太福音》11：29。

② 语出《论语·学而》。

which old errors are excluded, can have anything like the effect on mankind of old rules and recommendations to which we have been long accustomed and with which our feelings and affections have become entwined. Pedants always suppose they can, but that these mistakes should be so commonly made, proves only how many of us have a mixture of the pedant in our composition. A correct scientific statement of rules of virtue has, upon the great majority of mankind, simply no effect at all. A new rhetorical statement of them, appealing, like the old familiar deliverances of Christianity, [or of the sacred books of China and even the Buddhist sermons in the *Okio hajimaru* in Japan] to the heart and imagination, can have the effect which those deliverances had, only when they proceed from a religious genius equal to that from which those proceded. To state the requirement is to declare the impossibility of its being satisfied. The superlative pedantry of Auguste Comte is shown in his vainly imagining that he could satisfy it. The comparative pedantry of his disciples is shown by the degree in which they adopt their master's vain imagination."

如同中国的神圣典籍,甚至日本古经里的《佛教训诫》)那样,吸引人心并激发想象力,从而产生效果,那么,它只能产生于一位宗教天才,且等同于他们旧式的陈述。可以断言,以--种新的雄辩陈述来传达必要的东西是做不到的。极端喜爱卖弄学问的奥古斯特·孔德,则自负地想象他能做到。而他的学生们的卖弄,则取决于他们对其师自负想象的承袭程度。"

APPENDIX D

The rich, idle, luxuriously-living class say to the working class, and they are supported in what they say by political economists: "We are very sorry, but what can we do? Don't you see that unless we drink champagne and live luxuriously trade will suffer ; and when trade suffers, it is you, the working class, who will suffer?" This is the logic and plea of the privileged class for upholding social inequalities.

Against this, however, the socialists justly answer: " Granted all that you say ; but is there any reason in the nature of things why we should not exchange roles? Any reason why you, idle, privileged class should not take a turn to work, and we, working class, should not take a turn to drink champagne and live luxuriously for your benefit? "

"But you cannot do that," answer the privileged class, "because you have no money."

"We have force and can take your money. "

"Oh, you cannot do that, because there is the divine right of property. "

"But who invested property with divine right?" ask the socialists.

"The law courts and lawyers," answer the privileged class.

"But what if we do not submit to the decision of law courts and lawyers ? "

"Then," reply the privileged class, "the policemen will take you to jail. That's all."

The basis of society in modern Europe, therefore, is the lawyer and policeman — force and fraud; it is not a moral basis.

附录 D

富裕、有闲、生活奢侈的阶级这样对工人阶级说（而且这些话受到了政治经济学家们的支持）："我们非常抱歉，但又能做什么呢？你们没看到吗？如果我们不饮用香槟和奢侈地生活，贸易就会变糟；如果贸易变糟，遭殃的正是你们工人阶级。"这是特权阶级维持不平等社会的逻辑和托辞。

然而，与此对抗的社会主义者们却这样回答："诚然如你们所说的那样，但我们为什么不调换角色呢？难道事物的本性中有这样的道理吗？有什么理由，为何是你们有闲的特权阶级不应该去工作，而我们工人阶级不应该为了你们的利益去饮用香槟并过奢侈生活呢？"

"你们不能这么做，"特权阶级说，"因为你们没钱。"

"我们有武力，能抢你们的钱。"

"噢，你们不能这么做，因为存在神圣的财产权。"

"但是，谁授予财产以神圣权利呢？"社会主义者又问。

"法庭和律师。"特权阶级回答说。

"但是，如果我们并不服从法庭和律师的决定呢？"

"如果这样，"特权阶级回答说，"警察就会把你们扔进监狱。就这样。"

因此，现代欧洲社会的基础就是律师和警察——武力和欺骗，

It must, however, be said that the socialists who claim political power and enjoyment of luxuries for the people, also base their claim, not upon justice, but upon love of power and love of enjoyment. The socialists' argument is that as the lower orders have as much love for power and appetite for luxuries as the privileged class, they therefore have as much right to the enjoyment of these things as the privileged class. Thus the socialists in Europe who want to break up social inequalities are as immoral as the privileged class who want to uphold them, i.e. they do not recognise any moral basis for social inequalities; do not know and acknowledge that there is such a thing as moral obligation which should form the basis of social inequalities.

这并非是一种道德的基础。

然而，不得不说，为人民提出政治权力和奢侈享受要求的社会主义者，他们的要求同样基于对权力和享受的喜爱，而非基于正义。社会主义者争论的是，作为与特权阶级一样热爱权力并对奢侈充满欲望的底层阶级，他们也跟特权阶级一样，拥有享受这些事物的权利。因此，想打破社会不平等的欧洲社会主义者们，与希望维持这种现状的特权阶级一样不道德，换言之，他们并未认识到社会不平等的道德基础，也没有认识到并承认存在道德义务这样一种东西将构成社会不平等的基础。

后 记

对我而言，翻译并解读辜鸿铭的英译《中庸》与《大学》，与译注其英译《论语》，初衷是不同的——如果说，我翻译其英译《论语》，主要是为读者提供一个诠释《论语》的独特版本，并借此展现辜鸿铭的一些相关思想，那么，翻译并解读其英译《中庸》《大学》，则是为归纳其所包含的哲学体系，并为我们当前所遇到并在思考的"现代化"过程中的诸多问题，提供一种哲学意义上的参考。

而本书的参考意义就在于它非常系统地归纳了"古典"精神。杜维明先生在《〈中庸〉洞见》一书中提到辜鸿铭时，称之为"古典学者"（classicist）[①]，我认为这是对辜鸿铭的准确界定。并进而想到，不单单辜鸿铭，包括他所尊崇并承袭的莎士比亚、歌德、爱默生、卡莱尔、阿诺德等人的思想，也都代表着"古典"精神，而且他们之间表现出了深刻的"共性"，那就是：在"现代化"发生之初，他们对人类的"古典"精神遗产所进行的挖掘、阐发、归纳、整理与发散（这也是辜鸿铭在著作中频繁引用他们观点的原因）。他们认为万物都带有某种灵性，并统之于活泼泼的宇宙精神与秩序之中。这截然不同于我们"现代"意义上的对宇宙万物及世界的理解。

[①] 杜维明，《〈中庸〉洞见》，人民出版社，2008，第16、17页。

而当我们看到在现代化中所产生的种种人类精神生活层面的问题及其所导致的种种不良甚至严重后果时，并不难发现，我们需要来自"古典"的精神滋养，这是必不可少的。至少，"古典"精神可以教给我们如何更尊重我们所生存的世界、更能够从道德意义上来审视我们自己，从而，让我们获得一种更加"人性"的生活体验与结果。因此，我认为，在我们思考现代化并从事现代化建设时，应该能够了解"古典"，并延续某些珍贵的"古典"精神，以使我们的"现代化"更加完善，令我们的世界与社会更适于人性本身的发展。

幸运的是，在我看来，辜鸿铭所英译的《中庸》与《大学》恰恰比较系统、完整地归纳了这种"古典"精神。——其中，《中庸》主要是揭示了宇宙万物与人性的本质，而《大学》则主要是阐述了人类社会应如何去合理地发展这些本质。打开这本书，我们可以走进辜鸿铭通过英译、解读这两本书而给我们描绘出的一个气象恢弘的"古典"精神世界——而我希望我的工作更完整地呈现了这一点。是为记。

王京涛　于北京

写于2015年11月21日下午

修改于2016年2月1日晚与3月12日午